FREDERIC RAPHAEL

BYRON

SPHERE BOOKS LTD

Published by the Penguin Group
27 Wrights Lane, London W8 5TZ, England
Viking Penguin Inc., 40 West 23rd Street, New York, New York 10010, USA
Penguin Books Australia Ltd, Ringwood, Victoria, Australia
Penguin Books Canada Ltd, 2801 John Street, Markham, Ontario, Canada L3R 1B4
Penguin Books (NZ) Ltd, 182–190 Wairau Road, Auckland 10, New Zealand

Penguin Books Ltd, Registered Offices: Harmondsworth, Middlesex, England

First published in Great Britain in 1982 by Thames and Hudson
Published in Cardinal by Sphere Books Ltd, 1988

Made and printed in Great Britain by
Richard Clay Ltd, Bungay, Suffolk

CONTENTS

BYRON'S WAS A LIFE which, as the movie trailers used to promise, had everything. No one, he was to boast, lived faster than he. In thirty-six years, he covered a prodigious amount of ground, and paper. One has to cut briskly from this scene to that, from one drama to the next, in order to accommodate his careering career. He was more often like an actor (a brilliant performance here, a flop there, a flashing comeback somewhere else) than a reliable literary type. If his art concealed art, it rarely concealed him: his personality and his work are inextricably woven together. 'Do you like Byron?' can never be a question simply about the text; it is bound to concern the man himself. Though he has been dead for well over a century and a half, he still demands to be taken personally, as he himself took the world. He requires not only a straight account but also an emotional response: how can you do him justice and be impartial at the same time? He was not merely a poet, but also a star, the first modern celebrity, the artist as performer and publicist. If there were famous writers before him, none was ever famous in quite the same infamous way as George Gordon, sixth Lord Byron.

Once notoriety had been achieved, he lived always in the glare of publicity, and if he sometimes glared at it, he could not do without it: even his private life was lived in public. He shared Oscar Wilde's view that if there was one thing worse than being talked about, it was not being talked about. Probably as much has been written about him as about any other English poet except Shakespeare, of whose private life little is known, though more has been said. He is both revered and reviled. His influence was as wide as that of any man of his time, but he has been no less often denounced as pernicious than celebrated for his humanity. Although he appears in every anthology with some of the most quoted lines in the language, a Provost of Eton could say, and not without backing, that he was popular because he was a Lord and wrote badly. He himself admitted that at times he lowered himself by pandering to the base tastes of his public. Alone of all English authors, he has a chapter to himself in Bertrand Russell's *History of Western Philosophy*, but few philosophers salute his presence. (They say, knowingly, that Russell was really keeping a niche warm for himself, since he too was a Whig, a peer, a libertine and an egotist.) Even Byron's place in the poetic pantheon remains questionable. Though often readable, his poems are not much 'taught'; his flippancies disconcert those who confuse literature with morals. He was debarred from Poets' Corner in Westminster Abbey until recently and even now it harbours his bust, not his bones. When his heartless body was brought back to England in 1824, the doors of the Abbey were closed against it. It still lies in a vault under the chancel of Hucknall Torkard church, near the Byrons' ancestral home, Newstead Abbey, in Nottinghamshire.

If Byron's name is associated with lordly excess and romantic adventure, he began without titled prospects or gaudy circumstances. He was not in the direct line of succession to the peerage held by the so-called Wicked Lord, his great-uncle, a misanthropic recluse living a life of penurious self-indulgence on his rundown estate at Newstead. The place had been a monastery until the time of Henry VIII, after which its new tenants broke ostentatiously with monastic restraints. The Wicked Lord's own son had made an unsuitable marriage, for love and not for the money which the estate and his father so badly needed. He was accordingly disinherited, not that there was much left for him to inherit. After his son's departure, and early death, the embittered father abandoned himself to the few pleasures he could afford. He played with model ships on the large lake in front of the dilapidated abbey, firing at them with a miniature working cannon mounted on a small fortress he had had built on shore. His servant, old Joe Murray, kept his head down in a rowing boat as he towed the Lilliputian battle fleet within range. His trigger-happy master was neither of a reliable temper nor conspicuous for the maturity of his entertainments.

After dark, the Wicked Lord repaired to the great hall, where the same dusty bottle of claret was placed on the table every night; appearances, of a seigneurial kind, were maintained, but the cellar was not. To pass the time, he conducted 'horse-races' with cockroaches. Female company was supplied by one of the servants, who came to be called 'Lady

Betty'. His own wife had long since left him. Lurid stories of his unmarital behaviour (he was said to have shot and killed her ladyship's coachman) added to his scoundrelly reputation, though like his heir he seems to have had the knack of keeping the loyalty at least of his servants. His unofficial title for wickedness he owed above all to a fatal episode in a tavern in Pall Mall in 1765. He had disagreed with a Nottinghamshire neighbour and distant kinsman, William Chaworth, over the vexed question of the best means of preserving game. His Lordship had the last word, in a murky upper room, where he shortened his sword and ran Mr Chaworth through the belly. His neighbour died next day, without reproaching Lord Byron, at whom he had himself made the first thrust. However, there followed a sensational trial for murder in the House of Lords, which was packed for the occasion (scalpers got six guineas a seat). Although the defendant was acquitted of the capital charge, he was convicted of manslaughter and was never welcome in London again.

The Byrons, or de Buruns as they were originally called, traced their lineage back to the time of William the Conqueror, though there was no evidence that they assisted in the conquest. Henry VIII, having evicted the monks, installed more amenable landlords. The Byron family always depended on largesse rather than industry for their richer hours; if they were often handsome, or at least virile, they worked only at their pleasures and at striking attitudes. In Elizabeth's reign, one of them maintained a private band of actors at Newstead. It had been the scene of dramatics and debauches long before the Wicked Lord (or his successor) added his name to its tenants.

Byron's grandfather, his great-uncle's brother, was a naval man. He was known as 'Foul-Weather Jack': his crews seemed always to be at the centre of a storm. He was an able navigator (he went to the South Seas) and rose to be a Vice-Admiral. A renowned womanizer, he was no stranger to vice on land. The Byrons were generally hot-blooded: it was one of Foul-Weather Jack's attractive daughters, Juliana, who caught the unapplauded fancy of her cousin, the Wicked Lord's son. The family saw no virtue in moderation, and very little, it seems, in virtue. The admiral died in 1786 (only just before Byron's birth), which gave him ample time to observe the outrageous behaviour of his own first-born, John. It so much displeased him that he too disinherited his son, whose nickname lacked nautical jauntiness: he was known simply as 'Mad Jack'. Lady Caroline Lamb was to say that Byron was 'mad, bad and dangerous to know', but quite a number of ladies must have said the same of his scapegrace father who, soon tiring of his career in the Guards (though he retained the title of Captain and the dashing manners and accent he had learnt in a French military academy), preferred to mount his campaigns in female company. His own sister is rumoured not to have been exempt from his gallantry.

In 1778, he made a notable conquest in London society: the clever and bold Marchioness of Carmarthen, whose marriage to the Marquis was a love match that had turned sour. Captain Byron laid siege not only to her person, but also to her fortune: she had just come into £4,000 a year. The lure of a pretty face and a pretty penny combined in the same lady were not to be resisted, nor did the lady herself long resist. The lovers eloped (the Marquis obtained a divorce only after the outrageous event) and went to live in France, a favourite refuge for those for whom London was too hot or too expensive. Lady Carmarthen bore the Captain three children, of whom only Augusta, the last, survived into maturity, of a kind. The Marchioness died in 1784. There were rumours that 'Mad Jack' had maltreated her. It was as typical of the Byrons that such accusations should be made as that there may have been some truth in them, though Byron himself was to assert his father's devotion to his beautiful lady.

The Captain was broke, not broken. He came to England to repair his life and found what he needed, though not necessarily what he wanted, in the shapeless shape of Catherine Gordon of Gight, a Scottish heiress whose fortune, not her face, was her fortune. She was reported to be very rich when he met her in a ballroom in Bath, where the upper classes put their daughters on parade for likely, or plausible, suitors. Captain Byron had no difficulty in sweeping the heiress off her clumsy feet. Catherine was a callow Scots girl of twenty who believed as innocently in the Captain's love as he did in her money. Both were to be disappointed: he treated her scurvily and her endowment proved to be a useful but not an inexhaustible sum, some £23,000. Her family was both ancient and royal (Byron claimed descent from James the First of Scotland) and it too had its fiery and disreputable sons.

For a while the newlyweds resided at Gight, Catherine's ancestral home, but if it had come down to her from time more or less immemorial, it was quickly lost to her posterity.

The Captain had the knack of getting money out of his wife but no capacity for holding onto it. So helpless was she in the face of his handsome demands that she managed to retain a fragment of the money left from the rapid sale of Gight only by arranging for it to be sequestered in such a way that she could never sign away the principal, however persuasive the unprincipled Captain might prove. Fear of the duns drove the couple first to rural Hampshire and then to France, where they were living by the time George Gordon, their only child, was due to be born. When Catherine, without the Captain, returned to England for her confinement, she brought with her the young Augusta, now four years old, whom she delivered to the late Marchioness's mother, Lady Holderness, before going to London to be delivered of her son. One may picture the little girl held against Catherine's large lap lending warmth to the womb in which her half-brother lay as they crossed the English Channel. One day he would cross it on his way to exile, not least on account of her.

Byron was born in a caul, a membranous sac, which was easily removed and caused the infant no damage or discomfort, though he later associated it with the predestined curse on which he sometimes dolefully, sometimes gleefully, prided himself. He was also born with a deformed right foot; medical argument now holds that a dysplasia, a withered calf-muscle, distorted the foot. His father greeted the news of the deformity with a not unkind shrug: he had more pressing problems. They soon pressed also on Mrs Byron, for the dregs of her treasure were her husband's first objective when he consented to rejoin his family. Dependent on the inalienable vestiges of her birthright, Catherine removed to inexpensive Scotland, where she set up house with her infant son, George Gordon (named after her father), in Queen Street, Aberdeen. Mad Jack, proclaiming that she was impossible to live with, lodged at the other end of town, but he was not above calling on her for tips. Mrs Byron was never a balanced or a gracious lady, but the unmerry dance she had been led must partly account for the capriciousness of her temper during Byron's babyhood. Poor confused woman, she still loved the Captain (when she did not hate him), but motherhood excited only an unpredictable regime of alternate kisses and blows. The mother's temper cannot have improved the child's. He was said to be wilful. Now spoilt, now abused, he probably needed a strong will to survive. As he grew up, he had to endure both the uneven character of his mother and his own uneven gait.

He had to reckon not only with the derision of other children but also, more painful still, with his mother's insistence that he accept the ministrations of a series of quacks who, with outstretched palms and racking machines, promised the credulous lady that the incurable could easily be cured, given time, and money. More sensible and pessimistic early advice from the great surgeon John Hunter was long ignored.

When 'wee Geordie' was two years old, his father decamped once again, and this time forever. Having gone through the last of his wife's extractable money, he returned to France and resumed going through actresses and servant girls. In 1791 came the news of his abject death: it may have been suicide, it was certainly not an excess of prudence. The widow was free of his demands, and distraught. Being unlikely to find it anywhere else, she sought consolation in pious propriety. All her happy hopes were now dashed, except for those she fastened, with exasperated urgency, on the boy.

In 1794 Byron's cousin, William, a boy of eighteen, was killed at the siege of Calvi, in Corsica; in the same campaign Nelson lost an eye. It is one of the ironies of Byron's story that his name is popularly associated with dashing heroics, but that he would never have come into the title at all had not the original heir been killed in just such an exploit as he himself was never to achieve, though not for want of trying. It is a moot point whether his talent would ever have flourished had it remained the gift of the impoverished and untitled son of the widow Gight. Be that as it may, Geordie was now the heir of the Wicked Lord, not that the old man had either the means to celebrate or the inclination to acknowledge the fact.

Mrs Byron and her son continued their provincial life in granite Aberdeen. He went to school, and to the kirk. He had pretty curls and a pretty face. Only his dragging foot reminded him of the ugly fate to which he was shackled. If he was touchy, he was also brave: he faced down the bullies who called him 'Mrs Byron's crooked devil' and he made clumsy common cause with another lame boy. (One day, he and yet another crippled Caledonian, Sir Walter Scott, would be the most famous and successful writers in England.) The boy dreamed of raising a troop of his own soldiers who would be called 'Byron's Blacks' and would perform 'prodigies of valour'. The inexorable division between the damned and the saved, preached so regularly from Calvinist pulpits, bore heavily on him: was not his warped right foot the outward and visible sign of God's damnation? For such a child, in such a place, fantasy and freedom were likely to be much the same fugitive thing; reality was what was inescapable, a prosaic bondage. Only in the world of the imagination was there a playground for impossible dreams. The severe Sundays were as boring as they were intimidating. He is said once to have abstracted a hat-pin from his pious mother's hat and driven it into her plump arm, causing her to cry out in the middle of the sermon. But if his damned foot inclined him to associate himself with the ill-favoured, he now knew also that he must one day be a lord. Pride of family was a happy crutch for hobbled vanity. The motto 'Crede Byron' proclaimed a fierce sense of personal honour but it might also be translated, challengingly, 'Trust me!'.

Byron was already a keen reader, particularly of Roman history and Mediterranean legend. (Poetry he despised.) He was precociously romantic. He fell in heartsick love with a cousin, Mary Duff, who excited in the bookish boy all the daydreaming passion associated with adolescence, though he was not yet ten years old. His absurd mother, now smothering him with kisses, now pursuing him with blows, was scarcely a seductive object for his affections. His love for pretty young Mary was chaste and distant; the attentions paid to him by a young servant girl, May Gray, were neither. Did he later exaggerate the caresses she supplied? Exaggeration was hardly untypical of him, but May almost certainly did introduce Byron to sex, not that they were likely long to have remained strangers. He was a very attractive and also a very coquettish child. He craved affection and feared himself repulsive. Aberdeen could be a very cold place. A warm servant girl could be expected to furnish what he was too ashamed and too proud to seek elsewhere. The separation of sensuality and sentiment may be an inevitable part of growing up, but Byron learned abruptly to divorce them. The appetites of women may have fascinated but they also appalled him, not least because May Gray, however delectable her embraces, swore him to silence by promising him hell fire if he ever revealed their secret. She was pious by day and a devil by night. Cant and cunt revealed their proximity very early in Byron's life, though he was not free to remark the fact in quite such clipped terms until success licensed outspokenness. Calvinist preachers might warn their congregations to beware lest 'all give destruction that should give comfort', but as between Mrs Byron's smacking kisses and

13

the hot secrecy of May Gray's embrace, can Byron be blamed for choosing the latter, especially if he could persuade himself that he had no choice? Had he been a different sort of boy, he might have forgotten or made less of May Gray's initiatory fondling. Such domestic baptisms were surely far from rare. Turgenev recalled how a servant girl took him by the hair, when he was fifteen, and led him to bed with no more ceremony or lasting hurt than Christopher Robin might have endured when summoned for a hair cut. Guy de Maupassant told an almost identical story. When is the right moment? It is always too early or too late. May Gray should not be stigmatized for what was at least partly a kindness. If Byron could later see himself as a debauched innocent, put upon by a randy woman, the curly-haired lad had probably done his winsome bit to seduce his seducer.

When the Wicked Lord died, in 1798, the ten-year-old heir was translated from stony Aberdeen to the green estate of Newstead, on the fringe of Sherwood Forest. May Gray accompanied Mrs Byron and the boy southwards. The ride down the long drive to the Abbey took them through gently rolling, brackened acres – over 3,000 of them – which, but for that random shot at the siege of Calvi, Byron might never have seen. To say that he was now their undisputed master would be to take too blithe a view of the family's finances. The Wicked Lord had cut the saleable oaks, slaughtered thousands of the deer for market and mortgaged the property; his creditors had already been prompt to strip the place of whatever could be carried away, including the furniture. The ochrous beauty of the despoiled buildings remained; a boyish imagination already stimulated by romances like John Moore's *Zeluco* must have caught fire at the sight of the roofless front of the Abbey church, its unglassed Gothic arches filled with sky. Legend (passed on by old Joe Murray) promised that the ghosts of dispossessed monks still haunted the cloisters.

Byron began to play the Lord with the swagger of any understudy cast by chance in a part he might never have obtained. Having been raised far from great houses, he had gained an impression of aristocratic behaviour more from books than from observation. Now he found the Wicked Lord's pistols to be just his kind of toy. But if no one could deny his title, there was something of the impostor about him, or at least of the *arriviste*: he had great expectations but no great experience. He had to be coached for his new role by

John Hanson, the family lawyer, who came up to Newstead from London to greet the heir. Hanson took him on the rounds of the neighbouring great houses and introduced the young Lord to a pretty girl called Mary Chaworth at nearby Annesley Hall. She lived with her mother, Mrs Clarke, whose first husband had been of the same family as the man whom the Wicked Lord once spitted on his sword. The girl was only a year or two older than Byron so Hanson suggested jocularly that he had better marry her. 'What,' replied the well-read boy, 'the Capulets and the Montagus intermarry?' He once said that all he ever wanted was to make a woman laugh, but how often he began by scowling at her!

Newstead was magnificent, and scarcely habitable. There was no money either for repairs or even to replace the confiscated furniture. Byron's mother took him to Nottingham where his foot was again cruelly manipulated, this time by a quack called Lavender who passed himself off to the gullible Mrs Byron as a scholar who could read eight languages. (He was careful to stipulate that he could not *speak* them.) Byron recognized the man as a fraud, but his mother was persuaded of his genius. A young American, 'Dummer' Rogers, who had agreed to act as Byron's part-time tutor, witnessed his brave agony. One day Byron took witty revenge. Possibly at Rogers' instigation, he wrote something on a piece of paper and asked the 'Doctor' to tell him what language it was. After study, Lavender pronounced it to be Italian. Byron burst into triumphant laughter; all he had scrawled on the paper was the alphabet broken up into the appearance of separate words: ab cde fghi jklmno pq etcetera. However, treatment continued and Rogers was sickened by what he knew the boy to be suffering on Lavender's rack, but Byron assured him, 'You shall see no signs of it in me.'

In July 1799, John Hanson took the young lord with him to London, conscious of the inadequacy of both his treatment and his education. Though Mr Rogers had taught him some Latin, he needed regular schooling and the company of other children. A London bootmaker, under the instructions of a practical Dr Baillie, built him a shoe which would enable him to walk as normally as possible and thenceforth there were no more quacks: his condition was admitted to be irreparable and he had to live with it. He went to school for a while in Dulwich, where his mother's visits were obstreperous and embarrassing. 'Byron, your mother is a fool,' said a fellow-pupil. 'I know it,' he replied.

In 1801, he was sent to Harrow, the financial situation slightly alleviated by a grant of £300 from the Civil List accorded to Mrs Byron to assist the boy's education. Surrounded by richer, and nimbler, young noblemen, he resorted to bluff as a necessary part of his performance: he had the manner but not yet the means, or the standing, appropriate to his station.

He proved a clever but not a diligent pupil. The classical education, despite the tedium of rote learning, did not lack appeal for a boy with his knack for rhetorical conceits. Byron's first poetic essays are associated with another innocent passion, for his first cousin, Margaret Parker, whom he idealized as 'one of the most beautiful of evanescent beings', but a discovered talent for mimicking Latin poets may have prompted his 'effusions' as much as any spontaneous passion: Byron's early work shows not a few signs of those precocious tropes which are designed to impress the examiner quite as much as the beloved. His adolescent style is sometimes sweet, but it is rarely artless; his feelings may have been genuine, the expression of them was often derivative. The verses of the young classical scholar are not expected to be either truthful or sincere: it is enough if they scan properly and pay homage to accepted masters. In the classics, deference to tradition counts for more than innovation. Byron's public school education inhibited a wholehearted flight into Romanticism.

His admiration for Margaret Parker's beauty was in sublime contrast with the earthier feelings May Gray had awakened. Having observed the power she had over her young charge after the silly Mrs Byron had deputed her to accompany him to London, Hanson eventually saw to it that the wayward servant girl was dispatched home to Scotland. Before she finished, however, May had instructed Byron not only in what happened between a man and a woman in bed, but also in the duplicity he so habitually and so conveniently wished on the female sex: it is not surprising that May took an adult lover as well as her boyish comforter, but she is said to have responded to Byron's complaints of betrayal by beating him black and blue. The evanescent Margaret was a chaste contrast to the muscular servant girl and Byron was happy to be unhappy in her distant contemplation. When she took evanescence to the limit by dying, the mournful Byron resumed his attentions to Mary Chaworth.

1. Castle Street, Aberdeen, in 1812.
'My cap was the bonnet, my cloak was the plaid.'

2. Byron and his mother.
'And thus, untaught in youth my heart to tame,
My springs of life were poisoned.'

3. 'Childe Harold had a mother.'

4. Captain John ('Mad Jack')
Byron, the poet's father.

5. Admiral The Hon. John Byron
(1723–86), the poet's grandfather.
After a painting by Reynolds.

6. *The lame brat; Byron at seven.*

7. *The only treatment.*

8. *The Old Grammar School, Aberdeen, as it was in Byron's time.*

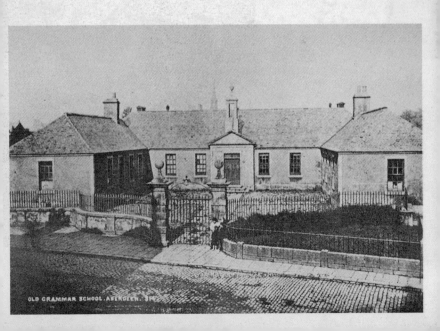

OLD GRAMMAR SCHOOL, ABERDEEN. 317

9. *Byron at Harrow, aged thirteen.*
'And friendships were formed, too romantic to last.'

10. Mary Chaworth.
*'A touch of hers, his
blood would ebb and flow.'*

11. Annesley Hall, the
Chaworth home.
*'And on the summit of
that hill she stood.'*

ANNESLEY HALL.

THE RESIDENCE OF MISS CHAWORTH

GRANDE SALLE, D'ANNESLEY.

LA RESIDENCE DE MISS CHAWORTH

12. The Big Schoolroom, Harrow.
'I will carve myself the passage to Grandeur . . .'

13. Byron's Elm, 'Spot of my youth!' Harrow Churchyard.
'Again I behold where for hours I have ponder'd.'

14. Neville's Court, Trinity College, Cambridge.
'We have eternal parties here.'

15. Byron, c.1804. Augusta wrote on the back of it:
'This miniature of my poor brother was the last token and given me on my birthday.'

16. 'I got 11 notches the 1st innings and 7 the 2nd.'

Annesley was only a good gallop away from Newstead and he often rode over to the Hall for company and pistol practice. Mrs Clarke was always welcoming, Mary often amiable. He would never forget an expedition to Derbyshire during which he and his pretty, no longer distant cousin were obliged to lie prone together in the bottom of a small boat while they were ferried under a low lintel of rock. A certain Jack Musters, who was considerably older than Byron, was also of the party, but it was Byron who pressed his body against the girl's as they flattened themselves under the overhang. 'You're trembling,' she teased. 'Not from fear,' he replied.

He was hardly the first young man to experience the sly panic of adolescence, the inadvertent touches, the gleaming glances, the exhilaration and disappointment in which desire and high-mindedness, exaltation and fretfulness were mingled, but he retained an exceptionally vivid impression of them. It is one of the oddities of Byron's life that comparatively little of it was out of the ordinary, though much was extraordinarily exaggerated by the rhetoric of his responses. The vividness of his reaction is often more remarkable than his experience; what would have grazed another drew blood from him. Not until Proust did another great writer make so much of what to a commonplace mind could well have passed for commonplace. His subject was always himself, not so much because he was egocentric as because *how* he experienced things was for him indistinguishable from the experience itself. (In this his 'philosophy' synchronized with that of Bishop Berkeley and David Hume.)

He had piqued Mary Chaworth with his very first words to her and there remained between them that flyting, flighty contest not uncommon among adolescents, at least until the eclipse of chaperones and chastity. He had promised Mary, as the stream took command of their little boat, that he would save her if they capsized. The Byron crest was supported by a chestnut horse and a mermaid: his Lordship sat a horse well enough and he was never lame in the water.

Harrow, at first, was as disagreeable as anything Mr Lavender had devised. The club-foot attracted those gibes at which schoolboys, especially those from the best homes, are always adept. Byron showed defiant courage: he not only defended himself, he was also the champion of other small boys whose education began, in the great British tradition, with humiliation. He earned and treasured their affection; many years later, on the road between Venice and Pisa, he would meet one of them, Lord Clare, for the last time. The overwhelming strength of his feelings, after such an interval, proves his capacity for retaining the flavours of the past. 'Friend of my youth! when young we roved/Like striplings mutually beloved . . .' sounds like a middle-aged lament, but the jejune lines about Clare were actually written (in imitation of Valerius Flaccus) when youth was still upon him. The fugitive sense of life made the apostle of youth into a premature sentimentalist, already looking back even when life was before him and already lamenting the loss of what he had yet to lose. Byron's constant unwillingness to throw things away (apart from women), his penchant for memorabilia, his tendency to live fast but to hoard the savour of every moment, fill even the apparently mundane corners of his life with a mournful intensity.

Despite Clare's status as 'Harmonious favourite of the Nine!', Byron's passion for Mary Chaworth grew so commanding that at the end of the summer holidays of 1803 he refused to go back to Harrow. One day, he wangled an invitation to stay overnight at Annesley by claiming that he was afraid once again of meeting a 'bogle' on the way home. He told the impressed (or merely straight-faced) Mary that bogles were spirits that cannot find their rest; just the kind of nocturnal revenant a Byron might expect to have to confront. What he did not expect was to overhear Mary's maid asking her mistress whether she was in love with her young visitor, to which the girl was heard to reply, 'What, do you think I could feel anything for that lame boy?' Hindsight could argue that her remark was possibly one more move in the taunting play between Montagu and Capulet which Byron himself had initiated. Was she being any more cruel than schoolboys who jeer at the unfortunate for the curious pleasure of seeing whether they can take it? But if Byron was usually slick with repartee, he could not now either see the joke or pass an appropriate jest. Mary may or may not have loved him, she may or may not have known that he was behind the door; the quick of the situation is beyond recall, though Byron often recalled it. Her words were unforgivable and he fled into the night, never to return. One day, too late, she would come after him.

He went back to Harrow. What had started as a harsh trial now began to offer the pleasures of friendship, and the safe perils of schoolboy rebellions: who could be surprised that when some Harrovians mounted an uprising against their headmaster, Byron was among them? But his genius for striking heroic or impertinent attitudes rarely drove him to harbour a grudge or to maintain a pose for very long. He was soon reconciled to Dr Drury who, whatever the shortcomings of his régime, intelligently defused Byron's Jacobinism by dosing him with sherry and alert flattery. Drury recognized the boy's talent and was not too mature to be amused by his immaturity. From the very first day he had seen him as 'a wild mountain colt' and had decided to lead him 'by a silken string', a programme he had the consistency to maintain and which earned him the respectful, if bucking allegiance of his pupil. Byron's affectations of solitary doom (conspicuously enacted on the Peachey stone, on top of a tomb in the little churchyard adjacent to the main school from which today one may enjoy a wide view of suburban Wembley) did not preclude enjoyment of his last term at Harrow: he revelled in patronizing the ducal 'shavers' like Lord Dorset to whom he addressed some lines as mawkish as any in the language. Despite his abnormalities, he was a normal enough school-boy. He even obtained a place in the cricket eleven against the 'Eton' in the year of Trafalgar. By then he had befriended sufficient members of the aristocracy to be confident of his social position. Robert Peel, the future Prime Minister, was a contemporary whose name appears close to Byron's, carved in the dark panelling of the big schoolroom. If Byron's penchant for self-advertisement is confirmed by the evidence of his name in several places, Peel's ambition advertises itself in the outsize lettering of his sole inscription.

The affection which Byron came to feel for Harrow was in contrast to the dismay with which he now regarded events at Newstead. Though she remained in residence, financial necessity obliged his mother to let the place to Lord Grey de Ruthyn, a young man of dissolute style. The latter not only behaved insolently and amorously towards Mrs Byron but, when Byron himself came home for the holidays, apparently made a gross pass at the handsome boy. One cannot be sure whether Byron's bisexuality was awakened (as he later intimated) by de Ruthyn's knowing assault or whether he was already aware of it from the homosexual habits not unknown in single sex boarding schools even within living memory. The most disagreeable thing about the tenant of Newstead may well have been his manners rather than his morals, but his presence undoubtedly served temporarily to banish the magic from the property. Luckily, there was another great and good place to which to repair. In the autumn of 1805, Byron went up to Trinity College, Cambridge. He had intended to go to Christ Church, Oxford, but no place was available.

At the Eton and Harrow match during that same summer, at Mr Lord's cricket ground in Dorset Square, he renewed what till then had been a distant acquaintance with his half-sister, Augusta, now a ringleted charmer, more perky than beautiful perhaps, and about to be married to her cousin, Colonel George Leigh, the owner of an uncommonly fine house at Six Mile Bottom, near Cambridge. The Colonel was often nearer Newmarket than his house was, for he was addicted to race-horses. As far as the cricket was concerned, Byron did not play a particularly distinguished innings (Harrow were most confoundedly beat), but – batting with a runner – he had the satisfaction of making more 'notches' than the chap directly above him in the order, a boy called Shakespeare. 'Oh such were the days which my infancy knew!'

Augusta's easy humour delighted her brother (or rather half-brother, though half measures are hard to maintain where Byron is concerned) and their familiar banter was untainted by any sexual complications: Augusta was neither a fool like Mrs Byron nor a tease like Mary Chaworth. Byron could be skittish and lugubrious by turns and all Augusta did was laugh. What more did he ever want in a female, unless it was the love Mary had denied him? Well, there were things, of course, and he was soon to find them in the ladies of the town. He was always prone to behave as fashion required, especially when it was badly. Modish debauchery never went against his grain; he was drawn to the cult of the dandy, though he always risked being too plump for the tightest exigencies of elegance. At Cambridge he preened himself in the special gown to which peers of the realm alone were entitled. He had super-excellent rooms in Neville's Court, Trinity, and was untroubled by any systematic course of study. His appetite for books could easily be satisfied by the proximity of the Wren Library at the end of the court overlooking the Cam, where his blanched statue can now be seen, pensive pen to marble chin, though there is no record of frequent visits to it. (He later claimed to have read 4,000 novels, but he would not have found them in College.) He stocked himself with the best provisions a wine merchant could supply, on credit, and proceeded to make new friendships, though it was not until his second year that he found a congenial set. At first he was rather short of company, apart from an Old Harrovian chum, Francis Noel Long, to whom he was particularly attached. Having shucked the layered society of Harrow, he recreated something very like a master-fag relationship with a Trinity Choir School boy, John Edleston, whom his aquatic agility rescued from drowning in the river.

Byron always maintained that his and Edleston's friendship was 'passionate, but *pure*'. If sexual favours were asked, or granted, they were not the only ones. Edleston may have recognized a good thing when he saw one (Byron was generous with tips), but he was not merely on the make. One day, Byron was touched when it was his turn to receive a gift and he was later pleased to compose some frankly sentimental lines about the cornelian heart the choirboy gave him. As they took tea and buns in Byron's expensively decorated rooms, Edleston may have been surprised to see a bust of Napoleon in a place of honour. England's war with France did not inhibit his lordship's early admiration for his 'little Pagod'; indeed it gave it a smart touch of heterodoxy, the most consistent of all Byron's doxies. The blissful dawn which had thrilled the young Wordsworth still enlightened the dreams of those who sided with Fox rather than with Pitt. Byron looked forward to the discomfiture of the Tories and the advent of a more progressive social order, assuming always that lordly robes could still be worn. His admiration for Napoleon may also have owed something to such gestures as the parade of ancient gods which attended the Emperor's triumph; Buonaparte was an apostatic apostle of the new who, like Byron, liked to strike archaizing attitudes. The causes of liberty and of self-advancement were wonderfully reconciled in the career of the iconoclast who became an icon.

Byron declared Cambridge to be a conspiracy to put excessive flesh on a man's bones and idleness in his heart; an early collection of unremarkable juvenilia was entitled *Hours Of Idleness*. In his spare time, Edleston was deputed to bowl to him. Before swinging the bat, his lordship – ever afraid of corpulence – put on a wealth of waistcoats, with a top coat over them, to induce a slimming sweat. Cambridge, he observed, tolerated any indulgence, but scholarship was a vice to be practised, if at all, in secret. The sensualist is often shocked by the sensuality of others. Like many rebels, Byron may be suspected of craving the discipline of strong masters, or mistresses, and perhaps most of all he craved the firm dominion of the all-powerful God whose omnipotence – and existence – he doubted. When others took scepticism too far, he was not above calling them damned atheists. His unconventional gestures were excited not least by a barely concealed respect for convention, if also by the desire to test its authority. Impertinence is often deference in the form of a snook. Wit itself depends on there being a limit, or how shall one overstep it?

Just before he went up to Cambridge, Mrs Byron told him that she had some news: Mary Chaworth was married. He took it as he had the ministrations of those whom she had hired to twist his foot. ('Is that all?' he said, and went very pale.) If she hoped that her news might bring him closer to her, she scarcely chose the most tactful means of breaking it. Mrs Byron had removed to Southwell, a few miles from Newstead, having abandoned the latter to Lord Grey de Ruthyn, whose attentions to her were too shocking (or too infrequent?) to be endured. At first, Byron found an agreeably Arcadian refuge among the inhabitants of the small town, dominated by its magnificent, honey-coloured cathedral in the shadow of which he encountered the nicest kind of provincial society: pretty girls, intelligent clerics and domestic comforts. The Pigot family was particularly welcoming. Their daughter, Elizabeth, was one of the first of a series of older women, ineligible either for marriage or for dalliance, on whose encouragement he was able undoubtingly to rely. However, Mrs Byron's incompatibility with the habits of the Byron males soon declared itself and, pursued by her nagging, he fled the chaste charms of Southwell ('now the place I abhor') in favour of *louche* metropolitan attractions. He was not short of bad examples: the young aristocracy took little seriously apart from its frivolities. During his now frequent absences from Cambridge, he immersed himself eagerly in hot water. Byron always maintained that he preferred the intensity of what the modern cant calls meaningful relationships, but he proved precipitate in slaking adolescent appetites. His sexual gluttony was marked enough for even a seasoned French procuress to advise him to season ardour with delicacy. Initiation into the joys of what the French call *plaisirs tarifiés* seems to have been without traumatic consequence, however much it jarred his higher sensibilities; he celebrated his newly acquired carnal knowledge in some explicitly appreciative stanzas about 'love's extatic posture' which might be expected, or even designed, to scandalize the Reverend John Thomas Becher of Southwell, and his parishioners, when they read them in the privately printed little volume Byron entitled *Fugitive Pieces*, his first manifest, over-myrtled advertisement for himself. Even at this early stage the 'infant' poet can be observed worrying about his auburn hair thinning to silver: the cult of youth begins with the dread of age.

Byron not only savoured Piccadilly trollops, he also learnt boxing from the famous pugilist 'Gentleman' Jackson (lesson one was the unsubtle maxim, 'Mill away right and left') and took fencing instruction at Henry Angelo's Rooms, number 13 Bond Street, where fashionable bucks quizzed the passers-by and compared debts. Byron was prompt to adhere to the mode of mortgaging oneself to the Jews. If he was later to be the author of *Hebrew Melodies* and a friend of their composer Isaac Nathan, as well as something of a Zionist *avant la lettre*, he was as scornful as any man of fashion towards those whose cash he did not scruple to borrow, not that the Regency money-lenders, to judge from names like Thomas Riley, were all of Semitic origin. Mrs Byron, outraged by his extravagance, finally prevailed on her son to return to what she assumed to be the cloistered propriety of Cambridge. His absences had grown so prolonged that his rooms had been re-allocated to the brilliant and witty C. S. Matthews, who disarmed the returning tenant's indignation by declaring his apprehension of what their tutor had described as Byron's 'tumultuous passions'. Matthews' homosexuality, no less than his free-thinking opinions, may have endeared him to Byron, not because they were lovers but because they were in the same camp. Matthews and his circle, which included the earnest, ambitious John Cam Hobhouse (Byron's lifelong, unlikely familiar) and the stammering Etonian dandy Scrope Berdmore Davies, a fellow of King's and a gambler by addiction and necessity, made light of Byron's satanic pretensions and dubbed him 'the old English Baron'. The others liked to provoke the slower Hobhouse, whose Whiggish opinions and satirical compositions did not preclude a decorous attitude to religion. For all this new intellectual stimulus, Byron's flashy side was undimmed: he kept a coach and pair and acquired a Newfoundland dog, which he brought into College. Reminded that the statutes specifically forbade canine company, he is said to have paraded a bear before the outraged Fellows. He declared that he had brought the beast up to sit for a Fellowship: it was not specifically forbidden, was it? Joke over, he boarded the animal out, the first of many outlandish creatures for whose dumb affections he had an unusually soft spot: he was happy to bait the dons with his bear, but bear-baiting at least was wholly foreign to his taste.

If his return to Cambridge resulted in enduring friendships, it did not itself last very long. Mrs Byron was horrified, but powerless, when once again he found London and the moneylenders irresistible. He put up at Dorant's Hotel and renewed his expensive subscription to the delights of the town. He returned to Cambridge later to collect his M.A., but there is no evidence that it was preceded by any formal test of his intellectual credentials. 'Thoughts Suggested By A College Examination,' however, show that he did not wholly neglect the curriculum and they contain a nice jibe at academics: '. . . Prizing Bentley's, Brunck's or Porson's note,/More than the verse on which the critic wrote.' Yeats, on Catullus, made the same point more than a century later: too much scholarly attention suffocates the very poetry it affects to treasure.

Caroline, Byron's first fully-fledged mistress – not to be confused with Lady Caroline Lamb, who was neither his first nor his last – had a trim figure, at least at the beginning of their association, and it amused them to pass her off, in boy's clothing, as his brother when he took her on an excursion to the Prince Regent's glittering Brighton. Rumoured to have paid a hundred pounds to ransom her from the life of a common tart, he grew fond of her, though he probably more postponed than averted her commercial career. If the saucy couple had a good giggle on the fringes of smart society, they were denied the entrée to its stylish centre. Byron affected the sneering hauteur of those not quite at the top: society, he proclaimed, was the four thousand persons who stayed up when everyone else was in bed and who stayed in bed when everyone else was up. He kept their hours; he was hardly yet of their number.

Beau Brummell, the least dumb of tailors' dummies, is unlikely to have given Byron's new clothes an enfranchising glance from the window of White's (a place to be seen in, no less than to see from). The dandies had succeeded, for a precious season, in making the cut of a man's coat more important than the blueness of his blood. No *arbiter elegantiarum* was ever more superbly or more perilously poised than Brummell. By the time Byron himself became the most modish (though never quite the best dressed) celebrity in St James's Street, if not in all England, the almost bankrupt Brummell, having quarrelled with the Prince Regent, was reduced to a reach-me-down remnant. Soon he was heading for exile in Mad Jack's old refuge, dun-free France. Yet Brummell's fastidiously impertinent style left its mark on Byron. What enviable folly to have called out to Lord Alvanley, as he was being spoken to by the Prince Regent who had just cut Brummell, 'Alvanley, who is your fat friend?' To rise to the height of fame and favour and to throw it all away with one reckless quip, what could be more stylish than that?

By and by, the androgynous Caroline proved that her sex was, after all, unambiguous: she was pregnant. Byron is alleged always to have carried a contraceptive in his top pocket (not the kind of utilitarian bulge Brummell was likely to tolerate), though it must be said that it was rarely a very effective one: his sword outwore its scabbard with inconvenient regularity. Caroline's condition did not excite in Byron that calculated cold-heartedness which a seasoned Regency blade might have considered appropriate: his Cambridge friends heard with alarm that he had declared himself ready to marry the girl, and with relief that it was no longer necessary. Caroline miscarried and her hopes of an aristocratic connection did not long survive: Byron bid his best belov'd adieu, counselled forgetfulness and was quick to take his own advice. His sugary farewell to Caroline found its place in the next slim volume and that was that.

Authorship at this point was a matter of vanity, not of royalties: no member of the upper class, however poetic or penurious, could deign to soil himself with anything that smacked of literary trade. Only grubby fellows like the Irish poet Tom Moore composed for cash, hence perhaps the sneers the young Byron directed towards his immorality. For a gentleman, the only acceptable way of repaying one's debts was to contract new ones. Byron was now nearly twenty-one and he assumed that the attainment of his majority would release new funds and bring about a cheering change in his financial circumstances. Mr Hanson was deputed to disencumber his Rochdale estate (rich in coal-mines) from the mortgaged mess in which the Wicked Lord's high-handedness had landed it, and to procure a shower of gold by its early sale. Men like Scrope Davies were obliged to gamble if they were ever to make enough money to live like the lords they chose to emulate and even patronize, but Byron had no talent for gaming and was ready enough to settle his debts and live on his revenues, though it was to be a long time before such an option became fully available to him.

The publication of *Hours of Idleness* was intended to announce Byron's entrance into the literary arena. He was galled by its largely contemptuous reception. Naively, he had relied on his Whig sympathies to secure him a good press at least in the *Edinburgh Review*, but either his opinions had not reached the reviewer before his verses, or they failed to seduce him. The anonymous critic (later identified as Henry Brougham) declared that 'the poesy of this young lord belongs to the class which neither men or Gods are said to permit: his effusions are spread over a dead flat and can no more get above or below the level than if they were so much stagnant water.' Byron was later to scorn John Keats's supposed inability to take a critical lashing without crying out, but his claims to have taken his own medicine without whimpering scarcely square with reports that he was loudly contemplating suicide, the self-dramatizer's revenge. Alternatively, he announced that he would go mad. Cambridge friends like Scrope Davies declared that his problem sounded more like silliness than madness and Byron's frantic pistol was indeed levelled at no more mortal target than the bottle-tops he liked to remove with a bang. It would, he decided, take more than 'paper bullets of the brain' to put paid to the old English baron and he proceeded to mill away right and left with a lively volume entitled *English Bards, and Scotch Reviewers*. If he could not yet join the charmed circles, he could at least try to give them a licking. Though he identified his Edinburgh critic wrongly as Francis Jeffrey, with whom he was later reconciled, he made not a few palpable hits. What maligned author would not applaud the suggestion that critics have a mind 'skilled to find, or forge a fault'? Alone at Newstead once more, he penned some quick quips that have not lost their snap: 'Care not for feeling – pass your proper jest/And stand a critic, hated yet caress'd'. The solitary, often sozzled, loafer toyed with drowning himself in an underground pool in the abbey precincts, but could not finally resist staying alive long enough at least to see what the *Edinburgh Review* made of his riposte. He sighed that he had not a friend in the world, but he knew very well that Hobhouse and company would not fail his feast. In the autumn of 1808, they joined him in the partly refurnished mansion, from which Lord de Ruthyn had finally removed himself.

They found Byron in mourning, no longer for himself but for Boatswain, his Newfoundland dog, for whom he composed a winsome epitaph. His friends attended its consecration, hooded and cowled in monkish robes in which, before and after the amorous pursuit of female domestics, they chose to garb themselves. Hobhouse played the parson and intoned, 'Here lies Bo'sun, a dog,' after which C. S. Matthews tripped him and announced, 'Here lies Hobhouse, a pig!' In the evening came claret and horseplay. Byron had acquired a new page from among the tenantry, Robert Rushton, who poured wine into the skull which Byron had had mounted as a drinking cup. ('In me behold the only skull/From which unlike a living head/Whatever flows is never dull.') The young shaver slept in the room next to Byron's coroneted and canopied apartment. A new lightweight but fairly entertaining friend had accompanied the old Cambridge chums, James Wedderburn Webster, nicknamed 'Bold', whose goatish appetite for the 'Paphian' servant-girls presaged a farcical episode in later years.

Blasphemous lightheartedness could not entirely banish satanic gloom. Byron talked of ending up by marrying a 'Golden Dolly' or blowing his brains out; they amounted to much the same self-destructive thing. Hobhouse assured him that he had it within his power to achieve much more than that, but such assurances only goaded him to seek further flattery by insisting that he was a lost soul. His friend retorted that he did not believe in lost souls, whereupon the mischievous Matthews frightened John Cam half to death by rising, sheeted and shrieking, from an antique sarcophagus on Hobhouse's dark and draughty way to bed. Before the Cambridge circus had left Byron to pass the remainder of the time until January, and his twenty-first birthday, in the mournful if not wholly monkish contemplation of the cavernous abbey, he and Hobhouse had made a compact to go on their travels in the New Year, if they could raise the wind.

His twenty-first birthday, 22 January 1809, brought no remarkable improvement in his circumstances, but the planned tour of the Mediterranean had become an obsession: he had to get away, though it was not quite clear what from, unless it was his creditors. A winter in Newstead was perhaps harsh enough reason to yearn for warmer skies. To mark his majority, he came to London and took his seat in the House of Lords, though he refrained from speaking. Disappointed in his hopes for an early end to his financial problems, he now set about adding to them. If Hanson failed to disgorge any new funds, new debts were easily arranged. A noble gesture, the gift of £500 to the widow of a Harrovian friend, Lord Falkland, who had been killed in a duel, was covered by further indebtedness to a money-lender. Money from less extortionate sources was damnably slow in coming. Hanson raised a couple of thousand at last and then there was a windfall of more than twice that sum from an unlikely source: Scrope Davies had been solicited for a loan, but he was as broke as John Cam (who had temporarily fallen out with his father) or as Byron himself, until one night in London, gambling at clubs such as the Union, the Cocoa Tree and Almack's, he had a prodigious run of luck. The friends found him, dead drunk, beside a chamber pot brimming with winnings. Legend promises that a note was pinned to the snoring Scrope's lapel: 'Take what you want, but don't wake me up.' More punctilious sources, like T. A. J. Burnett, in his *The Rise and Fall of a Regency Dandy*, an invaluable study of Scrope Davies, tell a more prosaic tale of Byron's indebtedness to Scrope, but it is certain that Scrope did largely fund Byron's excursion and was markedly generous in awaiting repayment. It is a pretty subject for literary speculation to wonder how *Childe Harold* would have turned out had Scrope himself, wit and punster, been Byron's travelling companion. Perhaps they would have had such a hilarious time that the poem would never have been written at all.

At the end of June, Byron, Hobhouse, old Joe Murray, young Robert Rushton and William Fletcher, who was to be Byron's Sam Weller for the rest of his life, set off for Falmouth to board the Lisbon packet. While they waited for the right tide, Byron wrote to his old housemaster, Henry Drury, Dr Drury's son, that he was proposing to contribute a chapter to Hobhouse's new book which was to be entitled 'Sodomy simplified or Paederasty proved to be praiseworthy from ancient authors and modern practice.' Hobhouse, he went on to say, 'further hopes to indemnify himself in Turkey for a life of exemplary chastity at home by letting out his "fair bodye" to the whole Divan.' If the allusions to homosexuality were a confession in the form of jocularity, Byron also had time to boast to C. S. Matthews, the wit who stayed behind, that

Falmouth was not short of the more usual sort of coital opportunities. They also saw a woman flogged at the cart's tail, a local diversion. On 2 July 1809, the *Princess Elizabeth* stood out for Lisbon.

Childe Harold's Pilgrimage was to make almost every step of the friends' fairly Grand Tour into the stuff of best-selling legend. The image of the doomed youth, cursed with some congenital blight and obliged to go into exile in order to purge it, loads the comparative banality of tourism with the hectic chiaroscuro of a Romantic illustration. In commonplace fact, Byron and Hobhouse were proceeding in privileged comfort (the sea was rough, but the crossing swift) to a peninsula where not a few of their fellow-countrymen were still fighting a long and cruel war. Sir Arthur Wellesley, not yet the Duke of Wellington, was slogging his way towards Madrid, in command of the scum of the earth. The British Army had saved Portugal without wholly pacifying it. When Byron and Hobhouse went sightseeing to beetling Cintra, they were advised to beware of bandits and marauders. Tourism was thus spiced with dangers, without proving dangerous.

The Moorish palace of Monserrat impressed Byron with its outlandish beauty but he found the Portuguese an insanitary race. Hobhouse, who had brought prodigious amounts of paper, a hundred pens and two gallons of Japan ink, was diligent with his diary. Byron had shipped out a positive library, including fifty volumes of Parliamentary debates as well as *Gulliver's Travels*, Dallas's *Constantinople* and Barrow's *China* (one never knew, presumably, how far one might eventually go), twenty-five volumes of *British Theatre*, Gifford's *Baviad* and *Maeviad* and *Elegant Extracts*, an anthology that included Spenser's *Faerie Queene*. Wisely, he still saw himself as an apprentice. *Robinson Crusoe* was another of his books: the chronicle of the great solitary whom he was often to affect to envy, with his cry, 'I wish I were in mine island.'

Byron swam the estuary of the Tagus (more impressive, in Hobhouse's view, than his later heroic crossing of the Hellespont) and then the two friends ventured across country, *hidalgos* on horseback, to Sevilla, leaving the servants, their considerable wardrobe and the library to go on to Gibraltar by sea. The handsome white houses and the beautiful dark girls of Sevilla delighted them. They took modest lodgings with a couple of tantalizingly immodest (but never profligate) Spanish ladies, the frankness of whose admiration did no harm to Byron's vanity. The bullfight so zestfully described in *Childe Harold* took place in Cádiz, though Byron was a good deal more sickened than his chosen metre and dégagé tone obliged him to maintain. If the cruelty to the horses (in those days neither padded nor doctored to appease the tourist's conscience) was repugnant to him, he could not deny the charm of the plangent ritual or of blanched Cádiz itself, a clean contrast with scruffy Gibraltar which they reached early in August, having boarded a Royal Navy frigate, the *Hyperion*, for the short voyage past Cape Trafalgar. At Gibraltar it became obvious that Joe Murray could not, and Robert Rushton should not, accompany them any further. Old Murray was now more suited to boating on the lake at Newstead than to seafaring, while young Rushton was too pretty to be exposed to the lascivious Turk, to whose domains they were bound. Fletcher would gladly have gone home with the others; abroad was not to his taste and he was recently married. When, in due course, Byron was to point to a distant shore and observe, 'That is Greece, are you content?' the unromantic valet would reply: 'I shall not be content, my lord, until *that* is England.' He would have quite a wait.

First, however, they headed for Malta, where there was a British presence: ships and society and a famous beauty, Mrs Constance Spencer Smith, who was alleged to have been courted by Napoleon. When the Military Commander's A.D.C. smirked at Byron's susceptibility to the lady, a duel was mooted, though an apology averted pistols at dawn. Constance was a little older and a lot more experienced than Byron and she had the wit to lead him on while giving the impression that he was well ahead of her. A hectic romance was in prospect, if not consummated. Byron blamed the outbreak of peace for the curtailment of their fugitive plans: they had talked of eloping to Friuli, which now fell into French and hence unwelcoming hands. It is hard to estimate how important this 'everlasting passion' really was to Byron, or to the lady, but it neither damaged his confidence nor long impeded his eastward progress. Though he eventually was to say of her (as of so many), 'The spell is broke, the charm is flown', Constance lent a touch of class to his amorous experience and gave him a deceptive impression of the undemanding poise which a woman of standing could bring to such dalliance.

Byron and Hobhouse sailed for the Greek coast aboard the *Spider*, a brig-of-war escorting some British merchant ships bound for Patras, the big entrepôt on the north-west shore of the Peloponnese. Almost opposite it, across the Bay of Lepanto, Byron was able to see, on his very first day in Greek waters, the low-lying town of Missolonghi, from which his body would be brought back, fifteen years later, to England. From Patras, they coasted north along the Adriatic to Prevesa, on the Bay of Actium, where they disembarked for the ride up to Janina.

Byron seems to have felt at home (or happily *not* at home) the minute he set foot on Greek soil. When he felt insecure, he consoled himself by donning proconsular finery and was almost at once drenched by a cloudburst for his plumed pains. An exaggerated sense of his own importance (the failure of the Maltese authorities to salute his rank had considerably vexed him) led him to imagine that an English peerage would open every door and redden every carpet. However naive his expectations, they were not infrequently met, though not always for the reasons he assumed. If he and Hobhouse were handsome travellers, with their cumbrous baggage and their look-who's-here uniforms, they also paid handsomely for the hungry deference they enjoyed. Byron was disposed to accept the Greek style somewhat more tolerantly than his friend, who wrote copiously and complained vociferously, in much the same tones as Fletcher, despite having left no pretty Sally behind him.

Outside Prevesa, the travellers passed through the unimpressive ruins of Nicopolis, the city Augustus had founded to celebrate his victory over Antony and Cleopatra at Actium in 31 BC. If Byron was moved by seeing in three ruined dimensions the vestiges of the classical world which he had studied so flatly on the page at Harrow, he gave no literary indication of it. The local sights and sounds (the sheep bells, the frogs, the native accents) excited him more than traces of imperial grandeur. The decline of Greece to a state of servility appealed to his condescending sense of irony, but he was never tempted to the pedestrian pieties of map-in-hand archaeology. He revelled in what was colourful and vivid; solemn accuracies he left to Hobhouse, his pens and Japan ink.

The tourists advanced into the Pindus mountains and arrived, after no easy trek, at Janina in early October 1809. The domes and minarets of Ali Pasha's capital, its orange and lemon trees, its sconced setting beside the islanded Lake Pambotis, the mountains towering over its northern shore, were beguiling indeed, though the harsh facts of quotidian life under the Turks were brought home, as they entered the city, by the sight of a human arm hanging from a tree, brutal advertisement of what happened to those who crossed their picturesque rulers. The arm was all that remained of a Greek patriot called Evtinnio. He had been tortured for three months after conspiring against Ali Pasha until he was at last quartered and hung in the four plane trees at the entrance to the city, *pour encourager les autres*. Ali Pasha was pleased to be called 'the Mohametan Napoleon', but if he aped Buonaparte in military efficiency, he exceeded him in cruelty. Theoretically, he held his authority from the Sultan at Constantinople but he was as ambitious as he was autocratic and, Albanian-born, he was bent on creating a separate kingdom. He combined tactical agility with shameless diplomacy, while his local birth and his remoteness from the Sublime Porte, whose emissaries he scorned and even murdered, gave him the taste for independence which led eventually to his downfall. When the Greeks finally rose against the Sultan, Ali Pasha took his chance to follow the same course, though scarcely for the same motives. In 1822, he was unlucky enough to be defeated by a loyal Turkish force before the Turks were themselves evicted from Greece. He fled to the island monastery of St Pantaleimon which he had converted into a harem, and was there shot to death. Kyra Frossyni, the local folk heroine whom (among many others) Ali Pasha was said to have raped and then drowned in Lake Pambotis, was thus appropriately avenged.

However, as the Cambridge men arrived in Janina, nothing seemed less questionable than Ali Pasha's authority. The sly despot nevertheless deemed it prudent to keep in with any representatives of the British, whose hold on the Ionian islands gave them considerable local influence. A certain Captain William Leake was the courteous and vigilant British resident in Janina. When Byron and Hobhouse rode on into Albania, where the white-bearded, hot-blooded autocrat was 'finishing a small war', they were received with ingratiating ceremony. Remote and minareted Tepelene was garish with an army picturesque enough for Delacroix: Albanians in white kilts and gold-laced jackets, Tartars in high caps, turbaned Turks, their glaring horses attended by black slaves. Drums were beating, the muezzin called from the minarets of the mosque; an operatic throb of adventure was in the air.

17. Byron in travelling costume.
'And e'en for change of scene would seek the shades below.'

18. 'If there be any gemman so ignorant as to require as traduction, I refer him to my old friend and corporeal pastor and master, John Jackson, Esq., Professor of Pugilism.'

19. High Life at Almack's, seen by I.R. and George Cruikshank, 1823.

20. The House of Lords where, according to Sir Francis Burdett, Byron made 'The best speech by a lord since "The Lord knows when".'

HIGHEST LIFE IN LONDON. Tom & Jerry "Sporting a Toe," among the Corinthians, at Almacks in the West.

21. Newstead Abbey.
'In this print may be traced the profiles of the late Lord Byron, Ada [Lord Byron's daughter], Theresa, the Maid of Athens, and the Countess Guiccioli.'

22. Byron's bedroom at Newstead Abbey. 'Monastic dome! condemn'd to uses vile!'

23. 'Here lies Boatswain, a dog.'

24. The young Boatswain, erect, 1803, from a painting by Clifton Thomson.

25. 'Prepare for rhyme – I'll publish, right or wrong!'

26. *The Temple of Poseidon, Sounion.
'Where'er we tread 'tis haunted, holy
ground.'*

27. *The Capuchin Monastery, Athens.
'We have nothing but riot from noon till
night.'*

28. *'I hate a vandal worse than a critic.'
Byron inscribed his name on the temple at
Sounion in 1810.*

29. *'Maid of Athens, ere we part,
Give, oh give me back my heart!'*

30. Byron at the court of
Ali Pasha.
'Here men of every clime
appear to make resort.'

31. Byron resting in a
fisherman's house after
having swum the
Hellespont. Detail of a
painting by Sir William
Allan, 1831.
'What maid will not the
tale remember?'

The travellers had ridden through thunder storms and sheltered in cow-stalls, passed the gorgeous cataract of Zitza and dallied in the remote convent (monastery) of St Elias, where the poverty of the people had not stinted their welcome. If Ali Pasha was already disposed to be courtly, Byron seems in addition genuinely, even embarrassingly, to have taken the old scoundrel's fancy. Ali declared that, even if he had not been told of it, he would have known Byron to be of great family, merely at the sight of his small ears, curling hair and fine white hands.

The Pasha further confided that he was very partial to Englishmen: he particularly loved English sailors. When he solicited Byron to visit him at night (they would then have more time), the dormitory invitation was ducked with politeness and difficulty. On the other hand, Byron was glad to give a good report of his reception at Janina by the despot's grandson, Hussein, who was twelve years old but had a dark-eyed gravity that appealed to Byron's taste for the pubescent. (The dusky lad had wanted to know how someone as young as Byron could travel so far from his own country 'with no one to look after him.') When the friends left Ali Pasha's capital, there was a ritual exchange of gifts in the Homeric style. Byron presented the tyrant with a gun and a telescope; in return, he received a gold-embroidered tunic and a jewelled headdress. The Englishmen were also provided with a kirtled Albanian escort whose leader's head depended on their safe journey. Byron was flattered by the tyrant's favours even as he deplored his tyranny.

Before the party took the long, steep road through the passes from Janina back down to Prevesa, Byron had started work on the poem which was to contrast the gallant scenery of his travels with the gloomy introspections of adolescence. He called it, at first, *Childe Burun*, but was wise or lucky enough eventually to change the title to *Childe Harold*. The Spenserian stanza was borrowed from *The Faerie Queene* – thanks to his anthological volume, *Elegant Extracts*, he had the maquette with him – and the metre was gravely suited to the alternations of self-pity and self-deprecation, of locally colourful enthusiasm for the Mediterranean and British dismay at its unlovely cruelties. The picaresque narrative combined an apology for youthful debaucheries with a spicy enumeration of them. There can come a sudden moment in a writer's life when his apprenticeship ends; experience and technique are matched in the abrupt discovery of his own voice and style.

Byron became unmistakably Byronic in the last weeks of 1809, clopping down to Prevesa with his brash barbarian escort. They took ship from there for Patras, but a storm blew up as they were coasting towards the Peloponnese and the Turkish captain and crew lost control of themselves and of their vessel. Byron, wrapped in rhyming thoughts and a newly acquired Albanian capote, kept his head while most of those around were losing theirs. (Fletcher was sure they were destined for a watery grave.) Some of the Greeks on board managed to restore order and an even keel and the ship was finally run safely aground on the wild shore of Suli, not far from Parga, a notorious nest of bandits since the days when pirates held Julius Caesar to ransom on the same coast. Hobhouse was apprehensive, Fletcher terrified, as they lurched ashore under the greedy eyes of the flashily armed Suliotes. Luckily, and courageously, the escort commander, Vassily, succeeded in commanding obedience in the name of Ali Pasha.

After a welcome and welcoming feast around a camp fire, Byron was enchanted by the wild dancing of the Albanian warriors and by the vigour of their singing, especially of their shameless song 'Robbers all at Parga!' The outlaw, conscienceless and free, was an emblem of liberty and of liberation, the living alternative to half-measures and half-truths. 'Men to die with,' he called the circling dancers. Why, even Fletcher looked comfortable at last, lolling on gaudy cushions with a jar of wine! The sozzled servant declared sullenly that he had not met anything he could call comfort since leaving England. As part of the valet's job was to crush the lice in Byron's clothing, one can excuse his unheroic view. (The wine, he remarked, tasted more of turps than grapes, a view of retsina not unknown among insular travellers to this day.) The Suliote chieftain proved more to Byron's taste than the grabby Greek baggageman, Yorgo, whom he discharged with ignominy after they had reached what passed for civilization. When Byron went to pay off the Suliote, Vassily explained that the man wanted Byron's love, not his money, a precedent with few sequels in the venal East. 'Men to die with', the Suliotes, and die with them he would, in marshy, mosquito-ridden Missolonghi, to which the friends were escorted in romantic style by the affectionate brigands, before they crossed the gulf on their way to Athens.

As they loitered along the coast of the Peloponnese, they came to a town called Vostitza (now Aigion) where Byron was invited to dine with a young man called Andreas Londos, a well-to-do, well-connected twenty-year-old Greek of the Phanariote class, who had been appointed governor of the place by the Turks. Until that night, Byron had had no great respect for the native Greeks. Who could be surprised that an intelligent man like Londos had chosen to make his career in the service of the virile Turks? However, when the after-dinner discussion turned to the case of a Greek political martyr, Constantine Rhiga, executed in 1798 after an unsuccessful uprising, the 'chimpanzee-faced' governor leapt up and, tears in his eyes, gave a passionate rendering of Rhiga's rallying call, *Thefte pethes ton Hellenon* (Arise, You Sons of Greece), sung to the tune of the Marseillaise. Abruptly, Byron awoke to the loathing concealed under the enforced proskynesis of the enslaved Greeks, whose ancestors had resisted to the death rather than crawl in like fashion to the Persians. Byron's arrogant fellow-feeling for the Turks was converted to sympathy with the maltreated Hellenes. C. M. Woodhouse illustrates the Greek humiliation by observing that the Turks referred to them as 'cattle' (*rayah*). Elie Kedourie is less indignant and assimilates *rayah* to 'flocks', indicating a protective concern. The Turks, he notes, were a master race concerned largely with collecting tribute and left their subjects substantially to their own devices. The 'Franks' had no amiable reputation in Greece and experience of the Roman Catholic hierarchy led Greek Christians to prefer 'the Muslim turban' to the 'Latin mitre'.

Andreas Londos not only recruited Byron to Philhellenism, he himself had the courage to be one of the first to rally to the standard of national liberation when, at last, the Greeks took arms against their hated masters in 1821. It was while Byron was at Vostitza that he shot a young eagle and succeeded only in wounding it. He tried to save its life, but it died. He never went hunting again. Since it was also possible to see across the Corinthian Gulf from Vostitza to Mount Parnassus, the home of the Muses, the manuscript of *Childe Harold* gained a few tributary stanzas.

The travellers reached Athens on Christmas Day, 1809. A place of some 15,000 motley inhabitants, it was so fallen from its finest hour that the Greeks referred to it simply as *to chorio*, the village, a place like any other. (The city, *ee polis*, was always, and still is, Constantinople.) There was nowhere more elegant to stay than lodgings in what is now the loud and plastic Plaka. They found rooms with a Mrs Macri, a widow with three pretty young daughters, whom Byron, with more spontaneity than wit, dubbed 'the Three Graces'. His penchant for conspicuous cheek had already led him to jeer at Lord Elgin, who had begun in 1802 systematically to strip the Parthenon and send home its marble metopes, statues and friezes, but only now did he take full and scathing measure of Elgin's vandalism. He had sneered before; he raged now at Elgin's 'Gothic' insensitivity and was not mollified by Hobhouse's rationalizing arguments in favour of the benign influence of the marbles on British architectural design. The protection of the weak against the depredations of the powerful was grateful alike to Byron's sense of fair play and to his lordly vanity: *Crede Byron*, and watch this space.

If atmosphere meant more to him than accurate attribution when it came to visiting the great sites of antiquity, he could scarcely fail to be impressed by the temple of Poseidon on the sounding cliffs of Sounion at the rufous south-east corner of Attica. As if to apologize for his lofty verses, he had teased Hobhouse by comparing the Parthenon, unfavourably, with the Mansion House in London. When Fletcher was asked what *he* was thinking about, the honest fat-head replied, 'A plate of roast beef, my lord.' As for the temple, it would make a fine lot of chimney pieces, if properly carved. On a later trip to Sounion, the vandal-hating Byron saw to it that his name was incised in one of the columns as clearly as Peel's on the panel of Harrow big schoolroom. Now the company headed for the battleground of Marathon, where Hobhouse sought to square Herodotus' account of the great battle with the terrain (at least there was no mistaking the great funerary mound, where, even in gallant victory, the democratic Athenians distinguished the bones of the free from those of the slaves who had fought beside them). Byron's genius for combining self-centredness with magnanimity found one of its enduring images in the dream of a new Marathon which might once again liberate Greece from the barbarian. On returning to ordinary Athens, he continued to flirt with the daughters of Mrs Macri's house, especially Teresa, to whom he proved his new capacity to coin pretty phrases in the demotic. When he and Hobhouse departed on an excursion to Constantinople, he left Teresa, the Maid of Athens, with the words 'Zoe moo, sas agapoh' ('My life, I love you'), a fair sentiment and fair enough Greek, though a declaration of passion would normally employ the intimate 'se' rather than the formal 'sas'. However, there is no reason to question the tenderness of Byron's feelings or his delight in making love in a new tongue. Turkish he found more difficult; he could boast of his knowledge only of a range of oaths.

Early in 1810, the friends landed at Smyrna, where Byron finished the first draft (Cantos 1 and 2) of *Childe Harold*, and inspected the ruins of Ephesus, after which they boarded the frigate *Salsette* for the voyage to Constantinople. Before entering the Hellespont, Byron visited the site of Troy, though in those days, before the inspired literal-mindedness of Schliemann brought the toppled towers to unquestionable light, Priam's city was assumed to be a figment of Homer's imagination. There was no doubt about the reality of the Hellespont, however, and Byron duly emulated the aquatic gallantry of Leander by swimming the four cold miles from Sestos to Abydos. (Some Byronists say the distance was but a mile, though all agree the water was chilly and the current tricky.) He was accompanied by a Lieutenant Ekenhead, of the *Salsette*, who actually landed some five minutes ahead of him, thus standing out as the first non-mythical figure known to have managed the crossing; it was the second man ashore, however, who popularized the fashion for famous swims. Byron was soon to receive unhappy news from England of his other erstwhile swimming companion Edleston, the darling choirboy. He had been accused of indecency, a charge which may have touched Byron's conscience. About this time, he wrote to Francis Hodgson in England that he proposed to leave off wine and carnal company and betake himself to politics and decorum.

As they passed the Dardanelles, the guns of one of the forts on shore fired a salute in their honour. Hobhouse remarked that Byron should be gratified by the tribute (in Epirus his lordship had chided Hobby for attaching insufficient importance to nobility), but the ever-contrary Byron retorted that the Turks had broken out the flag of tyranny to welcome them and twitted his friend, not improvidently, on the feebleness of his liberal principles. Not long afterwards, however, he was vexed to find that his title afforded him no precedence in official diplomatic circles in Constantinople; though later he was handsomely shrugging, he became quite sulky about it for a while. Increasingly disgusted by Turkish callousness (the friends saw dogs snarling over a human corpse as they landed), he nevertheless insisted, with his neat aptitude for the outrageous, that the only difference between 'ourselves and the Turk, is that we have foreskins and he does not'. The remark was not merely flippant; travel had alerted Byron to the diversity of human morals and the uncertainty of human supremacies. If he was revolted by the tyranny of the Turk or appalled by the venality of the Greek, he saw that British conceit was based more on ignorance than on merit. The blazing devotion of his Albanian bodyguard was an amiable contrast to the belly-aching Fletcher, with whom he was considerably out of patience and whom he eventually sent home ahead of him. He and Hobhouse had been travelling together for a good year and in July it was agreed, not without relief, that after leaving the minarets and monuments of Constantinople, John Cam would sail directly to England, while Byron returned to Athens and the Three Graces, and their mother. On the quay at Colonni, on Keos, the two Cambridge friends broke a posy of wild flowers in half and so ruptured their joint pilgrimage, if not without quarrels at least without a breach. Hobhouse kept his half until it fell apart.

Byron was sentimental about Hobby, 'this singular young person', once he had gone, but he was not sorry to see him go, well-filled notebooks and all. It was not only Teresa to whom Byron was returning in Athens, but also Nicolo Giraud, a boy of fifteen with whom, before embarking on the tour of Asia Minor, he had struck up one of his sentimental, nay *passionate*, not entirely pure, friendships. Homosexuality was a commonplace with the Turks, nor did the Greeks show any large distaste for it. Nicolo was the young brother of a French woman married to a Neapolitan painter, Giovanni Battista Lusieri, who was working on architectural drawings for Lord Elgin. The boy returned Byron's feelings and also taught him Italian. Hobhouse's departure licensed indulgence without embarrassment; politics and decorum were postponed. Greece not only taught Byron to be a poet but also revel in a sensuality untinged by furtiveness or remorse; the great god Pan was not dead yet. Why go home? The privileges of a British peer were still largely valid (Athenian society, such as it was, was ready to lionize even a comparative cub) and money went further than it ever could in England, where the duns were giving Mrs Byron a bad time, not least on her absentee son's overdue account.

Byron and Nicolo were often together, but he did not keep exclusively male company, even when the daughters of Mrs Macri had lost their freshness. The widow was now bent on marrying Teresa, or at least selling her (the asking price was

£600), to her lordly tenant and her house began to throw a heavy shadow. Byron and Nicolo went riding (often eight hours a day) and they swam in the warm, unpolluted waters off the Piraeus. One day, on their way home, they met a party of Turks hauling a wriggling sack down to the sea in a cart. The Waiwode, or Governor, of Athens had condemned the girl who had been sewn in the sack to be flung into the Aegean for sexual infidelity. Byron remarked that if every faithless woman in England were thrown into the sea, they would pave a causeway from Dover to Calais. He insisted, first with useless threats and then with useful money, that the execution be delayed. He succeeded finally in having the woman smuggled out of the city. Folklore claims that it was only when the sack had been opened and the cat was out of the bag that Byron recognized, with alarm, that the condemned creature was one of whom he himself had had carnal knowledge, but can the encounter with the terrible tumbril have been entirely accidental? Byron had to use charm as well as cash in order to bend the Waiwode's will and he supplemented his blandishments with not a few glasses of rum, to which the Turk, being a Mohametan, was unaccustomed. He was assured that what he was enjoying was not wine (nor was it, after all) and Byron's spirited gall remained unpunished, just.

His amorous activities were not impeded, even by an attack of the piles. He had an appetite for all available pleasures and a lack of discrimination in its satisfaction: he soon added the clap to his other medical problems. When he and Nicolo went on a journey through the Morea, partly to escape the heat of the Attic summer, partly to be free of the demanding company of Lady Hester Stanhope, a visitor whose virile character he did not appreciate, Byron was taken sick of a violent fever; its cure probably owed more to the strength of his constitution than to the skill of his doctor, though the threats of his Albanian servants to kill the physician if their master failed to survive may well have concentrated the medical mind. The fever may have been malaria and proved recurrent.

The winter of 1810 was sunny enough: there was cosmopolitan company in Athens, a flow of quite grand tourists with whom Byron was pleased to pass the time of day. Nor were his nights without company. Yet the chronic canker of boredom was again working in him. He moved from Mrs Macri's to the Capuchin monastery, found amusement in riotous adolescent company, and regaled himself on a diet of mullet and woodcock. However, Attic life, enchanting before, was merely acceptable now. He toyed with an excursion to Egypt, but his funds were as low as his spirits. In the spring of 1811, laden with memories, mementos and manuscripts, he took ship at last for England.

There were painful partings with his devoted Albanian servants whose anguish appears to have been uncorrupted by avarice: they loved him. Of all the qualities which Byron possessed, his charm is perforce the most fugitive. He may be accused of self-centredness (but where else should a poet have his centre?) and of a lack of self-control; he may be said to have traded on his title and his treasure (even when it had to be borrowed) and to have found an appropriate spiritual home in the land of Narcissus, but neither his pouting profile nor his aristocratic largesse can wholly explain his hold on a heterogeneous range of casual acquaintances and hardly less casual lovers. He had an inexhaustible desire and ability to make himself desirable. His physical lameness was compensated by mental agility. His larkiness may have jarred on Lady Hester, but his jokes were typical of a man who always needed laughing evidence that his wit and his presence had been appreciated. And to be the source of laughter is to be sure that one is not being laughed at. He was capable of seriousness, and even of modesty, in intelligent (usually male) circles, but he was endowed with a seductive charm which, like his remarkable sexual appetite, he could not resist gratifying. His melancholy may seem, as melancholy always does, more sincere and more poetic than his facetiousness, but it is typical of the actor to experience a sense of let-down after he has delivered his best lines. Byron the solitary and Byron the entertainer are two sides of a coin: it would be witless to suppose one genuine, the other counterfeit. However, while on the subject of coin, the influence of money problems even on the poetic psyche should not be underestimated: to think of England was also to think of debts, which may explain his woeful opinion, on quitting Greece, that old age began at twenty-three.

On the way home, Byron left Nicolo Giraud in Malta, where he arranged for him to go to a good school and where he presented his return ticket, as it were, to Mrs Constance Spencer Smith, though their romance dwindled into a matter more of ardent marivaudage than of passionate demonstration. He left the hot island early in June and once again reached England (he landed at Sheerness) in the middle of July, just over two years after leaving Falmouth.

The conventionally unconventional young aristocrat was now a man of the world. If he had a new, and belittling, perspective on his native land (and the habit – soon lost – of chewing tobacco), he was heartened by the resumption of old friendships. Scrope Davies was as natty, bibulous and mordant as ever, Hobhouse as sensible and loyal. The Reverend Robert Dallas, who had appointed himself Byron's literary representative even before he went on his travels, showed fawning eagerness to peddle the new manuscript to publishers (Hobby had been talking). Of other friends there was soon less pleasing news: the brilliant C. S. Matthews was drowned in the treacherous, reedy waters of the Cam and, almost more painful still, young Edleston had died of consumption. Travestied as a girl, Thyrza, he would be the subject of an elegy that could not quite exorcise a ghost about whom Byron remained both sentimental and guilty. A wit has seen that Edleston is anagrammed 'Lost Eden', but the boy's decline from Edenic innocence (there were rumours that he had become a manifest tart) had perhaps been initiated by Byron's own reptilian overtures.

Within a fortnight of his landing in England, Byron's mother was dead as well. He was so broke that he had to touch the dilatory Hanson for a loan before he could race to her bedside. He arrived too late to comfort her, though in time for a spasm of remorseful self-pity. She was said to have had her first seizure when faced with yet another set of bills, poor lady. (Her son had spent, but not paid, a small fortune on refurbishing Newstead.) Byron was too distressed to follow the hearse when the body was taken to burial at Hucknall Torkard. Instead, he sent young Rushton to fetch the boxing gloves: 'Mill away right and left' was the order of the sorry day. Always more constant in retrospect than in the flesh, he mourned his 'one friend in the world', forgetting, or ignoring, how often he had fled her embraces or been repelled by her rage. He consoled himself with the accessible affections of the Newstead servant girls and, despite attempts at economy, imported three new graces into his seraglio, one of whom, Susan Vaughan, temporarily engaged his sentimental as well as his sexual attention. Fletcher had resumed his service; the availability both of roast beef and of his wife Sally rendered the valet's presence less lugubrious. More sophisticated consolation, and reviving wit, came from

Scrope Davies, whose resumed companionship was a happy reminder of happier days.

Baronial life at Newstead did not preclude ambitious interest in what was happening in London: Byron was eager and apprehensive about the publication of *Childe Harold*. Hobhouse feared that the flagrant immorality of the poem would damage his reputation; Dallas was as disconcerted by the evidence of free-thinking as by that of free living, but Byron was encouraged by the good opinions of William Gifford, a critic whose taste he was always to value and who was, as luck would have it, chief reader for the publisher John Murray, from whose house, in Albemarle Street, the poem was destined to appear. Gifford had been an admirer of *English Bards, and Scotch Reviewers* and proved a shrewd and trusted editor of Byron's poetry for many years.

Childe Harold was not published until March 1812. The preceding months were the last Byron would enjoy, if he found them enjoyable, out of the limelight. He was hardly unknown, however. *English Bards, and Scotch Reviewers* had not made him famous, but it was now into its fourth edition and its satire had not failed to find its mark or its audience. Tom Moore, the amorous and fashionable poet of *Lalla Rookh*, had felt himself slighted by Byron's jejune satire (insolence, as so often, had been the ambitious young writer's visiting card) and had actually challenged him to a duel, by post, before the pilgrim's departure for the Mediterranean. But now what had begun in antagonism ended in the warmest of new friendships.

Moore was an *arriviste* who had succeeded in arriving (from rather further away) in the very circles to which Byron was still aspiring. The son of a Dublin grocer, he had, unlike Frank Harris in Oscar Wilde's sally, dined in all the great houses of London more than once. 'The heaven of each,' he once said, 'is but what each desires,' and he desired nothing better than teasing fashionable ladies. He was naughty, but he was nice; the rapier of his wit was swift but always buttoned. Nor did his social climbing inhibit him from giving others a leg up; he introduced Byron to the circle of Samuel Rogers, the affably sarcastic banker-poet who once remarked that whenever he heard of a good new book, he rushed out and bought an old one, but who nevertheless bought – and distributed – Byron. It was he who gave a copy to Lady Caroline Lamb.

Moore and Byron became constant companions and indeed the Irishman grew jealous of long-standing friends like

Hobhouse and Scrope, who lacked either the passport of genius or the patent of breeding. Scrope was a life fellow of King's College, Cambridge, but university appointments were not as socially impressive then as they can be today. After accumulating too many debts, Hobhouse had been reconciled with his father only at the price of accepting temporary service in the militia and was stationed at Dover. However provincial his old friends might seem and however much attracted he personally might be to the centre of any new stage, Byron never abandoned loyalties, while Hobhouse's affection was unshaded even by the fact that he still owed Byron some £800 which he had borrowed in the East. Thus there was little truth in Byron's here-we-go-again lament that his only friends were a newly acquired greyhound and some tortoises he had brought home with him. If he lacked someone with whom to be unguardedly himself, he had a host of good companions. Augusta Leigh, his only close blood-relation, had written to him to commiserate on the death of Mrs Byron and he was glad to resume epistolary contact with her. Not only was she house-bound as a result of having borne Colonel Leigh several children in the intervening few years, but her visits to London were also restricted by her husband's having incurred the disfavour of the Prince Regent. She was a lonely, lively lady.

In February 1812 Byron made his maiden speech in the House of Lords. He chose to lose the last of his virginities, as it were, by speaking against a Bill which proposed savage penalties against the Nottingham weavers who had employed Luddite tactics in breaking the mechanical frames which were threatening to put them out of business. Nottingham was virtually his constituency and the issue gave him an opportunity for both genuine indignation and orotund Ciceronian counterpoint. He posed a posse of rhetorical questions: 'Are there not capital punishments enough in your statutes? Is there not blood enough upon your penal code that more must be poured forth to ascend to Heaven and testify against you? Are these the remedies for a starving and desperate populace? Will the famished wretch who has braved your bayonets be appalled by your gibbets? When death is a relief, and the only relief, it appears, you will afford him, will he be dragooned into tranquillity?'

The speech had been thoroughly, perhaps too thoroughly rehearsed and it was delivered in a theatrical style which, no doubt, concealed a measure of stage-fright. The elaboration of its periods may have detracted from the sincerity of its tone, but Byron was pleased to believe that Lord Eldon, the Lord Chancellor, had been vexed, just as he was flattered by the compliments of the leading radical in the House of Commons, Sir Francis Burdett, a rich and influential friend of Scrope Davies, who took the trouble to come up and hear him. Byron was proud to declare that he was born for opposition; his humane scorn no doubt incensed the government, yet his speech was as much an advertisement of his talents as a blow for justice. Everything he said rings true, but its genuineness was compromised by artificial delivery; he decked indignation with a frieze of classic pretentiousness which would have done credit to Regent Street. Lord Holland, the patron of the Whigs, offered congratulations more to Byron's taste than those of Sir Francis Burdett, since they implied social as well as political encouragement. Holland House was the centre of a circle to which Byron had so far scarcely even been tangential. In the event, he did not have long to wait before he made his electric, limping entrance, though it was not his politics that opened the tall doors.

The impact of *Childe Harold* exceeded all John Murray's expectations, and Byron's. Indeed, who could ever have expected such a success? All London was said to be pelting the booksellers with *louis d'or*. Within three days, the five hundred copies of the first edition were sold out. Though it was never to sell as hugely as legend implies, the impact of the poem certainly made it the talk of a talkative town. In the window of a Piccadilly bookseller was displayed a copy of the poem 'specially bound for her Royal Highness, the Princess of Wales', a gesture of patronage which Byron may well have remembered when, on account of her morals, the royal lady fell into disfavour with her husband, whose own had never troubled him.

Byron disdained royalties, in the sense of financial rewards (for the time being he made his literary revenues over to the receptive Dallas), but he drew delightful dividends in a flood of invitations; toadying visitors beat a path to his temporary door in St James's Street. On that unforgettable morning when he woke to find himself famous, the carriages of the *gratin* jostled to present cards and compliments. All those elements about which Hobhouse and Dallas and Murray had been so apprehensive proved delectable to the modish. Adolescent *angst* and Eastern promises, the call of liberty and the hint of libertinism, technicolour escapades and doomy forebodings offered a stimulating elixir of youthfulness. The poet's dexterity announced a talent at once precocious and well-schooled. A desire to please chaperoned an urge to shock; glum sentimentality was trimmed with casual cynicism. The freshness of the author's eye was nicely at odds with the melancholy of his vision; *Childe Harold* offered candour without innocence and originality without innovation. Byron was the man of the moment. The cause of the Nottingham weavers was left to the untender mercies of the government; politics and decorum yielded to poses and dandyism, the studied cult of the unnatural.

Byron was only twenty-four, but he had waited ardently enough to be fully rehearsed for fame. The lame boy had accumulated a quiverful of fancied slights to feather his wit; his arrows were tipped with a venom for which the dimpled darlings of smart society proved positively cupidinous. Hostesses begged him to name the day on which he would consent to visit his impertinence on their guests. What and whom else would they have come for? He dressed in black, hellishly pale and poetic, a metropolitan Hamlet who specialized, he soon served notice, in country matters. When the girls at Lady Westmorland's, and at other fashionable rendezvous, asked him what sort of woman he liked, he fired back that he was an admirer of the harem principle. Ali Pasha may have been an appalling Eastern tyrant in the flesh, but he gave Byron a superb model for West End tyranny over the ladies. Which of them would not happily have been sewn into a sack for his sake? His 'under-look', which would have been more ham than Hamlet in anyone but an accredited celebrity, made every virgin feel like a potential adulteress and every adulteress a vulnerable virgin. Lady Falkland, the young widow to whom, with obliging *noblesse*, he had once given £500 he could ill afford, was convinced that *Childe Harold* was really a love poem to herself and became one of the first of many women whose determined identification of themselves with his heroines would first flatter and then exasperate him.

He had fresher fish to fry, though in public he made a great show of liking neither meat nor fish. There was, it seemed, very little of anything he liked. Having maintained that his diet was nothing but hard biscuits and soda-water, he was once caught in a low chop-house eating mutton and potatoes mashed with vinegar. Set upon doing nothing that was expected, he soon found that only the unexpected was expected. He honoured his naughty reputation by declaring that he hated children so much that he had always had the greatest respect for the character of Herod. In the midst of the richest marriage-market in England, and probably in Europe, he spoke scathingly of being forced to marry 'some wealthy dowdy'. He would, he said, 'ennoble the dirty puddle of her mercantile blood' in order to redeem his estate. Meanwhile, if his fortune was still uncertain, his fame secured him almost unlimited credit.

Male friends watched his revenge on the female sex with a measure of complicitous humour. He was doing little more than give voice to their standard attitudes, though in mixed company they were rarely declared so uninhibitedly. Coaxing ladies might accuse him of 'having it in him to make some woman very happy', but his answer was that a woman had no need of him to be happy: 'It's quite enough to give her a looking glass and a box of sweets.' Of all the women who coveted either his affections or his name, the most reckless was Lady Caroline Lamb, the young and wilful wife of William Lamb. She was seduced at first neither by the under-look nor by the beautiful pale face which she later declared was her fate, but by *Childe Harold* itself, which Samuel Rogers brought for her to Melbourne House, in Whitehall, where she lived with her husband, the son of Lord and Lady Melbourne and a rising Whig politician. In his maturity, William Lamb would be Queen Victoria's first and beloved Prime Minister, Lord Melbourne, a worldly wise man whose wisdom had been tempered and tested, not least, by the follies of his wife.

Caro Lamb's education had hardly been conventional: she belonged to the Devonshire House set, amongst whom precociousness and self-indulgence went together and where the only rule was unruliness. The young rarely stayed innocent there: they soon learnt that adultery was the great game of the aristocracy; if discretion was demanded, self-restraint was simply unsporting. (Lord and Lady Holland themselves had been married only two days after her Ladyship's divorce had come through, yet their house outranked even the Melbournes' in smartness.) Samuel Rogers was quite possibly laying bait for Caro Lamb; he had a reputation for both open-handedness and trouble-making. He said of himself, 'I have a very weak voice, and if I did say ill-natured things no one would hear what I say.' When Caro asked him what Byron was like, his low tones told her that he had a club-foot and bit his nails. Nevertheless, she was soon writing the now pampered poet an anonymous fan letter and, having decided that he was 'mad, bad and dangerous to know', it was, of course, only a matter of time before she made his acquaintance. However, at Lady Westmorland's one night, she adopted the dangerous preliminary tactic of turning her back on the opportunity of an introduction (Byron was surrounded by too much competition) and the glowering young lion read her diffidence for contempt. If she hoped, by these means, to become his meat, she underestimated his vindictiveness once he caught up with her, a process that did not take long, since she made most of the running in his direction.

When they did meet face to pretty face, he promptly chided her for her earlier indifference. She made a neat excuse, but it was the least amiable of Byron's characteristics to appear to forgive while not forgetting. It may be that Caro's infatuation was partly modish – she wanted to be seen to possess what everybody else so clearly dreamed about – but it was not wholly capricious. Her education was disorganized but she was not lacking in either talent (she wrote tolerable verses) or taste.

Her husband was a man of conventional ambitions and indulgent morals, neither passionate nor censorious. Other members of the upper classes might regret her impulsiveness, but few were in a position to read her sermons. Her passion was, to begin with, as generous as it was imprudent: she offered Byron not only her affections but also her jewellery to pay his debts. If it was none too subtle to appear to be proposing a down payment on his attention, it would be a mistake to deduce that the slim, blonde hoyden lacked other means of attracting it. By a coincidence of fate's prognostication, Caro shared with Caroline, Byron's earlier, humbler mistress, a penchant for dressing in boy's clothes. She often trousered herself like one of the pages she was pleased to employ. Such androgynous antics doubtless intrigued Byron; they catered to an appetite which, whether or not she was conscious of it, at once made Caro more enticing than the normal run of golden dollies and put her at considerable risk. The fact that she was both Byron's senior by three years and a married woman excited a comfortable consciencelessness in his never very conscientious character: she was the shameless older woman, he the reluctant and guiltless, if scarcely innocent, follower. No spider could be more fly than he.

When Lady Bessborough, Caro's mother, poured on her routine charm in an ill-judged effort to dissuade Byron from pursuing the affair, she merely added fuel to the flames she was seeking to douse. By suggesting that Caro was provoking Byron merely in order to wound the husband whom she really loved, her ladyship encouraged his spite without procuring his discretion. It suited him to believe that Caro was a treacherous and cynical libertine, when the truth seems rather to have been that she was a vulnerable and unpremeditating fan, unused to frustration and averse to half-measures. The hot-pressed darling of society responded to her loving protestations with racy repartee, though he clearly loved receiving them. Her outrageousness sponsored pranks that surely appealed to his own undergraduate taste: dressed as a pretty boy, she hid herself in his carriage when he was leaving a soirée at Lady Bellamy's. He repaid her audacity by challenging her to kiss him, on the mouth. What a rare moment of realized fantasy, obliging the female to play the male part, the initiative all hers! If Caro hesitated, hesitation was never her natural style. Byron may have been wary at first, but he was the kind of dandy for whom no cap was complete without another feather. When he literally tripped up the stairs of Melbourne House (he read the omen gloomily), holding a rose and a carnation for Lady Caroline in his bitten fingers, he may have been advertising a passion less for passion itself than for its counterfeit, sensation. Yet his affectations were no less the gauge of his apprehension than a hedge against naiveté. Mary Chaworth had put him on his guard; a year later, scorched by unhappy marital experience, she wrote him an old flame's regretful, rechauffé note, but the lame boy would always make her sex pay dearly for her devastating rejection and he made it clear that he felt nothing for her lame overtures.

Byron offered Caro his flowers with the flip observation that her ladyship was reported to like all that was new and rare, for a moment. The play between the lovers remained flighty, all unserious solemnities and deliberate casualness. Caro wrote to him in mock obituary of the death of Byron's rose, 'probably from regret at its fallen fortunes.' Her mother-in-law, Lady Melbourne, who had abstained wisely from Lady Bessborough's panicky stratagems, became Byron's favourite confidante. If she half-deplored, half-delighted in the mounting scandal, she set about controlling its worst extravagances with tactful tactics. Byron grew so susceptible to her poise that he declared that if she had been younger, he would have fallen in love with her. When, on his second visit to Melbourne House, he was introduced to Annabella Milbanke, Lady M.'s niece and the heiress to a substantial fortune, Byron may not immediately have been taken with her person (that dark earnestness was an unsmiling contrast to Caro's blonde vivacity), but he was not indifferent to her reputation for intelligence or unimpressed by her provincial self-possession. The close blood relationship with Lady M. may have given the young Annabella (she was only twenty in 1812) an intriguing resemblance to the aunt for whom Byron felt so much admiration. Nor, despite her Christian disapproval of his morals, did the ungushing heiress's interest fail to be piqued by the very rumours which, she declared, made her disinclined to make any offering at his shrine. Tom Moore told Byron bluntly that he should marry Annabella and repair Newstead, but there was, for the present, a mutual wariness that, in a happier story, might well have presaged a more joyful outcome than fate actually provided.

Byron was in no hurry to marry: why waste himself on one woman when he had the chance to waste himself on a dozen? If aristocratic practice promised that husbands could always have their cake and eat it too, had not many a good man been tricked into bondage by the promise of freedom, only to find his reward in a pair of horns? William Lamb was but the most conspicuous example. Some biographers have suggested that Caro and Byron never actually went so far as to make love, but how far, in the Regency circumstances, was that? They were neither of them renowned for refraining from whatever appealed to their senses or to their vanity; it is implausible, if not ludicrous, to argue that the affair remained unconsummated. Byron's taste for trophies was highly developed (he kept curls from his conquests' hair in annotated folds of tissue paper) and Caro genuinely excited his unreliable ardour, at least at the beginning. However, he was never so lacking in lovable qualities as in the later stages of his love affairs. Steadfastly loyal to his male friends (his devotion to John Murray for a long time led him to ignore, or tolerate, the publisher's squeamish attitude to an author who made his fortune), he prided himself on his mutability when he came to women, and especially when women came to him.

The unfluttered dignity of Annabella Milbanke at least gave her the allure of the one woman in the room who did not incline to the wind of fashion. Others might be learning the new-fangled waltz, but the limping Byron was pleased to find that Annabella did not dance, at least not in the morning, unlike more frivolous Melbourne House girls, who were to be found in a matutinal spin under the instruction of an imported German dancing-master. One had to respect a girl who was not ready to go to the devil as soon as he could provide her with a new tune. The waltz brought out a measure of Calvinist severity in Byron which Scrope Davies might have called silliness or humbug but which, given his present standing, none dared openly to deride.

One day, embarrassed by Caro's presenting to him not only her apparently complaisant husband but also their drooling child, Augustus, Byron inquired of Annabella, à propos society, whether there was one person among the company who dared to look into himself. Could Annabella fail to be flattered by the suggestion that she shared with Byron a perspicacity or a depth of character not to be found in anyone else? Perhaps she did not yet care to wish on him qualities that might make him 'the object of that strong affection which would make her happy in domestic life,' but can she have remained insensitive to his undomestic qualities? For the moment, she and he were united in contempt for London society: she despised its superficiality, he its veneration for himself. Despite all the appetizing applause, he knew himself to be a freak: how then could he merit idolization? The more society hounded him, the more elusive he became: he glowered, they cooed; he sneered, they cheered; he limped, they ran after him. Meanwhile, Caro Lamb's Jill-in-the-box ubiquity was degenerating into obsessive passion. If he had loved her skittishness, he was repelled when light-heartedness put on weight and became ponderous sincerity. During the spring of their great affair, they were clearly in love with love no less than with each other. One, it emerged, had taken on more than he had bargained for, and the other less. Byron's brief experience of Mrs Constance Spencer Smith had hardly made him an expert in the ways of wilful independent ladies and Caro's passion erupted with a dismaying, volcanic force. In the end she was the one who was scorched, and scarred forever.

On 18 May 1812, Byron went to Newgate Prison to witness the execution of John Bellingham, a demented tradesman with a grievance, who had shot the boring Tory Prime Minister, Spencer Perceval, in the lobby of the House of Commons. On the way to the hired room overlooking the gallows, Byron and his party passed an unfortunate woman lying in a doorway. When he offered her a few shillings' worth of charity, she repulsed him and, to the embarrassment of his companions, capered down the street in a parody of his crippled gait. (On another occasion, when the street boys greeted him by name, a companion sought to flatter him by remarking that even the London urchins knew who he was. 'They know *what* I am,' he said. 'Deformed.') Seeing Bellingham 'launched into eternity' was less a ghoulish pleasure than a test of a certain idea of manhood: one had to look at such things without blinking, as one had to endure the bullying of one's schoolfellows or the pain of Mr Lavender's machine. Byron's sadism was restricted, on the whole, to tongue-lashing the women in his life.

Caro Lamb forced matters to a whole series of climaxes. She waltzed to tease him and, when he reacted angrily, she astonished the company by stopping the music. Byron suspected her of loving her husband more than himself, though one may presume that he also loved his suspicions. He drove her to reckless and finally repellent demonstrations of devotion. However, his contempt was laced with desire and even affection. When she was larky, he could still enter graciously into her fantasies. There was even a mock wedding, at one point, with Scrope Davies playing the stammering parson. Caro was confident enough of her hold on him to agree to play the go-between for Annabella Milbanke, at least when that young lady sent Byron some of her verses for his appreciation. He offered the grave response that he did not think publishing at all creditable either to men or to women (did he not very often feel ashamed of it himself?), but that she had talents which, 'were it proper or requisite to indulge them,' would have led to distinction. (Scratch a critic-baiter and behold a critic!) He would like her more, he told Caro, who doubtless told Annabella, if she were less perfect. Caro's cousinly advice was that the girl should marry George Eden, a more suitable suitor.

The summer of 1812 ended with Caro's melodramatic disappearance from Melbourne House after a loud quarrel with the boozy Lord Melbourne, William's father. Lady Melbourne and Lady Bessborough (to whom Byron had given the discourtesy title Lady Blarney) rattled round to Byron's house in St James's to find out where the wild girl had gone. An elopement had more than once been threatened: had it now taken place? If so, it was not with Byron: he professed no knowledge whatever of where Caro might be. Typically, he chose to twit Lady Bessborough by asking whether, since Caro did not love him, she might perhaps have another lover. Even Lady Melbourne's usual sang-froid seems to have failed her, for she had not thought of the simple solution which Byron now proposed for resolving the mystery of Caro's whereabouts. Once Caro's hackney coachman had been primed with coin, he proved able to disclose that she was hiding in a surgeon's house in rural Knightsbridge, the first place 'off the bricks' of central London. Byron bluffed his way in by announcing himself to be Caro's brother, a piece of improvisation possibly borrowed from the games he played with his first Caroline, but one that the pattern-conscious may choose to see as premonitory.

Byron just about stemmed Caro's hysterics with reassuring speeches. The humiliation of discovery (but then why does a girl hide except in order to be sought?) and the loudness of the scandal bore upon the fugitive with sufficient force to persuade her to return to her home and her husband, who had been appointed to a government mission in Ireland. Byron hated scenes, especially those he had not scripted, and having promised Caro that he was thinking only of her, he made haste to find something, and someone, else to think about. The superbly mellow Lady Melbourne remained his confidante, even though the Prince Regent's sense of propriety was shocked by the mother's part in the imbroglio. (His Royal Highness himself, of course, saw nothing disreputable in being suspected, not without evidence, of having fathered one of Lady M.'s sons, George.) Annabella Milbanke was once again mooted as a reasonably pretty way out of the emotional thickets in which Byron was so thornily entangled. There were various problems, but Lady M. was sure that it would improve Annabella's eyes at least if she were to fall in love.

At the end of August 1812, Byron left the heat of London for Cheltenham, where all London was to be found: the Hollands, the Jerseys, the Melbournes were down there. During the summer he had been elected to the London Hampden Club, a liberal association of aristocrats, founded by Sir Francis Burdett, of which the beautiful and amoral Lady Oxford was the chief recruiting officer: her bed not uncommonly doubled for her office. Having met her again at Cheltenham, Byron had by the autumn succumbed, neither unwillingly nor inconveniently, to her seasoned embrace, though not before a less than ardent proposal of marriage to Annabella Milbanke, seconded by Lady M., had been unsmilingly rejected.

Jane Elizabeth, Countess of Oxford, was a woman who was used to pleasing herself, and others. The eclectic paternity of her children led them to be known as the Harleian miscellany (Lord Oxford's family name being Harley), in sarcastic allusion to the famous anthology compiled from the Oxford library by Samuel Johnson. Byron had begun by diverting himself at Cheltenham with an ample Italian opera singer, but when Lady Oxford persuaded him to become her guest at Eywood, a splendid country house near Presteign, he found her to be a mistress much more agreeable than the 'skeletal' Caro, who continued to badger him with letters and declarations. When she begged him for 'at least a picture or a lock of hair,' he treated himself to the cruel pleasure of sending her a lock of Lady Oxford's, nor did he refrain from impressing the wax on the envelope with his new mistress's seal. (A souvenir of Caro's pubic hair was already in his collection, but charity must assume that he spared Caro *'quei capelli'* when he honoured her request in so snippy a fashion.) Lady Oxford was autumnal, but autumn that year proved singularly enchanting. She was a woman of experience who could mother him without reminding him of his mother, whose demands were all favours and whose gratitude was pleasing, not pleading; she knew the rules of the game and she had the style to observe them. Her husband was complaisant and her daughters extremely pretty, especially the eleven-year-old Lady Charlotte, a nymphet much to Byron's pre-pubescent taste. He played games on the lawn with the girls, and with their mother elsewhere, and declared that he had never felt so much at peace in all his life. He only hoped, and asked, that Caro Lamb would now leave him alone, though alone was precisely what she knew him not to be; it was not only delicious to be in Lady Oxford's arms, it was also ostentatiously provoking. Had Caro been able to abide by such unreasonable logic, she should have been convinced that their affair was, by definition, at an end, since Byron had now told her that, alas (and hurrah), he loved another. But poor Caro's case could not be treated by reasonable recipes.

During that first year of fame, Byron was so lionized, so tumultuously passionate, that it would be unsurprising if his literary activities had been curtailed. In fact, his stamina was as remarkable as the demands made upon it; he could revel most of the night and then sit, sipping hock and seltzer until dawn, bent upon the compositions for which his travels had armed him. He had more than enough outlandish *données* to satisfy a public urgent for lurid tales. Only his political career, such as it was, lost impetus. He spoke a couple of times in the Lords and was wholly in tolerant character when he argued in favour of Catholic emancipation, but earnestness was somewhat inelegant for a man-about-town and he made light of parliamentary gravities. If he was still a Whig and still agin' the government, his high rating in high society (even the Prince Regent conceded that the Whigs made the best company) had sweetened the outsider's bitterness.

A personal introduction to Prinny, who professed himself an admirer of *Childe Harold*, did not inhibit Byron from making a butt of his royal largeness when the rhyme scheme demanded it, but it allowed him to see at close quarters a more likeable aspect of the Prince of Whales than any avowed, or unavowed, Jacobin would ever normally have acknowledged. Byron was a master of invective, but he often had a soft spot for those who had the wit to play on his vanity; flattery commonly turns the satirist into an entertainer. The Prince Regent scarcely converted Byron to Toryism, but Prinny's amiability rendered aggressive 'senatorial' ambitions less pressing than Lady Oxford, as opinionated as she was passionate, would have liked; their so far trouble-free affair threatened, during the first months of 1813, to become troublesome. Until now, she had handled things with patrician poise, but mistresses had a habit of taking Byron's handsome compliments at more than face value.

Whatever doubts may be expressed by the either/or school concerning his sexual preferences, he was evidently a very desirable lover. If he liked things both ways, or as many ways as might be available, none of his lovers is on record as disparaging his performance on the night, or indeed at matinées. Apart from his amusing and adroit tongue, he could recommend himself, with woeful conviction, as a fallen spirit desperate for a redeeming hand. A woman had only to lighten his melancholy, and evoke from him those high spirits which his male friends knew to be quite typical, for her to suppose that she had achieved some unique and gratifying miracle. Aware that she was coming to the end of her amorous career, Lady Oxford wanted to hold on to the very lover who would brook no such tenacity. She provided a memorable *bonne bouche*, but she was never his idea of a permanent diet.

He contrived as usual to be the wounded party and when the affair at last reached its term and the Oxford marriage regained its equilibrium on a Mediterranean cruise, Byron persuaded himself that he felt 'decidedly Carolinish' about his mistress's departure.

Meanwhile, Caro Lamb and her husband returned from Ireland. The menace of renewed hysterics filled Byron with alarm, and with malice. Guilt compounded aversion. At the Lambs' country house, Brocket Hall, Caro staged an elaborate and pathetic charade. Her pages in specially devised uniforms – their buttons inscribed with a parody of the Byron crest, *Ne Crede Byron* (Never Trust Byron) – and village girls in virginal dresses flung into the bonfire bundles of what Caro announced to be Byron's letters. In a final auto-da-fé, the volcanic lady burnt her erstwhile lover in effigy. When the patient William congratulated his wife on finishing with what had tried him to the limit and carried her beyond it, she rounded on him with the confession that the letters had been merely facsimiles. Did he think that, in reality, she could ever bear to lose a single word Byron had written? The originals would be with her till the day she died. Fireworks finished, Caro went into a decline, during which she swore that, young though she seemed, she would quit the world, and London, forever. Byron was more than ready to say amen to that, but her forever did not last long.

If Byron was always uneasy at the prospect of protracted attachments, he could never wholly let one go. No pool was too murky for Narcissus not to be tempted to take just one more look at himself in it. And though he had flung Caro from him as humiliatingly as he knew how, he knew also that their paths were bound to cross again, unless he set course for some far horizon. The devil and Medea and all her dragons were possessed of the little Maniac; flight from England seemed the only answer. Ah Naxos! What had been good enough for Ariadne and Dionysos, not to mention a Jewish Duke, would surely suit him better than the tight little island in which he was so narrowly, if glamorously, boxed.

But the thought of Lady Oxford, and the bitter-sweets of success, oh and Augusta, the darling goose who now came back into his life, detained and consoled him. Money troubles troubled him less than they had when he had little else to worry about: the sale of Newstead, apparently clinched when a Mr Claughton offered £140,000 for it, promised to keep the duns from the door. But the unfortunate Claughton, having forfeited a non-returnable deposit of £25,000, was unable to raise the balance. The final resolution of Byron's debts was further (and expensively) postponed. He still owed Scrope Davies the £4,000 he had borrowed before the Greek expedition and Scrope, whose gambling was eventually to drive him too into penny-pinching exile, could certainly do with his pot of money. The news that *Childe Harold* was in its fifth edition began to make Byron consider that perhaps the revenue from literature was too lucrative to be left to Grub Street scribblers or assigned to bores like Dallas. Walter Scott was making a fortune from his novels and poetry. Byron would have preferred to be an 'Aristides or a Washington,' to lead his country without being a tyrant, but if he was destined to be nothing but a rhymer, might he not as well be a rich one?

Augusta sympathized, and her geniality was as uncritical as it was endearing. She did not, however, take his seriousness too seriously; when he railed against the curse that lay upon him, she wagered that her children's measles were a good deal more vexatious. What might have irritated him in another amused him in her. Revelling in such unpretentious company, he even took her to meet Madame de Staël, the season's big literary tourist, when she held self-important court at Lady Davy's. The smug celebrity would insist on cutting off even such a wit as Byron's favourite Richard Brinsley Sheridan, before Sherry reached his punch line. Byron took straight-faced revenge by deploring the pernicious influence of her novels on contemporary morals.

Caro chose a small supper and waltz party at Lady Heathcote's, in the summer of 1813, to demonstrate, after several attempts to corner Byron alone, just how mad and bad she too could be. Invited to begin the dancing by her over-anxious hostess, she retorted, 'Oh yes, I'm in a merry mood just now!' When a young man asked her to waltz, she turned to Byron and called out, 'I conclude I may waltz now?' 'With everyone in turn, why not?' he replied, with a wounded bow. Lady M. begged Byron to be kind, but was it kindness when he expressed admiration for Caro's dexterity on the dance floor? His sarcasm prompted Caro to seize a knife from the buffet. Byron's aptitude for cutting remarks was quick on cue: 'Do, my dear,' he said. 'But if you mean to act a Roman's part, mind which way you strike – be it at your own heart and not at mine.' Lamely he added, 'You have struck there already,' and turned to go in to supper with Lady Rancliffe, while some of the guests attempted to disarm Caro. Either inadvertently or because she felt committed to a sensational gesture, she slashed her hand; it bled on her dress and she collapsed. Her reputation suffered more permanent damage than her person.

Byron was now not only tired of her, but tired of being tired of her: even the pleasure of wringing that 'obstinate little heart' had palled. He had threatened to be like marble to her fire; now he revealed himself at his stoniest. Caro's love had been reckless, but wholehearted; she never recovered from its rejection. Byron, flattered by her passion, had responded passionately, for a while, but his love, even at its height, was compounded of shame and vanity. Sincerity is ever the enemy of style and Caro's final performance was not only heartfelt, it was also gauche.

But if Byron was sick of scenes, he could not long do without female company. London was both loud and stale; Augusta offered peace and quiet and, very soon, a perilous kind of novelty. He visited her at Six Mile Bottom, in the absence of the Colonel, her husband, who was following the horses as usual. They went riding in the wide green fields; they had never had a cross word and there was no shortage of giggles. Soon he was to tell Moore of 'a new and serious scrape' with an unnamed woman.

His poetry was still selling prodigiously. Success had given the lame boy confidence but it had not expunged his boyishness: indeed, he traded on it. *The Corsair*, his latest tale of romantic adventure under Mediterranean skies, based on the life of Hughes Creveliers, the Parian pirate, was daring with dark doings and darker hints. He had learned to mix (and heighten) his colours to a nicety; hints of autobiographical revelation lent scandalous intimations to his gaudy heroes. His public image took a lot of living up to; respectability in the arms, and on the arm, of Annabella Milbanke, might seem an amiable consummation, but it did rather lack audacity, and it was perhaps as much the fantasy of retreat from society, no less than his flair for shocking it, that drew him, at some point, into making love to Augusta.

A writer often feels that he must match the nerve of his characters. The idea of bedding Augusta may have been frivolous, daredevil, puerile or passionate. It may have been all of them, for when did desire have a single motive? Sex was hardly a matter for solemn philosophy. Byron had already experimented with many forms of tooling and neither God nor prudence was likely to inhibit him now. As for Augusta, she had endured her husband's dull embraces dutifully enough. Why should she flinch from the much more amusing attentions of her famous and handsome half-brother? They had always had a secret language and now they could add spice to secrecy by forging an unspeakable bond between them. The trouble was that the unspeakable was the one thing Byron could not long resist talking about. Lady Melbourne was not merely a sophisticated but also a prurient woman: to titillate her, he whispered loudly of his latest foolery. Was his garrulous intimacy with Lady M. not a sort of love-making without physical contact or complications? She thrilled to his naughty news, even if she reproved his naughtiness.

At times Byron's biographers have found it incredible that he actually slept with his half-sister, but he had scarcely known the father whom he and Augusta shared and the fun of the thing lay in having found an outlawed pleasure in a world where pleasure was law and where what was forbidden was the rarest of all delights. Byron and Augusta elected to mock society by finding something new to laugh about, which might have been all right, had they managed to keep a straight face, but then where was the fun in an undisclosed secret? However, Lady M.'s alarm should have warned them that unless they were careful (Byron careful!) an abruptly unsmiling society would have the last laugh. The intimacy between baby B. and sister Goose began in a make-believe nursery for grown-up children. At first they had played at flirtation (Byron adored Augusta's 'damned crinkum-crankum', her infantile prattle), retrieving a childhood intimacy they had never had the chance to enjoy in reality. 'Camp' replaced innocence: they played at husbands and wives, as children do, but they did what children cannot.

Augusta was not his only diversion, though she was certainly the most diverting. He had fallen in again with James Wedderburn Webster, the silly ass whom Hobhouse and the others had brought to visit him at Newstead in the post-Cambridge days of the Paphian servant girls. The bold Webster had shopped successfully for a pretty and well-connected young bride, Lady Frances, the daughter of the Earl of Mountnorris. He now solicited Byron to meet her, manifesting the kind of silly pride that was likely to lead to the most obvious of falls. Webster persuaded Byron to come to his country house, Aston Hall, near Rotherham, in September 1813, and his wife, to whom he attributed the character of 'Our Lord Himself', proceeded in very brief time from piety (Byron averred to Lady M. that she was measured for a new Bible once a quarter) to infatuation. Byron had promised that he would be the 'living incarnation of rabid Platonism', but Webster's unsubtle pursuit of a German Countess, another guest at Aston Hall, combined with Lady Frances' naiveté – which led her to be remarkably forward without apparently recognizing the symptoms of her own besottedness – tempted Byron towards the usual trophy.

In the best tradition of Sheridan's farces, Lady Frances and he exchanged notes, blatantly hidden in improving books, under the eyes of her *marito*, though at first their commerce was conducted on a spiritual plane. Lady Frances chose to believe that Byron was capable of 'great goodness' and, goodness, he was willing to pander to such illusions, but as her sighs grew more languorous and her beauty more captivating, spirituality began to excite its physical correlative. When Webster formally requested a moment of Byron's time in private, it seemed that his host had at last taken exception to what was happening: but it was not the satisfaction of a duel he was so bold as to demand. Look here, he badly needed a loan of a thousand pounds (the Countess was proving no easy mark, d'ye see?) and could Byron help him? (He could, and did.) The virtue of his wife, Webster explained, had made it essential for him to seek carnal pleasures elsewhere: the Countess, it seemed, was a piece to perish in. Byron was soon able to report to Lady M. that, so far as he and the lovely lady went, though the seal was not yet fixed, the wax was prepared for the impression.

At the last moment, however, though all the circumstances were propitious (he and Lady Frances had an assignation at two in the morning), Byron 'spared her'. If she demurred becomingly at the last minute, she had scarcely come to their rendezvous for the pleasure of refusing him. No, something in her pretty confusion touched Byron's conscience. The rueful roué did not add her to his collection. He had pretended to suffer from her coyness, but now, when she promised that she was not cold, as her husband was pleased and stupid enough to believe, he could not bring himself to profit from his own subterfuge. He was rewarded by being told that he was the greatest man in the whole world and a saint compared to herself. Thus beatified, he left for London in the same coach as his host. A tearful Lady Frances waved them goodbye. Her husband observed complacently that she was absurdly fond, but Byron had a notion that the buffoon suspected something and speculated ironically on the possibility of dying in a duel with a man who owed him money and whose wife he had not, for once, actually dishonoured. The wits would have their laughs, the moralists their sermons and Caro Lamb, of course, would go wild with grief, that it had not happened on her account.

As winter came on, he and Augusta repaired to Newstead. Under heavy, isolating snow, they found themselves the only inhabitants (unless you counted the servants) of a cold, but comforting Eden. What was life? The summer of a dormouse! As he reached his twenty-sixth birthday, Byron was plagued by a sense of missed opportunity, as opportunists often are. The most he could now hope, he thought, was that some would say, 'He might perhaps if he would.' The examples of Sulla and Buonaparte, paradigms of action and resolution, haunted the conscience (and conceit) of a rhyming poseur who could not even find a buyer for his own property. He and his sister had toyed with elopement (what had they not toyed with?), but they were now faced with a problem to which flight could provide no romantic solution: Augusta was pregnant. Those icy, calm weeks at Newstead afforded only a temporary retreat from all the confusions in which Byron had so wantonly embroiled himself. What seemed like decided profligacy was also jaded indecision. The lame boy, once apparently excluded from the normal pleasures of life, the child whose father offered neither a reliable example nor even a reassuring longevity, had helped himself to a cornucopia of delights which now threatened to turn to Dead Sea fruit. For trivial example, Lady Frances Wedderburn Webster, that paragon of panting reluctance, could not take it that 'no' was really his answer: she pursued him with letters and an unappeased ardour to which his not ungenerous vanity was hardly less ardent to respond, though in the event he maintained his improbable halo while she set about jettisoning hers. The now bold lady's determination to acquire a famous lover was finally satisfied by a rendezvous with the Duke of Wellington in the corner of a foreign field, near Brussels, in June 1815. Lady Frances' hectic alternations of lust and shame continued to make her an alarming mistress as Scrope Davies' trunk, full of memorabilia, has recently disclosed. Scrope's failure to take Byron's advice to 'marry and beget some *scrooples*', made him an available, and evidently willing, lover of Byron's abandoned or rejected mistresses, including La Webster, Caroline Lamb and Lady Oxford.

As for Byron himself, only Annabella Milbanke seemed to offer some prospect of a life in which married rectitude would reduce the heat of sex and mitigate the cold wind of insolvency. She appeared also to be the one girl strong enough to work a transformation of his Luciferian character. Her measured concern with moral standards was at once impressive and, perhaps, mildly appetizing to a man of the world who had just seen, in the tearful comedy with Lady Frances, what could happen to chaste purposes and frigid reputations when they came to closer quarters. Annabella had all the public qualities of a proud and suitable bride, but might it not be amusing to humble her in private? Petruchio was a part he had not yet had the opportunity to play. Decorum also perhaps retained its attraction, even if politics did not. In the winter of 1813, he took the time and trouble to acknowledge a 'very able, and I believe very just criticism' of *The Giaour* which had appeared in *The Christian Observer*. He had not, he said, taken notice of any public criticism, 'good or bad, in the way of either thanks or defence', for some years. Why did he do so now? Common civility offers one explanation but so too does a certain hankering for the approval of the kind of decent people, like the Pigots, whom he had once known at Southwell.

In the spring of 1814, Augusta returned to Six Mile Bottom without any sign of panic or remorse. Lady Melbourne warned Byron that he was standing on the brink of a precipice, but then where else could one enjoy so dramatic a view? He seemed to be inviting society to give him a final push when, in his new poem, *The Bride of Abydos*, he flaunted the incest theme. Its extremely successful publication all but coincided with the birth of Augusta's daughter in April 1814. Whether it was he or she who elected to call the girl Elizabeth Medora, we cannot be sure, but if it was his idea, she patently agreed to it, either through arrogant frivolity or casual ignorance of the fact that the heroine of *The Bride of Abydos* bore the same name. Even Lady Melbourne gagged on the news: Byron, she decided, was 'lost forever'. If there seems little question that Augusta and he were indeed lovers, the paternity of the infant has never been established. Medora Leigh herself was always convinced that Byron was her father, but it is true that he never addressed himself to her with the fondness later bestowed on his illegitimate daughter by Claire Clairmont. He told Lady M. that Medora 'ain't an ape' – the form that superstition promised incestuous offspring would take – and though the remark may have been intended to draw boastful attention to the absurdity of the old wives' tale, it can equally be read as a disclaimer. Whether Colonel Leigh had taken enough time off from racing to be a plausible candidate for fatherhood it is impossible to tell, but he appears to have made no fuss, either because he was satisfied that he was indeed the infant's father or because he was indifferent alike to gossip and to Augusta's scatty humours. One thing remains certain: whatever his paternal role, Byron unquestionably helped to father the rumours.

Having already advertised his dislike of babies (he never recanted from his admiration for Herod), he stayed away from Six Mile Bottom after Medora's birth and did not see Augusta again until high summer. He spent the season in town and so, to his dismay, did Caro Lamb. Her haunting devotion was beyond exorcism; her gluttony for punishment fascinated hardly less than it repelled him. He resumed his bachelor life, even returning to Angelo's for boxing and fencing, but what had once been fresh and alluring was now corrupt and distasteful: he did not have to buy his women off the street, they trooped into Albany where he had taken a set of rooms, and sought him out; some he embraced, others he refrained from embracing. He went to Drury Lane to see Edmund Kean in *Othello* and was as excited by the electric talent of the man as by the poetic challenge of the theatre. One night he returned to Piccadilly to find that Caro Lamb had paid him a visit. Inside the flyleaf of a copy of Beckford's *Vathek* she had scribbled the message, 'Remember me!' As if in response to a challenge in a party game, he retorted with spontaneous savagery:

> Remember thee! remember thee!
> Till Lethe quench life's burning stream
> Remorse and shame shall cling to thee,
> And haunt thee like a feverish dream!
>
> Remember thee! Aye, doubt it not.
> Thy husband too shall think of thee:
> By neither shalt thou be forgot,
> Thou *false* to him, thou *fiend* to me!

As an improvisation, it was nice going, in its nasty way, and a perfect encapsulation of the double standard from which only the bravest or most brazen women could long claim exemption. Byron's debaucheries and seductions, his disdain for cant and his flair for impudence, seem to sort oddly with a growing conviction that marriage might still cure his malaise. Yet he had an abiding respect for the respectable, if only it could prove itself strong enough to bind him to a proper life. Why else should he have continued, as he had with sporadic enthusiasm, to correspond with his Princess of Parallelograms?

Annabella was up in Durham, at Seaham House, with her parents and not even the summer of the sovereigns, when London (though not Byron) was *en fête* at the defeat of Napoleon and his quarantine in Elba, could lure her to town. Here was virtue indeed! Such precocious dullness was a certificate, viewed in a certain light, of Annabella's sterling character; as for her physical attributes, they mattered less, at least at this remove, than the promise of domestic asylum.

She was not, of course, the only candidate for Byron's domestication. Lady Charlotte Leveson-Gower (Augusta's preference) was a more attractive proposition, but after a few assaying preliminaries, neither party was disposed to take the thing any further. Lady Charlotte skipped away like an antelope (an animal to whom Caro Lamb had also likened herself) and on 1 July 1814, Byron limped, solitary and sour, into the great masked ball at Burlington House where all Europe, it seemed, and certainly all London had come to pay tribute to the conqueror. For Byron, all the wrong heads in England had been crowned with laurel. He lashed out with an anonymous poem that roundly derided the Prince Regent and another that lauded his fallen idol, Napoleon. Affectations of anonymity guaranteed that the poems were talked about and that his name was attached to them. Hobhouse, back from the continent, regaled him with a thousand splendid stories about the defeated Buonaparte. Byron was particularly fond of his way with ladies who came to his tent: how masterful merely to say *'Déshabillez-vouz'* without even looking up! But the triumph of Wellington could not be smiled or smirked away. Byron, in monk's garb, observed that it was as if a stone were being worshipped because a man had stumbled over it and that London was ready to cheer any 'bloody booby who breaks heads'. But such insolence was the wine of sour grapes; he had been consummately upstaged and if he was to draw attention back to himself, he had to be more than cheeky or puppyish.

And so it is easy to suspect that he himself was responsible for the widespread canard that he had confessed to 'the foulest crime' a man can commit. Hobhouse, in the sceptical tradition, was prepared to believe that he meant deliberate and premeditated exaggeration; but gaping girls like Lady Charlotte obliged by guessing that it must have been murder, to which Byron was happy to retort that, had it been murder, the Burlington House Ball would as like have been in his honour. Did he whisper the word 'incest' himself? Did he who loved word-play anticipate Vladimir Nabokov's observation of the mere misprint that divides incest from 'nicest'? He was sometimes shameless enough and often drunk enough and always bright enough. At all events, by the autumn he was being propelled towards some kind of resolution: he must either go over the precipice or retreat into rectitude. He reconciled the apparently impossible and combined the two.

Byron's taste for memorabilia, which makes the quotidian jigsaw of his life so easy and so enjoyable to reassemble, was reflected in his inability ever quite to rid himself of anything that reminded him of the past. The apostle of ruthlessness and novelty was also addicted to sentiment and old memories. His willingness, however sighing, to spend time with people like Wedderburn Webster, posits an uncritical need for reassurance no less than a certain capacity for suffering fools, gladly or not. Revenge was the best way of living well: he was still tempted to pay out Mary Chaworth, who as Mrs Musters had failed to find happiness and to whom the strutting celebrity was not at all the same repulsive object as the lame boy. She had written many letters to him; she wanted passionately to see him and she had no wish, he could depend upon it, to treat him as badly as he was now armed to treat her, if he wished.

He was, however, either too sated or too busy to act on her invitation. Male companions remained those with whom he was easiest: Tom Moore, Scrope Davies and Hobhouse offered the unencumbering good fellowship in which he was most himself and most at his ease. With the exception of Moore, Monk Lewis and Sheridan, literary society bored him; that inky galère, with its trite malice and its rubbed elbows, had little allure. Though he was impressed with Robert Southey's profile, the Lakers as poets soon made him uncomfortable with their earnestness and finally disgusted him with their turncoat and toadying conservatism. The cult of nature was one to which, in due course, he would make effortful obeisance, but a poet with a gift for paradox, for punning conceits and for adventurous amorality never chimed with simple sincerities and po-faced piety. The most famous romantic poet was never entirely comfortable with Romanticism; though his life of sensational and egocentric excess appeared to make him the very instance of a Romantic hero, his writing neither disdained classical models nor avoided conventional tropes. Wordsworth's search for a new vocabulary was also an appeal to a new audience. The canker of aristocracy, which Shelley would deplore and the Cambridge men had already mocked in the Old English Baron, gave Byron's verse, even when it was selling very well in unsmart quarters, an allusive playfulness and an in-group cynicism which may have been as self-protective as it was self-regarding. Scornful or aloof, he remained the prisoner of his pretensions and the servant of his station. His astonishing facility leads to charges of superficiality (sometimes his own), but the manuscripts, so assiduously collected by, among others, J. Pierpont Morgan, reveal how unwise it is to assume that he never blotted a line. He often worked diligently at perfection, and he can hardly be reproached if it sometimes came without his having to work for it. It is tempting to make a correlation between his poetic flippancy and his frivolous relationships with women while his deeper, more painful work reflects darker and more secretive sexual tastes. His fascination with youths like Edleston and Robert Rushton makes it plausible to argue that he was 'really' homosexual all along, but his response to female beauty could be both ardent and apt. The sight of his cousin, the beautiful Mrs Wilmot, dressed in spangled mourning at a London party excited the ravishing 'She Walks in Beauty Like the Night' a lyric later appended to *Hebrew Melodies* and one which suggests how easily, in another age, Byron might have turned his hand to show business: would not George Gershwin have been as happy to have him as a collaborator as was Isaac Nathan?

The return of Augusta to London society was a comfort, but not so great a comfort as before. Still capable of her winsome crinkum-crankum, she now shared some of the alarm which her own garrulity had helped to generate; if not deliberately outrageous like Byron, like Byron she had little reticence. Caro Lamb was adept at getting her to talk and at using whatever she extracted for her own unpredictable purposes. In a situation without any reliable logic, when a hundred courses looked equally good or equally bad, Byron finally had recourse to luck, if you could call it that, and to superstition. While he was actually drafting one more letter to Annabella Milbanke, a Newstead gardener found a wedding ring in one of the flower beds. Byron recognized it as Mrs Byron's and, wearily or warily, elected to read it for an omen. He told Augusta that if Miss Milbanke accepted his latest proposal, he would become Lord Annabella and be married with that very ring. If not (and perhaps he still preferred this alternative), he would leave for Venice with Hobby.

Annabella was a studious and religiously-minded young person. She was also innocent, and not only in the worldly sense: she had many ideas but very little knowledge, not least of herself. She may have imagined that she was free to choose her husband for herself, but the money she would inherit and the expectations of her family circumscribed her choice. She had not been above teasing Byron with the correct qualities of George Eden, his putative rival, but Durham society offered no great range of possibilities and Byron's proposal, however lacking in passionate sentiments, presented, if starchily, the opportunity for a startling triumph.

It arrived, so the story goes, while she was indulging in one of her favourite childhood games, walking blindfold round the edge of the lake in the gardens of Seaham House. Boredom made her more skittish than her rectilinear reputation suggested. It has been wondered why Annabella accepted Byron now when she had been so cool before. Her moral fineness has been taken at its face value, but it entails no disparagement of a much disparaged woman to point out that, even in the most refined circles, Jane Austen-like judiciousness in the choice of a suitable partner, a nose for the subtlest nuances of character, rarely stood in the way of social and financial calculation when it came to assessing the chances of living happily ever after. Byron's tone, if often facetious, was never vulgar when conversing with a virgin. The rake was tactful enough (and had a sufficient appreciation of irony) to honour the terms in which the young girl wished to conduct their preliminaries, but both he and she, surely, knew precisely to what they were preliminary: the marriage bed may have held secrets of whose precise anatomical nature Annabella was not certain, but everyone knew to what practical consummation hesitant steps and high-minded formulae were leading. The enrichment of the line and the preservation of property, hardly less than personal happiness and emotional rapport, were the proper ends of marriage. Mathematical Annabella surely knew that the time must come in every heiress's life when the perpendicular would be dropped on the horizontal. If her parents still had misgivings, she showed no sign of sharing them.

It has been argued that Annabella had seduced Byron with a wholly unconscious skill, exciting his acquisitive interest by moves which could appear scheming though they were in fact artless: he read her for a minx when she was merely a rabbit. But may she not herself have been unconscious of how much she really desired him? Inhibitions obliged her to raise their courtship to a level of preciosity which was sometimes ridiculous, but that need not imply that she was always unaware of her artfulness. The desire to come out on top intellectually and the desire to possess (or to be possessed) are by no means always at odds, though one may well conceal the other. Objectively viewed, Annabella can be said to have waged a brilliant and patient campaign. Had Caro Lamb conducted herself with such teasing restraint, she might have been credited with positively Ovidian premeditation. After all, for whatever reluctant motives, the most desired man in England, perhaps in the world, was indeed now about to end in the arms of a not very pretty and entirely proper young provincial lady, hardly his usual destination. The issue of sincerity need scarcely come into the reckoning, for what was not artificial or venal in the mergers of the upper class? If we assume that Annabella did not crave Byron physically, we are taking at face value the cosmetic with which no young girl could dispense if she wished to give a correct impression of maidenly decorum. The truth remains that his lordship, tarnished or no, was the catch of the century and Annabella must have known it. She wrote ardently to accept his proposal, indifferent to the qualms of her family or of her old nurse, Mrs Clermont.

Byron opened her reply in Augusta's presence. He turned pale (did he not do the same when he heard that Mary Chaworth was married?) and then remarked: 'It never rains but it pours.' The omen may be read as darkly as hindsight warrants, but what rake, however fond, faced the end of his bachelorhood without a measure of distress? What fox likes to have its tail cut off? Whatever his emotions, he replied in a tone which lacks passion, but not seriousness; the overtures concluded, he can be seen to be trying to bring a measure of realism into the hitherto lofty and coy exchanges. He does not boast of his manifold sins and wickednesses, but alludes to them with a certain cleansing candour. Perhaps he was convinced that Annabella was indeed the paragon she had for so long made herself out to be, strong enough to keep him on the path of virtue, capable of a mature response to immaturities.

On a visit to Seaham, he played the apprentice son-in-law with as good a will as he might, enduring the cold appraisal of Lady Milbanke and the bumbling platitudes of her husband, Sir Ralph, with what he hoped would pass for endearing patience. He may be excused, when the time approached, for not looking forward greatly to another journey north for the actual ceremony, which was to be conducted quietly in Seaham House, at a safe distance – but what a distance! – from the London gossips. On the way, he and Hobhouse, still the reliable Horatio to his lordship's moody Hamlet, made a Christmas halt at Six Mile Bottom, where Augusta and child furnished a pretty reminder of why the long journey was really necessary; at length, the friends continued, through a hoary January landscape, to Durham.

Victorian writers were the first to make a full-scale cult of childhood, but Byron had done much to glorify youth. His own tendency to fat – he was one of the first compulsive slimmers – and his fear of losing his hair (and his teeth) made him particularly conscious of the brevity of life. His love of boys – he seems never to have been excited by males of his own age – testified also to his retrospective yearning for a lost Eden. *Childe Harold* celebrated, often mournfully, the heated vulnerability of adolescence. Had he not lamented old age when he was but twenty-three? Debauchery and irresponsibility, the adoption of surrogate mothers like Lady M., these things were – whatever else they may also have been – aspects of a decided desire to avert his eyes from the deciduous calendar of mortality. Marriage, never mind to whom, was the tolling of a bell he never wanted to hear. Was it Annabella in particular whom he now dreaded or the unprecipitous road which took him through the white gate of marriage along the common path to middle-aged banality?

He had scarcely arrived at Seaham House but he remarked to his fiancée that she had written him 'some powerful sermons'; he hoped he would earn sufficient marks to pass her examination. Annabella, on the other hand, was in a mood for amorous skittishness. She pointed out, light-heartedly, that the wedding cake made 'Ossa look like a wart', a nice classical reference, which a literary Harrovian should have appreciated. Byron's nervous severity made her burst into girlish tears which he assuaged, after his fashion, by saying that perhaps they would be as happy as if they had never been married at all. At the very moment when he wanted to be reassured as to her strength of character, he was faced with an over-excited and unfamiliar Annabella, all giggles and tears, while she, who had assumed, or hoped, that frowns and ploys would now be replaced by unaffected affection, was saddled with a resentful neurotic whose favourite classical tag at that moment might well have been 'Eheu fugaces, postume, Postume/Labuntur anni . . .' The imminence of marriage reminded him of the inexorable slip of time. And when he was reminded of something disagreeable, he rarely kept his resentment to himself if he could lay it on someone else.

On the day before the wedding, there was a gay rehearsal, during which Hobhouse appeared in drag in the part of Annabella. This camp parody was a good deal more cheerful than the actual ceremony. What Byron wished were over, or might never be, took place in an atmosphere of barely controlled misgivings. When, in due course, Hobhouse dared to call the wedding breakfast a very happy occasion, Lady Milbanke burst into tears. Oh dear, oh dear, how dire were the auguries! But it was not only Byron's youth which was ending; Lady Milbanke was losing her only daughter and she too was enduring a *rite de passage*. She might be forgiven for thinking of herself no less than of her daughter: had she not been given in marriage to a dullard and had she not been as naive as she now saw Annabella to be? Minor characters are not always thinking of the story which we know is about to unfold; indeed they are not always aware how minor they are. Lady Milbanke was neither the first nor the last mother to weep at her daughter's wedding and she should not be cursed with Pythian powers on that account.

True, Byron was not entirely at his ease and, in consequence, made others uneasy; it was not exactly tactful, when the wedding cake was being cut, to announce that 'it should have been eaten two years ago, when it was fresh.' He was obsessed with the feeling, or excuse, that Annabella had rejected his suit when he might still have been 'saved'. He treated her, both immediately before and after the wedding, with what sounds to be conspicuous caddishness, though the accounts of his behaviour, and their interpretations, came largely from the catalogue of Annabella's later disillusion-ment. Her promised determination to live for his happiness provoked him to deny that it was possible for him to be happy, which may have been less cruelty than honest dread. The tears that greeted his harshness also sweetened it; he promised that he hoped he could love her, though he had to add that Augusta had had more of his love than anyone else could ever have. Was this pointed play merely sadistic? It is as likely that he was trying to create a mood in which he could truly unburden himself. He told Annabella that her play-fulness sometimes reminded him of Augusta, to which she responded with a solemn undertaking to be playful. She sought to palliate his fear that the moment of redemption had passed by assuring him that she had loved him ever since he first spoke to her. In trying to win his confidence, she only confirmed his apprehension. Whatever naughty, curious or devilish appetite had driven him into his sister's arms and whatever folly had inclined him to advertise the fact, that love was now ineradicable. When he told Annabella that she reminded him of Augusta, it was perhaps not only to tease her but also to reassure himself.

The one aspect of Byron's personality which is always taken for granted is his sexual potency; not even those most con-vinced of his homosexual preferences have ever suggested that he had any trouble with the ladies. But marriage was something different from the venal or vicious affairs in which he had indulged. Respect for marriage had given adultery its tainted charm; a woman who will deceive her husband cannot expect much mercy from her lover, which is always convenient. When Lady Frances Wedderburn Webster offered herself so artlessly, he 'spared' her as he might have a virgin; she was offering less pleasure than responsibility, to which he was neither used nor, it seems, equal. By assimil-ating Annabella to his sister he sought to see her naiveté as the kind of insouciance which Augusta, at her crinkum-crankum best, so deliciously impersonated. Yet his affair with Augusta had been something no less scandalous than unforgettable. The apparently spiteful alternation of hints with endearments, during the last days of his bachelorhood, suggests also that he continued to angle for a chance to make a full confession to Annabella. If so, her timidities must have been appalling, blameless evidence that she lacked the kind of maturity so evident in her aunt, Lady Melbourne, a moral generosity (or indifference) which might have enabled him to put the past truly behind him. Doubtless it was unfair to expect so much of a provincial girl, but had she not herself encouraged his belief in her as someone of exceptional qualities? He was looking for that impossible combination of earth-mother and nymph which, in some obliging dream, might have furnished a blend of Lady Oxford and Lady Melbourne with Mary Chaworth or Mary Duff. As it was, too much had happened which could not be divulged, without shame or violence, for him ever to be on honest terms with his wife.

Regret was hardly distinguishable from disgust. When he told her, as they rolled away in the carriage from Seaham House, that she had once had it in her power to save him he was being as sincere as he was savage. And when he added that she was now in his power and he would make her feel it, the forecast may well have been no less rueful than tactless: he had no other prospect, if she could not now produce those rare qualities of sympathy and intuition she had appeared to advertise. He sought to amuse as well as to confound her by yelling some outlandish anthem learned from his Albanians; and neither her puzzlement nor her smiles furnished quite the right response. From her point of view, by now he must have seemed the most famous and self-assured man in the world, a buck now officially licensed to take her maidenhead whenever he fancied. How could she, in the midst of her own maidenly apprehensions, reassure him convincingly that he had done the right thing?

What might have been becoming in any other young bride was of little comfort to him; the prospect of possession was unalluring for one whose experience of the sex, though wide enough to be notorious, was of sex with the experienced. When, still in the carriage, he concluded (as report promises) that 'it must come to a separation', he was hardly conducting himself with the routine grace of a young husband, but then Annabella had not embraced a routine marriage. The impulse to experiment with repartee, to say the first naughty thing that came into his head, was part of his genius. (Had not the girls of London been enchanted by his impertinence and swarmed to match their wits with his?) Yet one may sympathize with an Annabella stunned by the violence of his psychological assault. She had spent her sharp shafts on their correspondence and now she was as good as disarmed, never realizing that such mum defencelessness might not be as fetching as she assumed it to be for a roué in mourning for his youth, still broke and with strange fruit on his family tree. Inexperience deprived her of the wit to read him with critical subtlety. She could never guess to what degree his remarks were parodies, or revisions, of what he had said to Augusta or Caro or a dozen other women, tests of her nerve and challenges to her temper.

The treacle-moon (Byron was not one to miss a punning opportunity) took place at Halnaby Hall, a residence lent them by boring old Sir Ralph. As they passed through Durham, the bells were ringing. 'For our happiness, I suppose?' Byron sneered. Yet for all the chilling reports which later swathed the occasion in mournful crêpe, the honeymoon was far from a frost or a wake. Indeed the only unquestionably black touch was a piece of material which Annabella inserted to keep fat Mrs Byron's gold wedding ring on her slim finger. Byron, the cynic and blasphemer, was unnerved by her careless gesture and insisted that she remove the unlucky ribbon. Unluckier still, as she did so, the ring flipped into the fire and had to be dredged out. Mrs Minns, an old Milbanke servant doubling as housekeeper, had arranged that they have connecting rooms, four-poster beds in each, one with red moreen curtains, which Byron elected to make his own. Adjacent to the fireplace in the sitting room was a sofa where, with his quirk for improvisation, he disposed of Lady Byron's virginity before dinner.

Arrogance and anxiety both make for abruptness. Caro Lamb, whose testimony can at best be termed wishful, had already forecast that Byron never would 'pull with a woman who goes to church punctually, understands statistics and has a bad figure', but Annabella seems to have found conjugal duties not too disagreeable. Soon she was conversing with Byron in those terms of nursery coyness which embarrass pundits but endear lovers. She became 'Pippin' or 'Bell' and he was 'duck' or simply 'B', the baby. In a letter to Tom Moore, written from Halnaby Hall, Byron referred ambiguously to marriage as 'the most ambrosial of all future states', but for the present the treacle-moon was clearly not as sticky as all that. Yet he was capable of threatening that he would be to Annabella 'as Caroline Lamb was to her husband's heart – a perpetually falling drop of water; it ruins and it petrifies.' He had, to say the least, an unreliable temper. He raised all the topics which haunted him, and haunted her with them. He even reacted with revulsion to the sight of her eating: it reminded him of his fat mother. When she wanted to spend the night with him, he announced that he hated 'sleeping with any woman'. Was his wife 'any woman'? Well, she could stay if she chose.

His charmless habit of putting the responsibility on the woman for desires he had aroused was not long in asserting itself. He had been a villain to marry her, he said, and when she contradicted him fondly, as she was surely meant to, he snapped back that he could convince her of it in three words. Yet if wifely optimism began to wane, he lost patience with her dismay and made light of the dark intimations with which he had depressed her. Why must she take him so seriously? He only wanted to make a woman laugh and 'did not care what she was besides'. He could make Augusta laugh at anything; hence she alone was able to make him happy. His bride could draw what conclusion from that she liked.

Yet he did reveal himself to her with a measure of unguardedness. They went climbing on the cliffs and he proved of what determined agility a cripple was capable when they raced up a set of steps in the face of the rock. She had the tact to give him a good race and to come second. He even showed her his 'little foot', his intractable secret. Yet whenever they seemed on the verge of unconditional intimacy, he would raise some barbed barrier. Money continued to preoccupy him; the marriage settlement was not unprofitable, but the income from it would accrue to him only after Lady Milbanke had died. Annabella could hardly be expected to look forward to her mother's death, but there was no doubt that it would come, was there? Byron affected to be doubtful: he suspected her entire family of possessing the secret of eternal life and declared them all to be 'at this moment cutting another set of teeth'. Even as he assured Tom Moore that, though an abiding enemy of any lifelong freehold, he was willing to renew the lease of his marriage, 'though the next term were for ninety and nine years,' he was soon soliciting news of what was going on in the way of 'intriguery and how the whores and rogues of the Upper Beggar's Opera go on – or rather go off.'

The quarantine of matrimony could not long isolate him from metropolitan contamination; Annabella would have had to be more resourceful than she proved in order to furnish sufficient understanding or entertainment to banish the memory of pleasures past and the lure of their resumption. Nameless vices had made his name; without them, how could he still be Byron? Unlike those aristocrats who had unencumbered lands and an acknowledged place in society, political prospects and a nexus of familiar duties, his status depended on an ability to invent and promote himself: if the scaling ladder of *Childe Harold* had elevated him to notoriety, he lacked any durable pedestal of wealth or lineage. It might be lovely to be a Lord, but it was scarcely enough. The idea of salvation at Annabella's hands was as alarming as it was comforting, for it would imply the collapse of his whole publicity-conscious personality, a kind of annihilation which would reduce 'baby B.' to a powerless and puling toy.

He was tempted, nonetheless, to settle for domesticity. One day at Halnaby, his wife came in by lucky chance when he was lying on the sofa semi-conscious, overcome by smoke from a fire so caked that, instead of drawing properly, it had funnelled suffocating fumes into the room. Annabella promptly kicked the coals into flame, doused a handkerchief with cologne and saved Byron from probable asphyxiation. As he revived, he was moved to tell her that perhaps he would 'try virtue after all – and go to heaven holding the hem of your garment.' (A few nights before, waking to see a light shining through those red moreen curtains, he had believed himself in hell.) The honeymoon may not have been a panacea; it was far from a catastrophe. As for his wife, given the manners of the day, she probably had a less traumatic time, in some respects, than many girls: her husband was neither as oafish as Wedderburn Webster nor as cynical as a routine fortune hunter. Priding herself on her ability to solve difficult problems, she had elected to marry a genius and a self-confessed 'fallen angel'; her vanity found itself faced with the knottiest psychological conundrum of the age, which was surely what had attracted her in the first place. In some respects she made him a model wife: she coped with his amorous propensities and copied his poems (he was working on *Hebrew Melodies)* with dutiful grace. As the honeymoon ended, he rewarded her with the conclusion that he believed that he loved her; not all she had hoped for, but no bleak verdict. Any sense of relief, however, may have been slightly dashed by the proposal that they call on Augusta on their way to London. Mrs Minns was distressed at the decline in Annabella's spirits and may well have reported so to the Milbankes.

How much had the bride now guessed, or cared to guess, about the incest? Byron, in his tart manner, assumed that she 'knew pretty well which subjects to avoid' when they arrived at Six Mile Bottom. Whatever she had been told or suspected concerning Medora's paternity, she could hardly fail to recognize Byron's inordinate love for Augusta. If she was to avoid offending her husband, she must show affection for her sister-in-law; if she was to keep him, she must supplant her. The mathematics of this particular triangle went beyond Euclidian definitions.

Byron had looked forward not only to the contest between his two ladies but also to the mail waiting for him at the Leighs' house. Unfortunately, it brought exasperating news of further delays in the sale of Newstead. More amusingly, he also opened a box containing three gold brooches which he had ordered, each containing two locks of hair, his and Augusta's, and each engraved with three cryptic crosses. He presented one to Augusta and one to Medora; the third, of course, the inveterate trophy-collector kept for himself. The crosses, it need scarcely be said, though it probably was, had no religious significance; they were the objective correlatives of a private language which was spoken only in loud whispers between brother and sister.

Augusta may have been flighty but she was not unkind; while Byron baited his wife with innuendo, his sister did her best to play the considerate hostess. Her children brought out Byron's amiable side; they goaded him into playing the bear with them and his grizzly growls, at least those uttered in their direction, were genial and entertaining. Annabella sought, either because she was still puzzled or because the truth, if it was true, was so unpalatable, to draw Augusta into her confidence. What was this secret agony which gnawed at Byron's vitals? Augusta volunteered the demystifying answer in a single word: indigestion.

Byron's dyspeptic behaviour may indeed have been egged on by his eccentric diet, the contradictions of alcoholic recklessness and weight-watcher's asceticism, though Annabella's anxiety can hardly have been dispelled by Augusta's facetiousness or by the giggles she overheard when brother and sister found themselves alone, or acted as though they were, the teases. She was needled by whispers about the meaning of those cryptic crosses; the three of them, one evening, played a rhyming game and Annabella, guilelessly or not, proposed marking her contributions, when they were passed to Augusta, with a cross, whereupon Byron said, 'For God's sake don't do that, you'll frighten Augusta to death!' The crosses, he thus hinted, with no marked subtlety, referred to some arcane activity whose nature he made very clear when, on another occasion, he ordered Annabella to bed with the words, 'We don't need you down here, my charmer,' adding that now he had Augusta, 'You'll find I can do without you – in every way!' He could be cruel and childish and not infrequently coarse; schoolboy sniggers about his personal knowledge that Augusta wore 'drawers' are hardly worthy of the poet Goethe admired.

The web of ambiguities is suggestive, yet awkward to unravel. Gracelessness towards those who had acceded to their sexual advances was so characteristic of Regency bucks that no singular stigma attaches to Byron's display of it; he could often be disappointingly conventional. Augusta alone seems to have been exempt from the condescension to which even his wife was soon subject; only with his sister could sentiment both precede conquest and survive it. Their liaison was privileged, and doomed, to fall into a unique category; his one remaining blood relationship, with all it implied of unconditional loyalty, held him in a sweet combination of the natural and the unnatural; it answered to the call of the sweet and of the corrupt side of his character. How could he be expected, in such circumstances, to transfer his allegiance to his stiff, stifling wife? Having married in order to escape the abyss, he was lured back to the edge by the delicious memory (and prospect) of forbidden fruit on a familiar bough.

At length the Byrons continued to London, where they rented an impressive house at 13, Piccadilly Terrace. In public they presented the very image of consecrated felicity. Lady Byron was appropriately pregnant, his lordship willing to parade his reformed character with enough amiability to spite Caro Lamb and Mary Chaworth-Musters, both of whom would have welcomed any sign of marital stress when the happyish pair came across them on the social circuit. Annabella was jealous enough to call Mary a 'wicked-looking cat', which must have been gratifying, but she was less wise when she expressed the wish that they could leave London because it was driving her mad; she should have known that if anyone was going to go mad, that star part would be reserved for her husband. Money would send him to Bedlam, if no more glamorous motive were available; the bailiffs were regular visitors and Byron could easily persuade himself that it was all Lady Milbanke's inconsiderate fault.

Annabella was too eager for her marriage to succeed for it to have much chance of success. The long-serving Fletcher, who had seen the ladies come and seen them go, declared that he had never known one who could not do as she pleased with his lordship, except her ladyship. Annabella remained less angry than confused; her pregnancy should have earned her some respite and some credit perhaps, in Byron's eyes, but it was also a reminder of his inescapable state. How could he respond save by escaping, at least temporarily? Delivered of marital duties, he was not long in seeking pleasure and oblivion elsewhere.

Ever since he had first seen Edmund Kean, the theatre fascinated him. The line between living a part and playing a part was thrillingly fine and the company of theatricals, at once remote from real life and full of vitality, relieved him of the need to impersonate the least regarded of all characters, the husband. Recruited by his friend, the honourable Douglas Kinnaird, to take a hand in the affairs of the revived Drury Lane Theatre (it had been burned down and rebuilt), he soon acquired an ambitious young actress, Susan Boyce, as his mistress and found her relaxingly broad-minded; another girl sometimes joined them as they rehearsed their pleasures. Buonaparte was 'chained to a rock' and Metternich's diplomatic arrangements had rigidified Europe in a reactionary mould, but *'Déshabillez-vous'* could still be the order of the day, and night, if one was discreet about it. Napoleon, he told the girls, would horsewhip those who disclosed the attentions he paid them, but the danger of a leak lay, as usual, less with his charmers than with his own garrulous self.

He was not the first husband to notice incipient motherhood glazing his wife with insipid complacency. He was excluded and he would punish her for it: was he there merely to pick up her fan at Lady Holland's and otherwise to live the life of an anchorite? Even – perhaps particularly – Augusta, when she came to visit them, was shocked by the coarseness of his speech and the violence of his address. He reverted to a wicked lordly way of brandishing loaded pistols. When, at last, he actually pulled the trigger in the drawing room, Lady Byron could be forgiven for jumping to the conclusion that he was mad. When she swore that she would never forgive him, he seemed appalled and flung himself at her feet, protesting that he was a fool and a monster. She hesitated as he grovelled before her, moaning that he had lost her forever. Perhaps 'keaning' would be the right term for his performance, for no sooner had she recanted and promised to forgive him than he put away his tears, jumped to his feet and burst out laughing. To her disconcerted outrage, he claimed that he had been 'conducting a philosophical experiment' in order to discover the value of her resolutions.

Was his remorse genuine and his explanation merely the gauge of his shame at having prostrated himself or was the whole performance indeed an 'experiment'? The choice is perhaps a false one; the dramatic artist is blessed and cursed with a sense of both sides of the question. Duplicity arms his vision; he is at once an actor in his own show and its observer and scenarist. The whole of his life is an 'experiment' of a kind; when he is most happy as a man he is often most anxious as an artist, for when was happiness a fruitful subject? (Childhood, since it is lost, is often gilded with retrospective blissfulness, but were it not irretrievable, what writer would be happy with it?)

Byron's anxieties were not only economic, they were also poetic. Some, if certainly not all, of the verses that made up *Hebrew Melodies* were proper enough to please Annabella when she copper-plated them, but an element of staleness marred his work. The danger of plaiting one's life into the work is that an unadventurous existence is mirrored in lacklustre verses. The autobiographical writer is obliged to a kind of cannibalism: when he can no longer go a-hunting, he begins to gnaw himself. Arguments about whether Byron really wanted to keep Annabella or not, whether he was a posturing sadist or a misunderstood genius, pose neat but impertinent alternatives. She complained that he blamed her for everything and, poor lady, she thought that she could avoid trial simply by being innocent. Love made her into a tearful scold and when she turned for help to her sister-in-law, who was kind enough and candid enough to confess that she too had been a victim of Byron's demanding moods, Augusta rather spoilt things by adding ambiguously, 'You don't know what a fool *I've* been about him.'

Lady Milbanke and Mrs Clermont come up to London for the accouchement. The old governess was quick to move into Piccadilly Terrace, where Byron took her for a sanctimonious spy. Lady Milbanke stayed at Mivart's hotel; she was said to be ill again. Could Byron resist hoping that it was for the last time? The management of Drury Lane Theatre having now co-opted him onto its ambitious sub-committee, he was not sorry to find himself out of the West End as frequently as its business and his pleasure could be confused. The duns vied with the doctors at the door of the conjugal home and Mrs Clermont's reproachful sympathy for her poor baby enraged the petulant father-to-be; prospective childbirth seemed to have united all the females in its exclusive club, Augusta included. Byron consoled himself with Susan Boyce (who soon became wearisomely fond and demanding) and with drink. When Annabella's labour finally began, he waited sulkily in the drawing room, in fee to the women who now commanded the house. Annabella would always believe, and proclaim, that he spent his time flinging soda-water bottles at the ceiling, so that they exploded under the bed in which she was suffering. It seems unlikely, though the trouble with Byron is that the unlikely is always possible. Probably he contented himself with scything the tops off the soda-water bottles with a poker. The agony of childbirth (Annabella did not have an easy time) may well have induced a near-delirium in which Byron's tantrums exploded in her subconscious like a literal bombardment. His jealousy of the infant (born on 10 December 1815) was so immodest that he had already threatened to go abroad as soon as his heir was born, 'because a woman always loves her child better than her husband'. Can he really also have said, at Annabella's bedside, during the course of labour, 'I hope you die and the child too'? And did he add, 'If it lives, I shall curse it'? Charges of exaggeration or downright fabrication are hard to resist; *our* Byron would never say such things and how can they be reconciled with other, more genial observations? When his daughter was at last shown to him, he was good enough to observe, 'Well, well, this is very fine indeed,' though it was hardly kind to continue, 'I should have preferred a boy, but it is very well as it is.' However exaggerated the list of Byron's vices or virtues, reticence never figured in either category. He missed no opportunity, in life or in literature, for spreading himself: what is a peacock without his tail? He could not inhibit the expression of whatever he felt without endangering the potency of his genius; when he was wounded, or even scratched, language flowed. He had manners, when it suited him (or the right people were watching), and he had sentiments which were often touchingly sentimental, but he had nothing which corresponds to that Freudian governor, the super-ego. It is not merely certain forms of behaviour which fathers seem to inhibit, but also the flow of words. Writers like Jean-Paul Sartre and one of his subjects, Baudelaire (a dandy remarkable for shocking similarities to Byron), testify to the eloquence which can accompany the early loss of one's father. Sartre was not only uninhibited in his sexual life, he was also addicted to voluminous verbalizing; he could never be silenced, rarely abbreviated. Byron's childhood was not happy, but the only child of a lonely mother seldom has to hold his tongue.

Above all, of course, Byron was Byron; no rules of psychology could predict or procure him. The range of his behaviour, from crude whoring to rare affection, and of his vocabulary, from gutter obscenity to Horatian refinement, testify to his Protean mutability. The egotist seeks to assimilate the whole world; even when disgracefully harsh, he can remain shameless, for the wound he inflicts is felt so deeply in himself that he may well resent the victim's cry of pain as a discordant interruption. When Byron went to the execution of poor Bellingham, he was sympathetic to the victim's plight, but he was above all interested to see how he himself would be affected. (He would display the same queasy detachment when he went to see three criminals guillotined in Rome.) The sufferings of others were experienced as if they were his own, which explains his magnanimity, but the anguish was also, as it were, filched from the victims and credited to his own pathetic account. The ghoul and the artist are often separated only by the latter's articulacy (Thomas Hardy went on horrified tiptoe to observe the distant hanging of a woman); the writer's skill lies in dressing voyeurism in the style of art, just as annotated slumming may pass for sociology.

Byron's humiliation when the Duke of Wellington, after Waterloo, displaced him from the centre of the London stage seems to have little in common with the neglect of an expectant father but what poet could fail to see ironic similarities? The glory of another degraded him. When, in his anything-for-a-laugh days, he said that he had the greatest admiration for Herod, he was not really giving approval to the murder of innocent children, but the phrase did not occur by chance: the spoilt and insecure child is, in a way, the enemy of all other children. W. H. Auden, a fellow spirit of Byron's, remarked how, even in his venerable years, he always had the illusion that he was the youngest person in the room: he never really accepted that he had forfeited the indulgence due to the precocious infant.

32. The meeting of Lord Byron and Sir Walter Scott in the drawing room of John Murray, the publisher; a watercolour of c. 1850.

33. John Murray II.
'To thee with hope and terror dumb,
The unfledged MS, authors come;
Thou printest all — and sellest some —
                          My Murray.'

34. Detail of a page from the autograph MS of Don Juan.
'I doubt whether it is not . . . too free for these very modest days.'

35. Holland House, head office of 'the
Upper Rogue's Opera'.

36. John Cam Hobhouse.
'Thou hast so many good qualities,
and so many bad ones, it is impossible to
live with or without thee.'

37. *Breakfast at Samuel Rogers' residence (detail), 1815. Around the table are
J. B. Sheridan, Thomas Moore, Wordsworth, Southey, Coleridge, Washington
Irving, the host Rogers and (in profile) Byron.*

38. *Lady Caroline Lamb dressed as a page.*
Painting by Thomas Phillips.
'What a little volcano!'

39. *'A Voluptuary under the Horrors*
of Digestion.'
The Price of Whales dans ses oeuvres.

FASHIONABLES of 1816 taking the air in Hyde Park!

40. *Melbourne House, in Whitehall, was taken over from the Duke of York by William Lamb (later Lord Melbourne).*

41. *Byron, with an actress on each arm, trying to out-stare Lady Byron, who is pregnant and accompanied by Mrs Clermont.*

42. *St James's Street, London, the heart of Clubland, as it appeared in 1792.*

43. *Byron in a miniature by H. Kearney.*

44. *Byron's wife, Annabella Milbanke.*

45. *Byron's gold betrothal ring, which bears the crest and motto of the Byron family, as well as the words 'sans peur' engraved on the inside.*

46. *Augusta Leigh, 1817.*
'Though human, thou didst not deceive me,
Though woman, thou didst not forsake.'

47. Halnaby Hall, Co. Durham.
'Our honeymoon was not all
sunshine; it had its clouds . . . but
it was never down at zero.'

48. Augusta Ada Byron, aged 4.
'Ada! Sole daughter of my
house and heart!'

49. Claire Clairmont.
'I do not complain of you dearest nor
would not if you were twice as unkind.'

50. Mary Shelley; a portrait of 1831.

51. Byron at Villa Diodati on the
Lake of Geneva, 1816.

Soon after his marriage, Byron said that he intended to propagate his kind and then 'put an end to his wormish existence'. The birth of his daughter was proof both of his displacement and of his capture; legitimacy had at once aged and ensnared him. Locked into parenthood, he was still deprived of a male heir, a miniature self; the mirror gave back the wrong image. To be sure, such ambiguities can be multiplied so fancifully that, losing discretion, they become a compendium of every available way of imagining his situation. Yet just such compendious immodesty is at the source of creation itself. Had Byron had the purity not to feel or the decency not to express everything he felt, he might have been a better man, but he would never have been Byron. His behaviour may have been inexcusable but his whole performance was based on testing the limits, on breaching barriers and taboos, both to announce man's freedom and to confirm his own bondage. Throughout his life, he dramatized incidents which, for another, might have furnished no large ground for anguish or excitement. The casual and the commonplace were, for him, charged with cosmic significance.

Now he became a kind of domestic Belshazzar; he could not look at a wall without seeing the writing on it. His letters are the facetious proof that he rarely failed to perceive how exaggerated were his own or other people's postures; the comedy of morals and the pretensions of literature could always be empressed for the diversion of his friends. Yet the poet, impious as he could sometimes be over poetry's solemnities, was dedicated, however furtively, to taking things seriously. Pascal's awareness of man's systematic alienation from any fixed or confident haven, the view that (without Christian faith) he is an 'incomprehensible monstrosity', is echoed in Byron's restless examination of himself as 'half dust, half deity'; his entertainment of opposites, his attempts to go one better than Jacob or Proteus and wrestle himself to a standstill announce the integrity behind his duplicity. To regret his choice of a wife is either to flatter Annabella or to vilify her without acknowledging that it was the condition of marriage itself, the logic of propagation and the ending of youth which it implied, no less than Annabella's particular qualities or defects, that goaded him to excesses he later claimed had never been intended to be hurtful. The pain was *his*, not hers, so what right had she to take it so personally?

Annabella had endured a laborious birth; she was weak and touchy after it. Mrs Clermont comforted her and infuriated Byron. Always the cat whenever he saw a pigeon, he proposed that they call the baby Augusta. Annabella seems to have made no objection: Augusta Ada were the names at the christening. After her recovery, Annabella sought to resume a normal life, but the wit is rarely an uncritical husband to the obvious. ('Am I in your way?' she asked, as she resumed her place in the drawing room. 'Yes, you are,' he replied.) Post-natal depression and his recent outrages – he may well have flaunted his infidelities and she had found hot books in his private case – undermined her strength to ride out his displeasure. Byron, mantled in his own obsessions (most of them financial), greeted the news of Annabella's proposed departure from Piccadilly Terrace with an outburst of self-pity which, had it not been for the 'experiment' he had conducted on her before, might have detained her. It was, he pointed out, exactly one year, 'almost to the minute', since they were bound together in Holy Matrimony. In an access of rage, he flung his watch into the grate and reduced it to cogs with the poker. After which he declared that he had cared more for it than for anything else he possessed. Lady Byron walked out, slowly. At the very last moment, she was tempted to curl up like a dog at the door of his bedroom to await his pat.

He may not have enjoyed her presence; her absence was humiliating. She told him, or so he told Hobhouse, that she meant to go only for a few weeks. The solemn complexion her family now put upon the tales told by their only child came as a surprise to him. Were his affectations of grievance wholly unwarranted? He had behaved thoughtlessly, but passion carried its own temporary licence and, after all, Annabella had no sooner gone than she wrote at least two cuddlesome letters promising that she could not bear to be without him. How could he believe that, faced with a choice between his own exciting company and that of her tedious family, his wife would prolong her pouting to the point of permanent separation? As her absence was extended, and advertised, Byron was in the untypical position of craving a quick and conventional solution. He was taking the consequences of his sharp tongue and louche habits, and he took them very badly. The master of words can often drive his victim to action, however illogical or inexplicable. For logic and explanation are the tools of the articulate; Byron so dominated the world of discourse that Annabella was driven to speechless retorts. She left the formalities to her advocates, Dr Stephen Lushington and Sir Samuel Romilly, for whom Byron conceived a violent antipathy: technically Sir Samuel was on a general retainer to himself when he accepted Lady Byron's case. They had once been parliamentary allies in opposing the repression of the Nottingham weavers. (Romilly's later suicide, soon after his beloved wife's death, came as a spiteful satisfaction, unworthily immortalized in a stanza of *Don Juan*.)

Annabella comforted herself, if she found it comfortable, with the decision that her husband was mad; her family and advisers were not prepared to find any such excuse: for them he was simply bad. It is doubtful whether Annabella gave voice to all she suspected of Byron's vices, but the highlights were enough to make Lady Noel believe that her daughter had married a monster. (The death of Lord Wentworth in April 1815 entitled the Milbankes to take the name Noel; Byron, always pedantic over matters of aristocratic nomenclature, did not fail to abuse his mother-in-law in accordance with her new style.) However monstrous Byron was now held to be, one aspect of the marriage had been far from unsatisfactory. Sexually, he had always had as little need or inclination to control himself as an ancient Roman grandee or a modern rock star; having whored where he fancied and having turned away as many women as ever he purchased, he cannot be accused of not knowing pretty well what he was up to when it came to bed-time. Annabella's case was different, but her desire, once aroused, did not lack ardour. However much Byron's drunkenness and violence alarmed her, she never seems to have repulsed or resented his advances. She loved him and she wanted him. She had not, perhaps, greatly excited him (though he was not inattentive), but he had been both husband and lover. His confidence that she would come back was based on his experience of women, who seldom relinquished him without a fight, or even after one. Lady Noel preferred to think that her daughter had been abused rather than pleasured; thus in the family's eyes even Annabella's fondness, what was left of it, seemed additional proof of her husband's degrading influence.

Seconded ably by Scrope Davies, Hobhouse played the diplomat; he had some credit with the Milbankes, as his good manners deserved, and he did his best to discover exactly how things stood or how they could be revised. As the accusations grew more mysterious and implacable, Byron convinced himself that mere tantrums and binges could never warrant so irreconcilable a rupture. Bemused by a barrage of innuendo, Hobhouse finally asked the Milbankes to itemize their charges. In the interests of precision, he listed every vice, sin, crime and horror of which a human being was, in his estimation, capable. When he challenged Lady Milbanke to tick those of her choice, as it were, she denied that Byron's unforgivable vice figured on the list. After this was reported, Byron had the wit to wonder whether Hobhouse's acquaintance with wickedness was wide enough for his list to be fully comprehensive, but he was also increasingly depressed, to the not unprecedented point of threatening suicide. He refrained, he said, because of the pleasure it would give his mother-in-law, though, if he could be sure of haunting the old bitch, he would willingly pull the trigger.

Death and exile (his father's solution) dominated his reflections. The dismal hiatus in a house denuded by the duns was the worst of all worlds. He was, he had been promised, the greatest literary figure of the day; Sir Walter Scott, his only rival, had but recently assured him, at a meeting in John Murray's offices, of his profound admiration. (It seems that Byron reciprocated, despite Scott's middle-class acquisitiveness and Tory sympathies.) London was still avid for his work, society for his company. Yet greatness eluded him, even as he was assumed to possess it. He was not yet thirty but how could a man with a galling flop of a marriage persuade himself that life was not past its climacteric? Lady Byron's absence was endurable as long as it appeared but a phase in some passionate contest between them, but when it dwindled into a shuttle of recriminations carried back and forth through intermediaries, it lacked either snap or spice. And once the issue passed irreversibly into the hands of the lawyers (for whom reconciliation would be bad business), remorse was supplanted by resentment, hope by bitterness.

During that first (and only active) year of his marriage, Byron was in a state of anguish which may seem more hysterical than justified. But to condemn him is not to understand him, even if to understand is not necessarily to pardon: he had brought his troubles largely upon himself, but they were no less troublesome on that account. The fact that his tantalizingly inaccessible riches were unearned does not make his dunned frustration less real. As a writer he was far from barren, but his well-travelled alter ego, *Childe Harold*, could scarcely muse on the journey from Piccadilly to Drury

Lane; nothing major, as the modern cant has it, was on the stocks. He might, had he been more of a trimmer or a diplomat, have attempted to repair his bridges to the Prince Regent and so bank some credit against the new and growing scandal, but he was too proud or too cowed.

Though the *dégringolade* of his marriage is usually taken to be the principal motive for his departure from England, marital disaster among the Regency aristocracy rarely entailed either obloquy or ostracism. Why was Byron's fall so Luciferian? His disgrace removed a menacingly witty tongue from the Whig counsels, but he is unlikely, as some have suggested, to have been hounded for political reasons; there is no evidence that he was involved in any serious seditious programme. Even if such a thing had been mooted, he would have been an improbable party to it. (He was to deplore Hobhouse's solicitation, as he saw it, of the mob.) Yet he had a reputation for posturing unreliability; he was not someone whom it was wise, or worthwhile, to defend. If he had no shortage of close friends, he had few others. He was a restless spirit upon whom too many had fawned for them not to be ashamed of their prostrations. And how often the vindication of mediocrity lies in the disgrace of genius! The vice now ruinously attributed to him, not least in the anonymous verses concerning 'Don Leon', analysed by G. Wilson Knight in his controversial *Lord Byron's Marriage*, was sodomy. Even the most wanton society can always arrange to be scandalized when there is a call for it; Regency London, accustomed to sensuality on a scale that might make Sodom and Gomorrah by-words for decorum, maintained certain taboos, if only, like the best silver, in order to utilize them on formal occasions. The Don Leon poems are a gleeful, quasi-Byronic satire on the depravities of his lordship, but private eyeful though they provide, they are unlikely to have been the origin of the now mushrooming scandal. Both Caro Lamb and Annabella, in their different ways, were likelier sources. How could Caro, still frantic with passion, resist attempting to make capital, or at least waves, when this last chance presented itself? The collapse of the Byron marriage encouraged her to play a double game: as a comforter to Byron, if he wanted that kind of comfort, and, when he did not, as an informer for Annabella. The latter, under the formal guidance of Sir Samuel Romilly, had small difficulty in converting a bad case into a good cause; nothing so blesses malice with self-righteousness as taking legal advice.

How true were the charges, and what exactly did they mean? Byron's sexual habits were certainly eclectic. For more than a century and a half, most writers – even, and sometimes especially, homosexuals – affected as great a horror of the very idea of sodomy as did moralists like George V, who presumed that men like that shot themselves. Our contemporary banalization of sexual anomalies may have had an unfastidious effect on literature, but at least it has eliminated humbuggery. Byron's own attitude to the perverse was neither whining nor egregiously sublime. It is hard to imagine him pining winsomely over the love that dare not speak its name: he knew its name, and used it. The sodomy charge was unquestionably convenient to Annabella and her legal adviser; which may be explanation enough of its currency. (One would not put it beyond her advocates to have solicited the scurrilous poems attributed to George Colman the Younger. The intimate revelations of Byron's disreputable life lead one to suspect that their author belonged among the rackety theatrical connections he had made at Drury Lane. Doris Langley Moore rejects Wilson Knight's attribution of the poems to Colman, though her arguments are more *ad hominem* than conclusive; there may indeed be no convincing conclusion to the matter. The slyest suggestion is that they are the ultimate act of self-destruction on the part of Byron himself.)

It may be that the whole notion of sodomy as a *criminal* performance came as a particular personal shock to Annabella, even before Caro Lamb volunteered hard, and fast, information. It requires a severe notion of natural proprieties to maintain a sense of outrage over Byron's erotic practices (though no one is obliged to like his morals), but Annabella lacked the knowingness of a modern virgin, prematurely primed by paperbacks. She had no access to those bland guidebooks which deal with anal intercourse as nicely as boy scout manuals illustrate the variety of knots available to the dexterous. Such clarity at least allows us to examine Lord Byron's crime without coyness. If he was tempted not only by boys but also by, in the words of the author of *The Story of O.*, what women have in common with them, he would be neither the first man nor the last. What shocked the Spanish missionaries in the sexual habits of the Incas may have been deplored by the Christian authorities but precisely what made it unacceptable to them has long made it attractive to others. As a means of birth control, in the days before Mrs Stopes, sodomy was more reliable than anything else; nor, it could be argued, would it 'hurt the baby' when pregnancy had already occurred.

Whatever strange or naive fancy brought Byron finally to marry Annabella, it would be unwise to assume that he did not find her at all attractive. He seems, in Caro's term, to have 'pulled with' her to fairly good effect, at least for a while; if he had to teach her the game, she appears to have been an unreluctant pupil. Would it be very surprising if he had managed to convince her that his own tastes were not in themselves distasteful? Annabella's virginity on her wedding day has never been doubted. Since she had no experience of men, whatever Byron proposed could be taken to be what men did. (Charles Chaplin was once accused, for vilifying purposes, of having persuaded one of his young brides to oral sex by offering the simple assurance that 'all married people do it'.) Annabella was, after all, in love with her husband. She knew his reputation and she surely guessed that what he was denied at home he would seek elsewhere. Furthermore, what was so terrible about it, or so much more terrible than any other form of sexual activity? We can rarely be absolutely sure what people actually do, or don't do, which is part of the justification of fiction: only by making things up can we conceive what is true. (Hence truth is stranger than fiction, but fiction is truer.) When Caro Lamb, in the umpiring presence of Augusta (herself now pregnant again, though not by Byron, or so we are promised), demeaned herself by muttering unspeakable confidences about her one-time lover, her disclosures may have shocked Annabella in two quite different ways. In the first instance, what Byron could well have sworn to be a gesture of unusual intimacy – what do we know of the patter of a poetic seducer? – was reported to be a gross appetite which he had been known to invite the venal ladies, and lads, of the street to satisfy. Secondly, Annabella was alerted to the criminal character of what, until the subject was raised in so formal a way, was unlikely ever to have been mentioned, albeit possibly practised, in her presence. Byron's possessive confidence, once the marriage had taken place, had been expressed with menacing glee; what better proof of his proprietary rights than peremptory sexual domination by any means he chose? (Did he not *have* Lady Byron on the sofa, quick as may be?)

When Byron persuaded himself, during the weeks when he sought to prevent the breach from widening into permanent separation, that Annabella and he had really been happy together, at least for some of the time, he was not necessarily lying, though he may well have been deceiving himself. What others call vicious or unforgivable is often both exciting and unforgettable; it is only when publicity demands that words be attached to acts that privacy is ruptured and debased. (The subtle argument against obscenity begins, and ends, here.) Annabella's sense of having been defiled, if there is any substance to the theory, need not have begun until either Caro or, possibly, her advisers, implied – perhaps without even knowing its dismaying personal relevance – that sodomy was worse than murder, a view that a self-dramatizing Byron himself may have put about, when he prated at Burlington House of a crime worse than murder, unless he was thinking of incest or unless, as is equally possible, he was not really thinking of anything except the giggling gullibility of girls. If, however, Annabella was suffering from a crisis of conscience over betraying her husband (after all those reassuring words she had written to B. above her lovey-dovey pip-pipping signature!), it was more than shocking to hear that his vice was chronic: it was extremely convenient. At first, she may not have had any notion of just what a liberty he had taken, but now that it could justify her flight from the task of mastering the husband to whom, in her now bruised vanity, she had imagined herself uniquely equal, how timely it was to be able to persuade herself that it would be wrong, as well as weak, to return to his bed! All the things that he had said (not least about not liking 'to sleep with any woman'), even the most light-hearted or endearing, could be conscripted as evidence of his mad corruption.

Surely his protestations of bewilderment about what the matter was, or could possibly be, would be out of character if they were nothing but hypocrisy. When he sent Scrope and Hobhouse back and forth to press for details, can he really have been all the time in no doubt concerning the fundamental charge against him? What he could not guess was how that conspiracy of two which takes place in the marriage bed could, once Annabella had defected from it, lose all its delicious complicity and be seen, by prurient eyes, as the diabolical debauch of a high-minded and credulous innocence. Annabella had indeed turned against him; hence the sexual awakening which had been her perhaps astonishing consolation was revised into a nightmare which Byron had foisted upon her: he had made her want what she should never have wanted and since she was not going to take the blame, he must.

Thus the situation deteriorated with a momentum which Byron, who could not believe sexual behaviour – especially when sanctioned by the special licence of marriage – to be of such heavy significance, was unable to comprehend. High society was so manifestly bereft of scruple that it was ridiculous to suppose that everyone did not know, and tolerate, what everybody knew, and did, especially after the conventional immunity of the virgin had been breached. The charm of Lady M. had lain in the elegance with which she combined being a woman with being ladylike; it may have been foolish of Byron to hope for similar sophistication from her niece, but was it singularly wicked or inappropriate? Comedy is full of plots which turn on the naiveté of the roué who imagines that his marriage will be an exception to the rule. When in the carriage Byron said, 'It must come to a separation' (if indeed he said it), he was, perhaps unconsciously, acting in concord with the heartless character who, in the first act, says the very words which will mock or torment him in the last.

> Fare thee well! And if for ever,
> Still for ever, fare *thee well*:
> Even though unforgiving, never
> Gainst thee shall my heart rebel.
> Would that breast were bared before thee
> Where thy head so oft hath lain,
> While that placid sleep came o'er thee
> Which thou ne'er canst know again . . .
> When our child's first accents flow –
> Wilt thou teach her to say 'father'
> Though his care she must forgo?

What an exercise in the alchemy of rendering brazen self-pity into golden memories! The famous lines are not unembarrassing to read, for they too clearly employ the unworthy stratagems of the wounded husband, who chooses to forget that he may not have behaved conspicuously well himself. The callousness of the father who would have 'preferred a boy' is sublimated into paternal tenderness which outlaws Herod at last. The rueful farewell of the heartbroken family man is in sorry contrast with the petrifying threats of the ensnared bridegroom. Lady Byron is not an easy woman to like, especially after the machinery of self-vindication committed her to an obduracy without respite or remorse, but the facile lines which allowed Byron at once to dab his own eyes and to put hers out are as calculatedly lacrymogenous as a sliced onion. No wonder she did not acknowledge their receipt or honour their claim upon her. Meanwhile he reserved his hatred for his mother-in-law and for Mrs Clermont, the convenient scapegoats. Since Mrs Clermont had lived at Piccadilly Terrace for a while, he had good reason to want to disparage her testimony, whatever it was. The erstwhile tribune of the people did not hesitate to use anything, including her lowly birth, which might undermine the witness's 'kitchen bred' reputation.

His debts were so unremitting that he was forced to sell even his library; there was no prospect of his means ever meeting his ends until Newstead was put successfully on the market. Despite his humiliations, emotional and financial, he proceeded to new involvements in both departments. Even as his household was being sold up around him, he produced plans for a new and elaborate travelling coach, along the same lines as Napoleon's, which Baxter's were commissioned to build on approval. It was to cost five hundred pounds and it would contain a large bed, facilities for dining and a 'library'; Byron was wary of appearing studious (he denied that he ever enjoyed *reading* poetry) but even as he got rid of one set of books, he made provision for acquiring another. What writer can think of going abroad without a last cull of the bookshops? Byron's coach was the earnest of his intention to quit the tight little island once more, and for a long time. His lease on the adulation of fashionable London, always tenuous in his own view, now patently lapsed. He tested the coldness of smart shoulders for the last time when he and Augusta went together to Lady Jersey's reception early in April 1816. Hobhouse accompanied them. The lure may have been less a chance to brazen it out in society than to meet Benjamin Constant, the lover of the garrulous Madame de Staël, and a novelist of notorious acuteness when it came to kissing and telling. (Byron would send *Adolphe* as a prickly present to his last mistress.)

The story of Augusta and Byron was now not only shocking, it was also over-long. If most of Lady Jersey's guests chose to ignore them, it may have been less because they were sickened than because they were bored; society's pointed lack of appetite for another portion of last year's lion furnished telling evidence that, like Caro Lamb, it loved all that was new and rare, for a moment. Augusta had been as loyal as she was unwise; nothing does her more credit than her affectionate efforts, until the last moment, to repair Byron's marriage and redeem his name. Yet once again ambiguities remain: was the show of barefaced cool in Lady Jersey's drawing room simply a case of dressing for the wrong social climate? Can one not sense a tincture of that zest for flashing their closeness which lovers often relish, even when they are not brother and half-sister? On the other hand, Augusta may have been persuaded (perhaps by Lady Jersey, too grand to be touched by the contagious high-mindedness of most of her guests) that people would be convinced that the sordid rumours were without foundation, were she and Byron to act as if they were; she was sufficiently spirited and loving to take the risk, but what they may have intended as a parade of their innocence was taken for a show of shamelessness from which there was no appeal.

Apart from Lady Jersey herself, only an independent-minded (and independently rich) young woman, the red-haired Miss Mercer Elphinstone, was bold, honest and vain enough to speak to Byron. 'You should have married me,' she said, 'and nothing of this would ever have happened.' Augusta and Byron never appeared together again in public. On Easter Sunday 1816 they had what turned out to be their last, unreproachful, meeting. The malicious cunning with which Annabella had begun to work on Augusta had not yet corroded her natural geniality or gorged her with the remorse which Annabella was to be so very Christian in provoking.

While Byron's furtive and ostentatious preparations for departure were slowly being put together in Mr Baxter's coach yard, he recruited a young doctor, John William Polidori, as his personal physician. Polidori was both a literary enthusiast and the youngest man ever to qualify at Edinburgh medical school. Once again, though there seem to have been no passionate undertones, Byron was enchanted by youth (Polidori was only twenty-three when they set off) and, probably, by flattery. It is hard to see why, at the age of twenty-eight, Byron felt the need for a medical man on permanent attachment; he had not been complaining recently of either haemorrhoids or the clap, though the former may have continued to depress his uncertain temper. (The dejected expression of chronic sufferers can allow a shrewd doctor to make his diagnosis without a word being spoken.) Polidori's enthusiasm for the projected journey came to John

115

Murray's ears and the publisher, not altogether charmingly, commissioned the young man to keep a gossipy journal, for which he proposed the fat sum of £500, an act of opportunism which, once discovered, cast early shadows on the sunny relations between Byron and his medical man.

In those joyless days between Annabella's departure from Piccadilly Terrace and his own from England, what began as a petty and reluctant adventure brought some variety into his life, with unsurprising and unwanted consequences. The self-styled Claire (*née* Jane) Clairmont was the stepdaughter of William Godwin, the liberal philosopher whose renowned *Enquiry Concerning Political Justice* maintained that government was the cause of the very injustice which it affected to counteract. The *Enquiry*, in fact, inverted Plato's *Republic*, which argued that rigid social institutions would automatically entail justice for all. Godwin's anarchy had impressed Percy Bysshe Shelley who, at the time when Claire first approached Byron, was already living with Mary Godwin, the philosopher's daughter by Mary Wollstonecraft, the founding mother, as it were, of feminism. (Claire's mother had had two children, of uncertain paternity, before she married Godwin, after Mary Wollstonecraft had died in childbirth.)

The domestic relations between the various children of earlier attachments and the Godwins' own son, also called William, seem not to have been unduly awkward; the household's main problem was money. Godwin's books had large influence but small sales. Shelley's veneration at first made him an almost unconditional subsidizer of his mistress's father (Percy was still married to the unfortunate Harriet, whose death, almost certainly suicide, at the end of 1816, would leave him free to make Mary his wife) but he soon discovered his putative father-in-law to be an insatiable financial leech. Although passionately excited by Mary's intelligence and even more perhaps by her blood tie with two of his libertarian idols, Shelley had been happy for the precocious, sixteen-year-old Claire to accompany him and Mary (who herself was only seventeen at the time) on their naively undertaken elopement in 1814. The almost penniless trio got as far as Geneva before returning to London, tamed by shortage of funds and a sense of anticlimax. Shelley's enthusiasm for non-exclusive emotional arrangements conformed with his campaign against the two-by-two limitations of marriage; his treatment of his first wife, whom he had married in a rescuing spirit when she was barely sixteen, is one more instance of the cruelties of magnanimity. Shelley's non-exclusive scheme probably did not embrace sexual relations with Claire as well as with Mary, at least in the early years of their tangled association, but he was a compulsive accumulator and dispenser of affection, though never a rake or a sexual statistician (one cannot imagine him matching Byron's tissue of amorous trophies). He was an idealist of entrancing sincerity who dreamed of reforming the world by poetic legislation, as noble in spiritual generosity as he was hectic in practical performance. He had been virtually cut off by his exasperated father, Sir Timothy, and lived on a pittance and his nerves. However, he remained the son of a wealthy baronet and though his finances were often stretched, he was potentially a very rich man, as Godwin remained graspingly conscious. As an enemy of convention, the latter displayed all the hypocrisy of the bourgeois parent in order to get the best possible return from his daughter's seducer. Shelley's patience bears the marks of a simpleton, a saint or an uneasy conscience.

In March 1816, when Claire first approached Byron, the author of *Queen Mab* was by no means as famous as that of *Childe Harold.* Shelley was finding difficulty in getting his work published at all and often had to pay the printer himself. His poetry was received with little more favour by the critics than by the public, though his convoluted private life made that the least of his worries. (In a nice phrase in a letter written some years later, he remarked, 'The man must be enviably happy whom Reviews can make miserable.') His passion for Mary – first declared when they were both actually seated on her mother's tombstone – may not have excluded Claire from his sentimental attentions (it would be typical of the man to feel that he had a positive duty to include her in them), but she undoubtedly took second place, which was not her favourite position. Mary was not yet Shelley's legal wife, but for all her bold breeding she lacked the experimental gusto which might have welcomed her stepsister's prettyish presence as a marital aide. The seventeen-year-old Claire's overtures were anonymous, rhetorical and intriguing: 'If a woman, whose reputation has yet remained unstained, if without either guardian or husband to control she should throw herself upon your mercy, if with a beating heart she should confess the love she has borne you many years, could you betray her or would you be silent as the grave?'

To beg for discretion was a nice way of promising it; to enjoin silence was no bad means of procuring a response. Claire was probably less scheming than apprehensive, but to begin with she struck the right note. She confessed her love, but she did not make it the sole reason for addressing Byron: she was also writing a novel and she was interested in going on the stage. Byron's connection with Drury Lane enabled him to introduce her to Kinnaird and to offer her the use of his box when she wanted to go to the theatre. Whether her acting ambitions were serious may be doubted; she seems never to have returned to them. Certainly, if Byron imagined that he had now rendered his dark and ambitious visitor all the service required of him, he was mistaken. She bided her time, but she did not have long; knowing his plans to leave the country, she offered herself to him with no strings attached.

An experienced womanizer should have known that hoops of steel can be concealed in such free offers, but his line of escape seemed secure and he was never immune either to the call of generosity or to the lure of flattery; both were accommodated in Claire's suggestion that they 'go out of town together' one evening and return the following morning. Byron was not disposed ever again to be in for a pound, but to be in for a penny probably did not seem too improvident. He honoured Claire's enterprise and entered one more prize in his roster, on the firm understanding that one thing should not lead to another. It may have affected Byron's judgment, and appetite, that the girl's surname was so nearly homophonous with that of Mrs Clermont, Annabella's wicked witch. At once to enjoy a clean young piece and to fuck *her* was a neat, punning economy. His aversion from Claire's last name was soon, if temporarily, remedied, when she told him that she would henceforth surname herself Clairville, another promise unkept.

Byron was indifferent to her future, under whatever title it might be conducted, but he was convinced by her recommendation of Geneva as a port of call on his projected travels. Whether or not a rendezvous was definitely agreed, he underestimated Claire's persistence if he supposed that he had seen the last of her. Having promoted the charms of Lac Léman, she went home to the Shelleys and persuaded them to repeat their earlier expedition to Switzerland. Plagued by Godwin's exigence and by his abandoned wife Harriet's distress (she had their two children, small means and ruined prospects), Shelley was as ready to leave England as Byron himself. His political activities, his quarrel with his father and with society in general, his atheistic and revolutionary verses rendered him even more objectionable to the authorities (who had already had him followed by spies) than Byron, whose heterodoxy was so often tempered by a lordly wink. Poets who show a high degree of wit, although capable of obstreperous contrariness, are seldom wholly disaffected from the societies they satirize. The man who likes to get laughs always has a soft spot for the audience, even when it offers him butts as well as applause. Those who have difficulty in achieving a pat pay-off have less of a stake in the social order which values polish. What Shelley called Byron's 'aristocratic canker' was due as much to his poetics as to his lineage: those who appreciated him best had to share an education and social background much like his own. Shelley's appreciation of the classics was in some ways more profound than Byron's but he did not lard his text with tags in the same allusive way; his reverence for Plato and Aeschylus reflected a radical desire to revise the whole basis of Western attitudes to Gods and men. Shelley was in some ways a finer spirit, but he lacked that snappy gift for spontaneity which both enabled Byron to twit his public and made him reluctant to break with it.

On the 21st of April 1816, the final deed of separation from Annabella was signed and the 'cureless wound' was left to cicatrize. Early on the 23rd, the great Napoleonic coach, cumbered with Byron, Polidori, Fletcher, Rushton and a Swiss servant called Berger, moved out before the bailiffs moved in. Hobhouse and Scrope Davies, loyal to the last, accompanied the disgraced darling of society down to Dover where, on the 24th, the 'dear fellow' went aboard, passing through hordes of celebrity-hunters in order to reach the Channel packet. Respectable ladies were said to have disguised themselves as chambermaids at the overnight hotel in order to slake their desire to observe him at close quarters. As the boat stood out, Byron pulled off his cap and waved it to Hobby and Scrope. Polidori, it soon transpired, was poor consolation for their lost companionship.

> Fare thee well! Thus disunited,
> Torn from every nearer tie,
> Sear'd in heart, and lone, and blighted
> More than this I scarce can die.

·The last words addressed to Annabella applied almost equally well to his native land. When the young pilgrim first left Greece for home, he had vowed to betake himself to politics and decorum. His belated attempt to be decorous had proved a calamity; his political career was stillborn, more through accidie than recklessness. In spite of these peripeties, he was now irremediably famous. He left England as a social outcast, but his stature on the continent had not ceased to grow. There was no choice for him now but to be a poet once more; careerism and prudence, the lineaments of mediocrity, had failed to suit him. With a sigh and a smile he recognized that he had nothing left but his genius. The rough crossing smoothed his feelings; water was his familiar element and, very Public School, he was often at his best when others were discomfited. By the time they reached Ostend, he was sufficiently revived, to Polidori's sneaking admiration, to 'fall like a thunderbolt upon the chambermaid'. Childe Harold was back in the soft saddle.

With certain talents, nothing succeeds like failure. Rejection restored his youthful vision of himself as an outcast and thus rejuvenated his poetic energy. He visited the field of Waterloo where his little Pagod had lost his last great gamble, and galloped across 'an Empire's dust', like Stendhal's Fabrizio del Dongo, in tardy tribute to a lost cause. There was already a regular trade in mementoes of the battle. He gazed on the skulls of unknown Yoricks whom pedlars labelled with the nationality of whatever side appealed to the purchaser's patriotism. Byron's loyalties were divided, for if Englishmen had won the battle, Napoleon had lost it. He compared the field with Marathon, of course, and found it no less fine. The division of his feelings alerted him to the dramatic possibilities of the occasion: Childe Harold's new travels were bound to touch on the Duchess of Richmond's ball on the eve of the battle. Battlefields indeed interested him a good deal more than the masterpieces of fine art which he was solicited to inspect; he always had a colourful ability to paint a scene in words, but little taste for pigment. His impatience with Rubens and the other masters displayed at once the prejudices of his class and the honesty of his responses.

From Brussels the overladen coach proceeded south along the Rhine, calling at historical sites and castles. Having divested himself, or having been divested, of nearly everything he had accumulated in England, the wanderer was soon in the market for fresh mementoes: he could not resist collecting a few bones 'as much as may have made a quarter of a hero' – at the site of the fifteenth-century battle of Morat. A reminder he might have chosen to be spared was waiting for him when, after a pause at 'the castled Crag of Drachenfels', he at last rolled into Geneva, by way of Lausanne. Polidori was probably no more irritating than any other unfamiliar travelling companion, but he was certainly no less. He was loquacious and bumptious and Byron cannot have been sorry when they pulled up at last outside the Hôtel d'Angleterre, on the edge of the lake, a couple of kilometres from the centre of John Calvin's city, already a commercial as well as a cultural enclave. The smartest class of visitor was able to call upon Madame de Staël at Coppet and savour her salon, before paying a pilgrimage to pick anthological flowers in the haunts of Rousseau's St Preux and the garden where Gibbon wrote the last words of his damned thick book. The less modish stayed at local hostelries and indulged in the relatively new sports of sightseeing and the contemplation of nature; there was a great deal of it about. Mont Blanc was in unclimbed prospect across the lake and the 'crystal waters' themselves were accessible for expeditions to Vevey and beyond, as far as Chillon. Byron was tired and when Mr Dejean, the *patron*, was Swiss enough to insist that he comply precisely with police regulations by adding his age to his surely sufficient signature in the register, he scribbled in '100', and be damned to them. It was not long before his joke was capped, though he was not amused. A note was delivered to his room: 'I am sorry that you are grown so old. Indeed I suspected you were 200 from the slowness of your journey. Well, heaven send you sweet sleep – I am so happy – Claire.'

Byron was less happy, and least happy when he discovered that that charitable night a few miles out of London, or its reprise, had resulted in Claire's pregnancy. The accumulation of souvenirs was all very well, but here was one he little desired and was expected to embrace. His new freedom was menaced by the very entanglement from which the girl had specifically promised to exempt him. Her pursuit had not only been perfidious, it brought with it the obligation to be sociable with Shelley and Mary, neither of whom was yet aware how far Claire's affair with Byron had gone. Mary had been introduced to him in London, but she had assumed that he was Claire's sponsor, not her lover. Mary is often blessed with a gravity beyond her years, the steadiness of her attachment to Shelley, and its tragic outcome, suggesting a mature wife rather than a still young mistress, but she was only nineteen (Shelley was twenty-three) and she was by no means impervious either to the Byronic charm or to jealousy at Claire's apparent triumph in attracting him.

Byron's tetchiness was eased when the new company proved by no means wholly disagreeable. Once a proper meeting had been effected between the two fugitives from propriety who, in the best British tradition, were embarrassed at never having been correctly introduced, Byron and Shelley hit it off very well. Byron may have sighed at the sight of Claire, but the sound of Polidori had already bored him to distraction. The puppyish young doctor, indignant at Byron's constant teasing, had gone so far as to demand what there was, apart from writing poetry, that Byron could do better than he. 'Three things,' came the neat reply, 'first I can hit with a pistol the keyhole of that door; second I can swim across that lake and, thirdly, I can give you a damned good thrashing.'

Apart from the vexation of Pollydolly, there was a horde of English tourists prepared to go to almost any lengths to get close enough to Byron to cut him dead. Worthy mamas believed that he had the devilish ability to impregnate or at least deflower their daughters at a glance. The Shelleys were a relief. Percy had all the shyness of a certain kind of pride, but Byron put him at his ease and, delighted by intelligent admiration, soon invited him to dinner in his apartments. It was not long before a boat was hired and the notorious group took to the water, not least in order to escape being jostled by cold shoulders. The Shelleys lacked Byron's stature as a target for gossip, but the young poet was not unknown and his morals were already debatable, and debated. The quartet became such a tourist attraction that life in the hotel was intolerable, and they had to seek lodgings elsewhere.

> Hard is his fate on whom the public gaze
> Is fixed forever to detract or praise;
> Repose denies her requiem to his name
> And folly loves the martyrdom of Fame.
> The secret enemy whose sleepless eye
> Stands sentinel, accuser, judge and spy,
> The foe, the fool, the jealous and the vain,
> The envious who but breathe in others' pain,
> Behold the host! Delighting to deprave,
> Who track the steps of glory to the grave,

Watch every step that daring Genius owes
Half to the ardour which its birth bestows,
Distort the truth, accumulate the lie,
And pile the pyramid of Calumny!

The pyramid was being heaped not only by tourists who swore that they had witnessed a sexual imbroglio of quadrilateral scope, but also, and more damagingly, in London. *L'absent a toujours tort* and the protective and protesting presence of Byron's musketeers – staunch Hobhouse, subtle Scrope, gallant Kinnaird – could not prevail against the forces of militant reproach. Lady Byron was rapidly reverting to that snappish smugness which had marked her girlhood. She was working hard through their mutual friend, the sanctimonious and prurient Mrs Villiers, at recruiting Augusta to the ranks of the penitent, and not in vain. When, presently, Byron sent home his heartfelt *Epistle To Augusta* ('My sister! my sweet sister! if a name/Dearer and purer were, it should be thine'), Mrs Villiers did her busy best to embargo its publication and sour its sense. Does anything make sadder reading at this point than the perkiness with which Byron's letters strive to maintain that intimacy with Augusta which he had so relished when it was a secret, or a near secret? He and she were, he said, the last persons in the world who ought or could cease to love one another. 'We might have loved so single and so happy – as old maids and bachelors . . .'

Claire was a poor substitute and he made her feel it; her brandished happiness struck him as an intrusion. Annabella's intransigence and Augusta's silence could not be mitigated by an ambitious dolly who would do anything he wanted, except leave him alone. Meanwhile Caro Lamb had brought her brick to the calumnious pyramid by publishing a naughty novel, *Glenarvon*, which was aggressively *à clef*, though Byron's life was by now so much of an open book that one hardly required a key to unlock its blemishes. Caro's spite was tempered by an inability to speak entirely ill of her demon lover, but the knowing public was in a mood to smirk at the satirist satirized.

Byron soon went into Geneva and found himself that local speciality, a banker. Charles Hentsch had elegant connections which gave his client immediate access to social and intellectual circles, though Byron was not, in the event, very keen to move in them. He decided to live outside the city and took a house, the Villa Diodati, high on the hill of Cologny. It was, and is, a substantial grey stone building, with a terrace, supported by an arcade, at the level of the first floor; its secluded gardens afforded a long view of the water and the old city. The Shelleys had already moved into a much more modest house at Montalègre, on the shore below the Villa Diodati which could be reached by a ten-minute walk through the vineyards. Claire was not long in finding her way, even though it was all uphill. Even here, spyglasses were trained upon the celebrities, but Byron, with his penchant for the grandiose, was happy with the house, while Shelley's presence seems to have stimulated his creative energies, though his never had quite the same effect on Shelley: the younger man was not an uncritical admirer of Byron's volcanic powers but the lava flow was as daunting as it was impressive. Shelley, conscious of the effort his own work cost him, had cause to envy Byron's apparently inexhaustible facility. The new stanzas of *Childe Harold* lacked the whining that disfigures the *Tristia* of that other famously immoral exile, Ovid, but their jauntiness is somewhat uninspired. Byron's rebirth needed a more mercurial *alter ego* than the refurbished Harold.

As spring gave way to early summer, the natural beauties of the lake inspired a Wordsworthian mood, seconded by Shelley's enthusiasm for the Lakers. During a moonlight excursion, in a small boat they had decided to buy, Byron treated his companions to a performance of the Albanian song which had bewildered Annabella as they quit Seaham House in their honeymoon coach. He was soon nicknamed 'Albé' either for that reason or in Frenchification of his initials 'L.B.' Mary and Claire continued to use it, affectionately, even when affection was lacking.

Claire's persistence had again won her a place in Byron's bed, though never his heart. He could not, he observed, very well 'play the Stoic with a woman who had scrambled eight hundred miles' to unphilosophize him. When the sexual state of affairs eventually became known to him, Shelley sought to persuade Byron that he owed Claire 'some kindness' at least: nobody, after all, had asked him to carry her off. Byron replied that no one had been more carried off than 'poor dear me': he had been 'more ravished than anybody since the Trojan war'. It was perhaps this aggrieved sense of being constantly drained which led him, during a rainy spell when they were confined indoors and had embarked upon a competition for a ghost story, to concoct a little fragment which added a fanged twist to the Gothick repertoire: he may not have been the originator of the vampire motif, nor did he use it to very memorable effect, but his image of the victim drained of blood by battening predators may well be a reflection of his own *épuisement* to which the duns, the ladies and peeping tourists' greed for sensation had all contributed. Polidori, whose silly jealousy led him to challenge the pacific Shelley to a duel over a trifle (Byron offered himself as surrogate) and to flirt with Mary, appropriated the fragmentary vampire narrative and inflated it into one of the first (not very successful) published tales on a theme which remains a staple of horror fiction.

The prize in the ghoulish contest was won by the unlikeliest candidate. Mary Shelley's *Frankenstein* proved as durable as it was unexpected, and with good reason: it is an extraordinary achievement for someone not yet twenty. The image of the unloved outsider who becomes a monster through a lack of human understanding bears no direct Glenarvonish resemblance to Byron, but the latter's disquieting presence looms over the book just as Shelley's excitable yet somehow inadequate genius furnishes something of the uneasy brilliance of Dr Frankenstein himself. (Shelley's experiments with 'galvanism' clearly inspired the pseudo-science that brings the monster to life.)

Shelley's own contribution to the ghostly evening was more dramatic than literary: overcome by the atmosphere, he went into an hysterical fit during which he had a vision of Mary with eyes in place of nipples. He screamed and ran from the room. Dr Polidori had to come into his professional own with the prescription of a sedative.

A few days later, towards the end of June 1816, the weather seemed to improve and the two poets took to their boat for an unencumbered tour of the lake. By now their friendship was secure even against Shelley's honourable, perhaps not wholly disinterested, advocacy of Claire's cause. While they were cruising along the lake, a sudden storm put the poets in peril. Byron, revelling in the danger, promised Shelley salvation when the latter disclosed, with equanimity, that he was unable to swim. Byron told him that he had but to strip off his coat and get hold of an oar and, provided he did not struggle, they would get to shore somehow. Shelley folded his arms and, surveying the storm as if it were a subject like the West Wind, announced that he had 'no notion of being saved'; Byron would have enough trouble saving himself. Luckily, the storm abated and the waterlogged boat was beached without either man being put to the test. With impressive indifference, Shelley observed that the solution to 'the Great Mystery' was evidently not to be revealed to them for the present.

They proceeded to the castle of Chillon on its spit of rock at the eastern end of the lake. Its pointed towers belittled by the mountains that rise behind it, its umber stone draped in perpetual shadow, Chillon seems to lie under a sullen and inexorable blight, for all its romantic appointments. The story of Bishop Bonnivard, the sixteenth-century patriot who had been chained for four years to a pillar in the vaulted dungeon below the keep, had all the dire ingredients required to fuel Byron's indignation. Freedom might be an indefinite concept, but the chain and the pillar were clear enough indications of what bondage actually meant. Byron, ever impatient with mundane accuracy, knew how to make Bonnivard stand for everyone who had the nerve to uphold the rights of conscience against the dictates of tyranny. At Ouchy-Lausanne, he composed his eloquent *The Prisoner of Chillon*. His sonnet on the same topic began with a plangent apostrophe: 'Eternal spirit of the chainless Mind!/Brightest in dungeons, Liberty!'

Shelley had the wit to see, and the gall to point out, the ironic contrast between Byron's poetic attachment to general rights and his severity towards individuals who had incurred his displeasure. The two poets differed irreconcilably in their attitudes to women; Shelley's happiest days, in his early childhood, had been passed in doting female company. If he too had a (probably repressed) homosexual side, his male friends, even the charmless Thomas Jefferson Hogg, were treated with an unpatronizing assumption of equality. Byron, even at his most affectionate, was disposed to wear his coat of arms, no less than his heart, upon his sleeve. Shelley was the more febrile, Byron the more insecure. Shelley's earnestness on Claire's behalf loses little of its admirable sincerity if one points out that he had what amounted to a fetish for sharing a woman's affections with another man. Soon after his first marriage, he had sought to persuade his young wife, Harriet, to make herself available to Hogg; his mission to make Byron face unwanted responsibilities may well have been spiced by the hope of recruiting a man who both impressed and disturbed him to the nexus of emotional triangles with which he liked to embroider his life. Byron infuriated him by arguing that women had neither souls nor rights, while he himself was sufficiently exasperated by Shelley's feminism to question whether an atheist had any warrant to make moral calls on others. (Shelley was enough of a self-destructive exhibitionist – or of a principled idealist – to inscribe himself 'Atheist' in the register of a Swiss hotel when they went to the mountains on a Romantic foray, thus provoking a fresh flight of scandalized tourists' reports to London. *The Necessity of Atheism* had, of course, been the book – more brash than blasphemous – whose publication led to his and Hogg's being sent down from Oxford.)

Byron finally offered to honour his obligations to the extent of bringing up the child of Claire's womb, on the provision that he never had to see the mother again. Shelley was not so easily placated and it is a testimonial to his other qualities that his persistence in so unpopular a cause never made his company unwelcome to the tenant of the Villa Diodati. Of course, exile often turns acquaintances into soul-brothers (Henry Miller describes how, meeting an old enemy on a railroad station in Poland, he and his *bête noire* fell into each other's arms), but the tie between the two poets was not merely adventitious; there were similarities that reassured and differences that stimulated them. Meanwhile, Claire's declarations began to have a woefully familiar ring: 'I shall love you to the end of my life and nobody else, think of me as one whose affection you can count on . . .' Shades of Caro's adhesive rhetoric! It was a comfort when, as the summer and the leases ended, the pregnant girl could be packed off, with the Shelleys and a bundle of manuscripts, to England. Percy, however, was eager to return in order to go to Italy, which he had not yet visited. The unharmonious quartet had not yet played itself out.

When good old Hobhouse – that loyal 'sow's ear' – and the gallant Scrope arrived in Geneva at the end of August, the little colony was on the point of breaking up. The Cambridge friends brought good cheer, but no glad news: Augusta was now almost wholly under Annabella's control and her willingness to take Lady Byron for her guardian angel was as unpalatable as it seemed inexplicable. Byron's hope that once again he could make Augusta laugh and that their conspiracy of two could have new life breathed into it, became more and more forlorn. The fresh company of old friends encouraged him to move on; though he took some of his troubles with him, especially that woeful sense of having ruined Augusta which expressed itself in *Manfred*. On leaving the Villa Diodati, he dispensed not only with Claire but also with Dr Polidori, to whom he gave his *congé* without rancour and with no little relief.

It is hard fully to reconstitute the charm of Hobhouse, but undemanding and unintimidated loyalty, the fruit of an intimacy that preceded the years of fame, gave the prosaic John Cam a lasting and well-earned place in the poet's heart. On Scrope's return to England, the two of them made a dutiful tour of the mountains in the Bernese Oberland, where the virgin snows were increasingly franked by tourists converted to the wonders of nature by the Romantic movement and its cult of the wild. The British were embarking on the great century of their conceit during which they assumed that it was their breeding and grace, not their money and vanity, which made them so remarkable to continentals. It is not surprising that Byron decided to quit Switzerland before winter iced them in. Boarding Mr Baxter's unpaid-for coach, he and John Cam and their servants proceeded over the Simplon to the plains of Lombardy. In early October, they were on the poplared road to Milan.

Shelley, London-bound, had acted as courier for the new cantos of *Childe Harold* and the other poems which Byron bade him deliver to Murray. The latter was uneasy at the autobiographical tone of the lines to Augusta, but happy enough to see the best-selling Childe's resuscitation. The £2,000 which he paid were pouched, thanks to Douglas Kinnaird's businesslike diplomacy and banking connections, without any lordly diffidence. (Kinnaird proved as good a friend and *homme d'affaires* as Shelley's excellent Horace Smith.) The exile Byron was no longer concerned with what his class might think of his mercenary manners. Nevertheless, he continued to find it difficult to be done with those from whom he had taken a final leave. There was a quasi-comic episode in the opera house at Milan when the recently dismissed Dr Polidori (attending La Scala separately from Byron and his party, who were the guests of Monsignor Ludovico de Breme in his box) was cocky enough to demand that an Austrian officer remove his hat. His impertinence went down badly with the occupying power: he was first consigned to the guardhouse and then expelled from Milan. Pollydolly's enforced disappearance may not have been entirely distressing, but Byron was affronted by the Austrians' arrogance and proposed to trump it with his own.

Announcing himself 'a peer of England', he was quick to vouch for Polidori's character, despite his own experience of it. The Austrians were inclined to be deferential, but Byron's protection of the insolent young doctor marked him as a man, literally, to be watched. He did not stay long in Milan. A meeting with another disappointed admirer of Napoleon, M. Henri de Beyle, alias Stendhal, does not seem to have given rise to any memorable dialogue between the novelist of seduction and the poet who practised it, though Stendhal later wrote that he was 'filled with timidity and tenderness'. He declared that 'Had I dared, I should have wept and kissed Lord Byron's hand.'

Early in November, Byron and Hobhouse set out for Venice by way of Verona, Vicenza and Padua. At Verona they visited what purported to be the tomb of the Capulets; it is unlikely that the recollection-monger did not recall how they had figured in the first words he ever addressed to Mary Chaworth, now a disillusioned, ill-used wife.

From Mestre they took an evening gondola to Venice and disembarked, on the bank of the Grand Canal, at the Hotel of Great Britain. The weather was foul and Venice itself, whose last, sorry doge, Ludovico Manin, had been ignominiously dethroned by Napoleon a bare twenty years earlier, was in the long, luscious autumn of her decline. Her once sumptuous social life had dwindled to nostalgic provincialism; 'the greenest isle' was less the drawing room than the backwater of Europe. Having lost so much, Venice was left merely incomparable. Byron had craved its dissolute charm before he reached it; having seen it he was immediately enraptured. He took lodgings in the Frezzeria, near San Marco, with a draper called Segati, whose young wife Marianna supplied the dark eyes and convenient passion which appetite and purse commanded. He soon made himself at home, always easier when one is abroad. He learned to lisp his Italian like a Venetian and interested himself in the language and history of the Armenians, another race oppressed by the Turks and burdened by the tragic destiny of those who combined pertinacity with lack of muscle. He was rowed out regularly to the cloistered Armenian monastery on the island of San Lazzaro and volunteered funds (and his personal services) for the composition of an Armenian dictionary.

The creative writer, in a trough, often has recourse to chastening study. San Lazzaro had, and has, an unpretentious dignity exempt from flashy Venetian worldliness;

the monastery seems to lie in the margin of time. The monks are hospitable and lack sanctimoniousness; the oldest of them today is convinced that when he first came to San Lazzaro he was introduced to an aged monk who had actually known Byron. A copy of the unfinished dictionary, with Byron's own phonetic entries, remains in the monastery library. The chastity of the place, with its modest quadrangle and unobstreperous campanile, gave him pause from the amorous tangle in which he so promptly enmeshed himself. Sometimes on his way home across the lagoon, he would slip into the water and swim back towards the Piazza San Marco and the goal of the two columns on the Piazzetta which once asserted, and now only commemorate, the Serene Republic's leonine domination of the Adriatic. (He always remained trousered when swimming, so as not to show his withered leg.)

He had lost any inclination to return to England, not least since Augusta had now been manoeuvred into an open declaration that she could never resume their previous intimacy. The exile stops his clock at the moment he leaves his native shore and Byron refused either to modify his affection for Augusta or to bring his busy imagination to bear on what might really be happening between her and Lady Byron; sentimentality and resentment persuaded him to see the past as always happy, true love as always betrayed. If he was oppressed by misgivings, his solution was to bury past delinquencies or present megrims in further adventures, just as his poetic method was to cover flaws with fecundity. Whether or not he had indeed forever renounced his native land, he continued to look to Murray to maintain his sales and his fame. Like all literary fugitives, he might shake off the ungrateful dust and become passingly proficient in foreign languages but, widely as it was translated, his work had little future unless those who had been left behind could be persuaded to read it. His peerage and his Muse were both English and it was in English eyes that he must finally vindicate his genius if not his behaviour.

For the present, morality took second place. He liked the company of the monks, but he conducted an unmonastic life. ('What I earn by my brains,' he was to say, 'I spend on my ballocks.') The salon of the Contessa Albrizzi afforded him a conspectus of the classy pleasures, both intellectual and amorous, on parade in Venice, while the ignorance, or complaisance of Signor Segati allowed Marianna both to make his bed, as it were, and to lie in it. Well-born Venetian ladies were not well-favoured; beauty was generally sought, and expected to be found, in humbler surroundings. Byron celebrated the revival of his spirits by a love affair at once passionate and slightly preposterous, since it required him to play the *galant'uomo*. Once again, albeit in a plebeian context and a foreign accent, he contrived to be the lover of a married woman. It was a position which the Venetian style more or less sanctioned, whether in the supposedly spiritual guise of a *cavalier servente* or in the straightforwardly adulterous form a rich patron like Byron might afford. *Table d'hôte*, or *à la carte*, it suited him to have pleasure without responsibility, the prerogative of the milord throughout the ages; though he announced his love for Marianna – the usual romantic excuse for doing as one chose, on the grounds that fate allowed one no choice – it was a passion which always had its term, and its terms. Marianna's freshness and sensuality were a fetching contrast to the squeamish Lady Byron and to the stratagems of Claire Clairmont, but she lacked the social position and intellectual adroitness necessary for a permanent place in his heart, or his bed. As for Claire, in January 1817 she gave birth, in England, to Byron's daughter, Allegra, whose happy name was to be no specific against an unhappy fate.

Marianna's attentions, however frequent (up to three times a day, at times) and however uninhibited, did not divert Byron from the sweets of the annual Carnival which took place during January and February. Venice was never a place of self-restraint; now, with the aid of a mask, what could not be proposed, or granted? Though Marianna afforded Byron the chance to advertise the regularity of his irregularities (his letters served to keep Murray, and posterity, informed), he almost certainly availed himself, more discreetly, of the pretty boys whose brief services could be enjoyed with little local risk of scandal. A Venetian woman with two or three lovers might be deemed to have gone too far, but though lovers ran the occasional, occupational risk of a genuinely outraged husband, no form of sexual indulgence *per se*, on the part of those with money to pay for it, was either shameful or reprehensible. The Venetians shrugged or whispered where the English winced or moralized.

Byron's announcement, 'So we'll go no more a-roving,' written soon after that first Carnival, may have been a sigh at the approach of the age of thirty, or possibly a confession of the futility of cruising as a cure for *angst*, but it was certainly as premature as it was memorable. Eroticism, André Malraux once remarked, is a way of escaping from one's era; it was a style of escapism to which Byron frequently had recourse. The chronic amorist is at once dominating master and put-upon servant: Byron managed to play both baby B. and lordly lover. Though his worst enemy could not accuse him of difficulty in recruiting partners, he often found pleasure in buying – or at least paying – them: thus he need have no anxiety about their feelings (it can be a relief to know that it is only money they are after) and no conscience if he treated them abruptly.

The news now came that Shelley's 'immorality' was likely to cause him to lose custody of the two children he had had by his unfortunate first wife (Harriet had drowned in the Serpentine in November 1816). Byron had reason to fear that Annabella, for whom his hatred had grown so unequivocal that he could not even bear to write the word 'wife', would be able legally to deprive him of the daughter he had scarcely seen but obstinately loved. Claire's bold coyness in suggesting, in a letter, that she might go and call on little Augusta Ada, just for the reward of 'kissing something that was his', cannot have helped matters. After the Carnival, he fell ill of a fever, during which Marianna nursed him. Given the climate of Venice, psychological explanations are hardly needed for an illness for which local bacteria were probably responsible, but his reversion to helplessness has a characteristic appropriateness in the circumstances.

By April he was better and travelled to Rome with Hobhouse, spurred on his way by the arrival in Venice of Dr Polidori. The friends are said to have put up in the Piazza di Spagna, where a few years later John Keats was to die of consumption and the critics, according to Shelley. The third canto of *Childe Harold* and the new collection which included *The Prisoner of Chillon* were both selling well; success restored cordiality to their author's relations with John Murray, but the reviewers were once again captious, perhaps because, for all his resumed facility, the new work lacked novelty. *Manfred*, on which he had been working in Venice, was an ambitious attempt to honour the attractions of the stage which had struck him so strongly when he frequented Drury Lane and marvelled at Edmund Kean in his season of electric stardom, though he swore he never intended it for production. Certainly, it never worked in the theatre, but the melodramatic treatment of a cluster of Romantic themes, including those shocking staples, incest and ungodliness, took heterodoxy to new lengths and he was apprehensive of its reception.

At the end of their stay in Rome, Byron and Hobhouse attended the public execution of three criminals who were guillotined after all the ceremony which masked priests and half-naked executioners could drum up. Byron confessed, in a letter to Murray, that the first decapitation turned him 'quite hot and thirsty', but the second and third failed to be equally horrifying. The fact that he 'would have saved them' cannot conceal a certain conceit at his quick imperviousness, the man of quality's determination not to suffer sentiment to sway his dignity. The exactness of his description – he remarks the attempt of the first man to draw back from the blade – is in line with his policy of avoiding cant; it renders voyeurism a form of honest witness. If he did not throw himself on the executioners, which would have been both inelegant and futile, he did not merely gloss the occasion with entertaining copy. His later efforts to import humane standards into the conflicts between the Carbonari and the Austrians, and between the Greeks and the Turks, are earnest of a distaste for bloodshed which is the more honourable since he never made it an excuse to avoid danger. While seeking to set a personal example of human decency, he always argued that no people could be free unless they themselves actually fought for what they had lost (his 'proto-Zionism' was based on the same argument), but he never promoted that degenerate Romanticism which had more appetite for slaughter than for the cause it serves. 'Prends garde à toi, Philippe, tu as pensé au bonheur de l'humanité,' the ironic remark of Lorenzo de Musset to Filippo Strozzi, could be equally applied to Byron, who lacked the malice of ideological particularism.

The determination to keep his poise at the execution may also be read as a rehearsal for his own death. In some ways Byron seems a sadist, deriving satisfaction from the humiliation of mistresses like Caro Lamb or Claire and from the purchase of sexual favours, but masochistic elements are also obvious in his fascination with pugilists like Jackson, from whom he solicited lessons, and in his almost wanton aptitude for scandal, with all the disgraceful consequences that at once humiliated and excited him. To attend an execution was less perverse, in those days, than going to a *Grand Prix* motor race might seem today, but Byron's morbidity, however wished for, dated from his adolescence and cannot be dismissed as modishness. It is true that his early death was due at least as much to mismanagement (or mistreatment) as to any fatal trait, but the appetite for adventure often fits suicidal temperaments with a bold coat. Byron, to us, inevitably implies a poet who died at the age of thirty-six and whose whole shortish life was pointed towards the need to bank some capital against oblivion; yet cushioned by fame and title, he must have felt that a soldier's grave, and the gravity of dying for a worthy cause, would never be attained. The famous as often dream of the freedom of anonymity as of the accumulation of greater glory. The death of the condemned criminal provided a spectacle at once exemplary and demanding; the petty quietus of the artist, at the hand of carping critics or the indifferent public, seems contemptibly soft when compared with the sharp and unique decision of the knife. When he later, and cruelly, jeered at Keats for seeming so broken by unkind words, was he not whetting his malice on an embarrassingly ample experience of crybabyishness? While it was true that he had toyed with duelling (his long quarrel with Henry Brougham, compounded by the latter's spiteful partisanship over the separation from Annabella, made it impossible, Byron had persuaded himself, to return home without claiming immediate satisfaction), his winning talent was for smiles and reconciliation, which was not the least reason why Lady Byron's obduracy was so bruising. Suicide at least would make her sorry, as he had fancied it would a variety of flinty critics or cold mistresses. To steel himself to the gory spectacle of judicial murder was to remind himself that death, if sickening, dizzied the spectator more than the sufferer. *'Avanti coraggio!'* were among his many last words.

Living illustration worked more vividly upon him than any of the great art which Hobhouse had insisted on showing him as they proceeded from Venice to Rome, even though Titian, Raphael and Michelangelo, viewed in their native circumstances, had convinced him for the first time of the power of visual art. The ruins of ancient Rome, and the irony of its contemporary pettiness, excited him to the new cantos of *Childe Harold* on which he was soon working. Rome also reminded him that his diabolical reputation with his fellow-countrymen had not abated. An English family, encountered on the unadorned roof of St Peter's, was so scandalized that the mother, a certain Lady Liddell, told her daughter to avert her eyes. 'He is dangerous to look at,' she said.

The sense of being a marked man, and marked by a fate as inexorable as Cain's, may have contributed to the glowering expression he adopted when Hobhouse paid for him to sit for his portrait-bust by Bertel Thorwaldsen. When the sculptor advised him that he need not assume such a care-worn look, Byron insisted, 'That is my expression'. The likeness was generally agreed to be excellent, but Byron maintained that his usual appearance was much more unhappy. However, the statue was well enough regarded by its melancholic subject for him to arrange for its conveyance to England. (It is now to be seen at the head of the stairs at the present John Murray's London offices at 50, Albemarle Street.) He saw his marble replica as a kind of premature stone obituary. Thorwaldsen, in the usual phrase, had 'executed' his bust; Byron was victimized by art as guillotined criminals were by life. He refused all attempts to garnish the statue's head with heroic laurels. No hero yet, he was resigned to the dream-like life of the exile who, whatever his willingness to side with the oppressed of other lands, knows that he is a privileged observer of what others endure as reality. It is one of the smallest ironies of Byron's story that Thorwaldsen shares some of the vandalizing guilt of Byron's butt, Lord Elgin; the sculptor agreed to 'improve' some of the fifth-century sculpture filched from the temple of Aphaia on the island of Aegina. The effect of this recension of genius by talent may be seen, if not enjoyed, in Munich.

At the end of May Byron was back in Venice, to find Marianna sick of the same fever she had nursed in him. Venetian nobility was not in the habit of summering in the city; the great Palladio – whose appropriate family name was della Gondola, though he was in fact Padovan, not Venetian – had set examples of neo-classical splendour along the banks of the Brenta whither those who could afford their pillared coolness were prompt to repair. The families who had conserved their wealth (or married into that of others) commissioned musicians to sweeten the riverside air with the undemanding patterns of Vivaldi, Monteverdi and the *petits maîtres* of Venetian Baroque like Galuppi. Byron, whose dandyism was a function of his uncertainty (to be the slave of fashion is a kind of tailored masochism), could always be trusted to do what was ostentatiously done and he leased a huge country house, the Villa Foscarini, near a village called La Mira, a few miles up river, where la Segati could find easy excuses to visit him, since she had relations there.

The routine of work and visitors was established; the Roman experience was put to paper in the fourth canto of *Childe Harold*, and Hobhouse and 'Monk' Lewis, another old literary friend, mocked for his Gothic predilections, honoured for his sociability, came and went. Marianna was all very well, and still very frequent, but in August, while out riding, Byron encountered Margarita Cogni, a peasant whose bold address and bolder figure (he was to say that it was made to breed gladiators from) enabled her to rival and then to supplant Marianna. She too had black eyes and was twenty-two years old and, happily, she was married, though childless and hence gratifyingly prehensile and un-'flumpity'. She was illiterate (a relief after all those reproachful ladies with their *cacoethes scribendi*) and she was tigerishly shameless. In due course, she saw off Marianna, whose proprietary quibbles were refuted by Margarita's assertion that they were two of a kind and that Byron was free, and doubtless well-advised, to prefer her. Curiously enough, Marianna's husband (whose status as a cuckold did not inhibit him from cuckolding a neighbour) was responsible for giving Byron the *donnée* for a new poem, *Beppo*. The frivolity of the anecdote released him from philosophical pretentiousness and from the corseting persona of the Pilgrim and so paved the way for the polysyllabic playfulness of *Don Juan*. It was a relief to adopt the lightheartedness of the *commedia dell'arte* and to abandon the heavy Romantic themes on which, in *Manfred,* he had expended so much clangorous rhetoric. He had never been a convinced admirer of the Lakers and their earnestness and he now resumed the snappy dandyism of Pope, another of nature's misbegotten wits, whose shapely spite harped back to Juvenal, Byron's favourite Latin and a particularly sarcastic observer of 'the sex'. The use of foreign characters, whether in verse or in prose, has often liberated English writers; they may be subjected to indignities and blessed with qualities of villainy or vitality which are less easily imputed to Anglo-Saxons. *Beppo* lays on the local colour – the gondola is here famously described as a 'coffin clapt in a canoe' – with a celebratory gusto that sets the tone for generations of more or less talented travellers who, having yielded to the *glissement vers le soleil,* send home their rhyming, or prosaic, thoughts from abroad.

Douglas Kinnaird had visited Byron in the early autumn of 1817 and due to his persistence Newstead was finally sold towards the end of the year, for £94,500, a sum which, despite the calls on it and the delays in laying hands on it, did much to consolidate Byron's finances, at last. He toyed with the idea of retiring to a rural house at Este, in the Euganean hills, which he rented from Richard Hoppner, the amiable, obsequious British consul at Venice, but as winter came on he preferred to return to his rather confined lodgings with the Segati. He stabled his horses on the Lido and would be rowed across to that largely deserted island in a gondola in order to have a good gallop before returning to nocturnal pleasure, and business (he liked to write late at night, after celebrating carnal vespers).

In January 1818, once again doing the right thing by attending the Contessa Albrizzi's *conversazione*, he was introduced to a young girl, Teresa Guiccioli, who had recently emerged from a convent in order to be married to the Count Alessandro Guiccioli, a man almost forty years older than herself. Byron was deputed to escort her into a private view of Canova's 'Helen'. She was small and had an attractive, fleshy figure and auburn curls (like Titian's mistress, whose portrait he had admired, and also like his own younger self). Though married, she had a virginal gentleness, as if not quite awakened from the cloistered piety from which an arranged but not unwelcome marriage (the Count was already twice a widower) had sprung her. It was again Carnival time and Byron, despite the previous year's rhyming promise to the contrary, had by no means abandoned the idea of going a-roving or of finding new scabbards for his sword. During the usual two months of licence he seems to have done little else. Marianna's jealousy probably provoked rather than restrained him; he had a greater liking for women than it was standard form to declare to his male friends, but little patience with them. Marianna's sale of his gift of jewels may well have excited that vengefulness so often consequent on unrewarding investments of emotion.

Disillusionment with his mistress (and the chance to flout any rule of conduct which might have been endorsed by Lady Byron) prolonged his saturnalia. He embarked on an orgy to challenge even the Venetian capacity to remain unshocked. As the Carnival ended, the roving poet decided to seek a permanent home in the city. Accommodation was as cheap as his tastes were grand and he finally settled on the Palazzo Mocenigo, on the left bank of the Grand Canal, with a view of the Rialto bridge to the right and just across from the Accademia. It was, and is, a massive grey building, more agreeable to approach from the Gothic landward side, where a shady garden dapples its heavy hull. On the front facing the Grand Canal, its Renaissance façade fails to embellish one of the least captivating of the decked *palazzi* that compete for the eye's attention as one reviews the stone fleet moored on either hand. An English ambassador, Lord Arundel, had lived in the *palazzo* in 1622 and Antonio Foscarini, suspected falsely of passing information to the English, was strangled by the Venetian authorities when he was discovered to have been visiting the place secretly. The gossip later alleged that Foscarini aspired to Lady Arundel's bed, also falsely. He was a dog who had been given an unwarrantedly bad name. If Byron was amused by the ironies of this cautionary tale, he made no known literary use of it.

The rent of the noble house (there had been six Mocenigo doges) was less than £200 per year; at that rate, with all his splashy habits, Byron could afford to spread himself. He took on Margarita Cogni as his 'housekeeper' and though the inverted commas are traditional (since her amorous activities, and her anatomy, are well attested by her master), she did indeed run a tight, if noisy, household. She could not read, but she could talk, and shout. To celebrate his installation as the tenant of a great *palazzo*, Byron also acquired his own personal gondolier, the bearded Tita, whose allegiance was to remove him from his native canals and take him, in Byron's service, and posthumous honour, first to Greece and then to chilly England, where he was found employment by that heterodox dandy, wit and Byronist, Benjamin Disraeli, whose father, Isaac, the indefatigable collator of literary curiosities, was once said by Byron to be his favourite author. The gondolier's loyalty was steadfast but he seems to have quit his native Venice not only because he was devoted to Byron but also because, since his father had been paid an agreed sum for his services, Tita regarded himself as literally his master's property. He was a gentle giant of hirsutely ferocious appearance and unquestioning honour. After many vicissitudes, he lived for almost forty-two years in England and his English widow, thanks to Disraeli, received a civil pension. Unlike the gondoliers who served other Englishmen through the years (A. E. Housman's was called Andrea), Tita seems never to have doubled as his master's catamite, but he was probably not above pimping.

The death of Lady Melbourne, in April 1818, was a further, small reason for Byron to wash his hands of England. His marriage with Annabella had been, in some respects, also a union with Lady M., a way of pleasing her and of allying himself to her family; her death meant that no quasi-maternal blessing could ever greet a return to propriety and his now hated lady. If he still had fatherly feelings for little Augusta, they were mocked by the arrival in Italy of Claire and the Shelleys. Shelley's diplomacy on Claire's behalf neither lured Byron to Lake Como, where they were proposing to stay, nor disposed him to welcome the mother of his illegitimate daughter. He agreed to see the baby, if she came with her nurse, but he was set against any resumption of the unphilo- sophical intimacies which had been more or less tolerable at Geneva. Claire wrote grovelling and sentimental letters, but they were not answered. However, when Allegra did indeed come to Venice, Byron grew fond of her blue eyes and her devilish spirit. (Recognizing his own traits, how could he fail to warm to her?) She made an innocent addition to the menagerie of pets, servants and passing trade which turned the Palazzo Mocenigo into so notorious a tourist attraction that strangers would bribe the servants for a view of its busy, vaulted vestibule, where two monkeys, a fox and a couple of mastiffs had made themselves a loud home.

Byron could not resist accumulating souvenirs, servants and sexual pleasure; his establishment expanded to absorb the funds available, though their availability, so slow were the mechanicals in charge of the Newstead sale, was once again postponed: when he was not complaining of losing hair, loose teeth and lost waistline, he bewailed his missing ducats. The exile's dependence on the post and on the good offices of those he has left behind makes him suspect that malice or malversation must be responsible for the long silences and longer delays to which he is prey. Byron's relations with Murray, whom he alternately flattered with chatty letters, which the publisher was proud to receive and flaunt, and berated for his pusillanimity, went once again into a reproachful decline, despite the success of the new canto of *Childe Harold* and of the saucy *Beppo*. Byron, who affected indifference to the critics, was wary enough of the latter poem's reception to publish it first anonymously, though few can have failed to guess its origin.

If little Allegra was a guileless presence among the calculating many who visited the Palazzo Mocenigo for this purpose or – more likely – for that, her Swiss nurse, Elise, took a primmer attitude and, preferring to change Allegra's habitation rather than his own habits, Byron decided to board nurse and child with Richard Hoppner and his wife, who was also Swiss. Claire was distressed at the arrangement and, although her feelings were possibly genuine, she took the maternal opportunity to accompany Shelley to Venice early in August in order to visit her daughter and lay tentative siege to Byron. Prudently, Shelley decided to call alone at the Palazzo Mocenigo, where Byron made no objection to Claire seeing her daughter, so long as he did not have to see Claire, whose presence in Venice was temporarily concealed from him. Her two parents never saw Allegra together.

The friendship between Byron and Shelley, though riven by contradictory estimations of the world and its prospects, and by their irreconcilable attitudes to Claire, was deepened, even under this stress, by the pensive profundities in which they indulged on the way to and from equine exercise on the Lido. Back at the Palazzo Mocenigo, they talked on and on into the lapping night. Shelley believed in the perfectibility of man; Byron in the incurable fallaciousness of his nature. Both agreed, roughly, on the need for a radical revision of English society, but Byron's ability to see both sides of a question prevented him from believing in any definitive prescription: his humour and generosity – aspects of the 'cheerful frank-ness' to which Shelley paid ungrudging tribute – precluded the unblinking severity of the zealot. It was, no doubt, on this account that Marx argued that had Byron lived he would have degenerated into a bourgeois reactionary ('Not so much of the bourgeois,' he might have objected), whereas Shelley had in him the stuff of an enduring revolutionary. Shelley located Byron's weakness in his pride, but for the rest he acknowledged the 'consummate genius' to which the preface of his poem *Julian and Maddalo*, an overt gloss on the time he spent alone with Byron during that summer of 1818, pays an un-qualified tribute rare among literary men who contend for the same limelight. Shelley's poem is among his most successful; the image of the two men on the glassy lagoon, passing the island on which lunatics are confined and musing on the brevity of human life, is a lambent reminder of how deeply Byron's personality impressed and influenced Shelley. (Charles E. Robinson's *Shelley And Byron: The Snake and Eagle Wreathed in Flight* is a stimulating examination of the tangled relationship and its literary consequences.)

Poetics to one side, Shelley was persistently anxious for Byron to abate his rage with Claire. If, as modern experts believe, Shelley was soon to embark, or had already embarked, on an affair with her, Byron's obduracy was much to blame for it, if blame is due. The more Byron rejected the girl (she was scarcely more), the greater Shelley's pity for her and, in some measure, his furtive debt to Byron. Though he lacked the random concupiscence he so deplored in his great rival, we have seen that Shelley was attracted by troilism; the more 'Albé' rejected Claire, the more likely it was that Percy would be constrained to console her. Thus Shelley's feeling for Claire did not rule out a certain tolerance for Byron's frigidity. The disasters which so regularly befell Shelley can sometimes be attributed to bad luck (or bad medicine), but his repeated if unpremeditated infidelities, first to Harriet and then to Mary, always for the best of affectionate motives, demand generous analysis, if they are not to appear as irresponsible as they were meant to be expansive. It would not be beyond Byron's intuitive powers to guess that there was something in his repudiation of Claire that did not altogether displease his guest, though for all his homosexual fancies, he is unlikely to have divined to what degree Shelley's growing involvement with Claire may have masked a kind of love for himself. Mary's unhappiness was at once a cause and a consequence of Shelley's increasing attentions to Claire, whose resilience and trust in him were alike attractive, especially after the death of the Shelleys' daughter Clara, at Venice, when they returned there in September 1817, had created a breach between Shelley and his grieving wife. It is possibly significant that part of Byron's hatred of Robert Southey, the poet laureate (with whom Shelley, early in his poetic life, had been on good, even deferential terms), derived from the slanderous remarks Southey had made about 'a League of Incest' compacted between the Shelleys, Byron and Claire during the Genevan summer. The canard was exaggerated tittle-tattle, but Southey's malice has a touch of intuition (as malice often does); it is apparent that a strong, if unrealized attraction did exist both between Shelley and Byron and between Mary and Byron. A web of jealousy and unexpressed envy laced them together in a cat's cradle of emotional tension, which was to persist even beyond Percy's death.

Byron, often generous to a fault, and sometimes generous when at fault, lent the Shelleys the farmhouse at Este which he had leased from Hoppner but never used. He was too well suited by Venice, too closely cossetted by Margarita Cogni,

La Fornarina (her husband was a baker), and too well served by those birds of passage who feathered his vanity and drove Margarita to comically terrifying descants of rage. Her jealousy made that of Marianna Segati seem positively restrained, though when the two of them clashed, it had been beyond the power of some passing Austrian soldiers to separate them. The two *Veneziane* broke off to make common cause against the invaders, before returning to the private business of scratching each other's eyes out. Byron observed that if Italy was ever to rid herself of the occupying forces, she would do best to rely on her women to do the job. On another occasion, when Byron was seen by Margarita to be yielding to the blandishments of a woman of quality, she did not hesitate to lay peremptory claim to him. He reminded her that the lady was of noble blood. '*Forsé nobile,*' retorted La Fornarina, '*ma io sono Veneziana!*' ('She may be noble, but I am Venetian!')

The melodrama and pageantry of life among the hundred islands, and the hired throne he had contrived for himself, might have been enough to confine Byron strictly to a routine of excess, but he was also working at a new poem in which he recognized the signs of a clinching renaissance: exit Childe Harold, enter Don Juan. Whatever questions may be raised about Byron's place among English poets, who can doubt the scintillating flexibility with which he handled the rigid demands of *ottava rima*? His colloquial impudence makes one wonder, time and again, how he can possibly find a way of finishing a verse or of sustaining its apparently reckless scheme. Though he never wholly renounced his more solemn mode (which, since it translated so impressively, made and makes his reputation more portentous in foreign countries than in his own), he now composed in a jingling lingo, almost untranslatable in its mixture of slang and satire. Having liberated himself from parochial poetics and afforded himself the freedom to create, in *Don Juan,* an irresponsible *roman fleuve,* he contrived a 'Mediterranean' poem of such linguistic resourcefulness that only his fellow-countrymen could ever fully respond to it.

Don Juan is a concatenation of episodes which, unlike those chronicled in *Childe Harold,* were paraded not as an advertisement for some dark destiny but as a skittish declaration of independence from all programmatic proprieties. (It is typical that Byron's scepticism over Leigh Hunt's real poetic ability was aroused by the latter's saying, precisely, that he wrote according to a 'scheme'.) The ideas of the Lakers had once seemed so powerful that he was tempted almost to acquiesce in them, but his temperament was wary, even scornful, of nature. The true dandy is dedicated to the unnatural, hence Oscar Wilde's remark that nature was 'badly lit and far too green'; he is committed to posture and adornment, the conversion of the body into its external decoration and of unkempt artlessness into perverse formality. Byron's invocation of Pope to authorize the stance taken in *Don Juan* confirmed his rejection of Wordsworth's cult of the commonplace. His fancy to have Allegra raised as a Roman Catholic, partly a spiteful joke at the expense of both Claire and Shelley, whose atheism smacked of an earnestness embarrassing to a gentleman, was also in character with the cast of mind which chooses a style for its strictness rather than for its comfort. The cripple renegade, half dust, half deity, devil and charmer, revels in taking lightly what will weigh heavily on others. When the time came to leave Venice (and later Ravenna), he trailed his menagerie with him, too soft-hearted to put down his pets or to leave them in unreliable hands, but he was prepared to be a petty Herod with his daughter and sent her to the Catholic kennel in which, at the age of five, she was to die. The early death of children, as the Shelleys' misfortunes with Clara and little William demonstrate, was not uncommon (nor was their capricious treatment by rich and idle parents), but Byron affected to stand for something extraordinary and he cannot be acquitted of faults because he shared them with a society to which, at other times, he is held to be the great and even Christian exception. (Professor Wilson Knight's attempt to equate Byron's character with that of Jesus is winningly straight-faced, but its partiality overdoes its hero's virtues by denying his vices.) In fairness, it must be remarked that when that notorious slow-coach John Hanson at last arrived in Venice with the papers to complete the sale of Newstead to Major Thomas Wildman, Byron took the opportunity to add a codicil to his will, leaving Allegra £5,000, no mean sum. And in the following year, it was paternal concern over Allegra's ill health that deflected him from quitting Italy for England, to which he was intermittently tempted to return, like an innocent man coming back to the scene of his crimes.

Everything that had once argued well for Margarita Cogni – animal spirits, brazen vocabulary, possessive deference to Byron's desires (and her bold initiation of them) – came later to work against her. He had seen her first, almost coy beneath her *fazziolo*, the traditional costume of the peasant girl, but she had acquired a taste for fancier fripperies so grotesque that Byron ordered his servants to burn her wardrobe. She wanted to be a lady; he liked her better as Medea, his singular choice for the woman he would have preferred 'to any that ever breathed'. (Did he see himself as Jason or as one of Medea's hapless children? Or as her mincemeat brother scattered like bread upon the waters?) Margarita's jealousy had a kind of ferocity he had found, for a time, almost protective. But her time was up when Byron discovered that she was learning to read, the better to spy on his commerce with other women. She had had the sovereign ability to make him laugh; now she was becoming a joke he had heard before. Given notice, she refused to leave, saying that her husband beat her, that she would sooner sleep on the stones and, of course, that she would kill her master rather than be without him. It was an old story, though more instructive perhaps, in Italian. Byron invited her to stab him if she really wanted to (unlike Caro Lamb, she cut his hand, not her own), but after flinging herself into the canal, from which she had to be rescued and 'refixed', she had spent her splendour. Her departure was doubtless well enough compensated to assuage her vanity and adorn that famous figure. She had made copious copy for Byron's letters – who would not laugh to read of her crossing herself, *in medias res*, if a church bell should happen to toll when she was making love? – and she had proved how an acquaintance with literacy can corrupt the most natural creature in the world.

Although the Carnival of 1819 returned him, inexhaustible, to the lists of love, Byron had been making such a habit of venal venery that Shelley, always appalled by prostitution, was disgusted; Venetian mothers and fathers, on the other hand, were uncomplainingly enriched. It is hard to believe that Byron could find any sexual sensation in the Carnival which had not been already procured for him by his personal pimps; during the previous year, ladies of quality and quantities of ladies had served his quick turn, for love or money. In the London days he recalled so nostalgically, he had often heard the chimes at midnight, but if his roistering with Tom Moore and others had been intemperate, it never equalled the sensual gluttony of his Venetian *passades*. He was apparently a man who lived only for the moment, but he knew that moments were fugitive and that life was running away. His nostalgia was of a piece with his debauchery: to caress the past is to be the miser of sensations. Love of yesterday is the horror of tomorrow, another day gone. When he crossed the lagoon with Shelley, and they heard the bell clanging the maniacs to Vespers, Byron remarked how conscience was the bell that calls mankind to virtue. 'We obey it like madmen, without knowing why, then the sun sets. The bell stops. It is the night of death.'

The sexual athlete defies *rigor mortis* by his stiff activity; he clocks a defiant quota of little deaths before the final, irrevocable climax. Modern statistical hedonism may find much that is reassuringly unsentimental – even exemplary – in his industrious playboyishness, but Byron's proleptic apprehension that the sword would outwear its scabbard was coming home to him. He had had his fill of sex, enviable as he might hope that others would rate him: the bedroom Corsair regaled worldly correspondents like Douglas Kinnaird with his jolly rogering of mothers, daughters, rich and poor. In April 1819 he chanced once again to meet Teresa Guiccioli at the gallant old Contessa Benzoni's *conversazione*. La Benzoni had been a sort of premature Isadora Duncan in her day, though now she was embarrassingly slow to recognize that its evening had come. She had danced half-naked around a Liberty Tree at the time of the French Revolution, though one may doubt that she welcomed the one which Napoleon had erected in the Piazza San Marco after poor Doge Manin laid aside his *corno* or ducal headgear. Byron was of a humour to be susceptible both to Teresa's beauty and to the uncoy naiveté of which she made so pretty a show. Having caught a clap (the first, he said, he had not paid for) from a supposedly proper lady not long before, it was a healthy change to fall in with a nice girl who, if married, was radiantly unspoilt. The reluctant Teresa had come to the soirée out of obedience to her rich husband's powerful whim, while Byron had no hunger for new acquaintances with women: 'If they are ugly because they are ugly – and if they are beautiful because they are beautiful.' Nevertheless, the formal brevity of their first meeting, a year before, was in contrast with the intimate protraction of their second. Teresa's convent schooling enabled her to converse intelligently about poetry; luckily, she had learnt her lessons about Byron's unlikely favourite, Dante, who was buried in her native city, Ravenna. Before embarking on secret meetings and curtained gondolas, Byron was refreshed by Teresa's girlish ardour and intelligent aspirations. His appetite for vapid persiflage and indiscriminate tupping had reached its term. As for Teresa, she succumbed dizzily to the melodic voice and the noble brow (nobler as the hair receded) almost from the first moment of this their second encounter. It was quickly followed by an assignation, during which she resisted the advances he had promised not to make (her husband was taking his siesta), and then by another, when she lacked the strength to deny her lover, or herself.

If Byron was 'not a man to confine himself to sentiment', no more was he a man to neglect it: even the most commercial of his sexual connections were often sweetened by gestures of tenderness. If he sometimes used sex as a form of assault (what virile man does not?), he had at least a sense of seigneurial responsibility; if the poor were his brothel, he was rarely a vicious whoremonger. Those he threw away often remembered him with affection. Even when he seemed to be straining every nerve to alienate them, he craved the good opinion of others, or dreaded the bad. (During his last days in Missolonghi, he feared his sickness might be due to the evil eye, the result of an enmity unwittingly aroused.) The child who doubts his mother's love – and who more than the cripple fears that he has disappointed her? – seeks to reassure himself of it by provoking her to the limit. The bad boy proves that his apprehensions were justified by making himself a pariah. To be sure, Byron's early life was not much more terrible, and in some ways incalculably better, than that of his contemporaries – the estate at Rochdale from which he derived his title, and no little revenue, thrust children down the coalmines for long hours at an age when today's mothers would scarcely trust them to cross the road – but that could never console him for the insecurity to which lameness added its unmetaphorical instability. The lame boy's affection for Venice must surely have owed something to its very wateriness; he was reported to have plunged straight into the canal after an evening out, and to have struck out for the Palazzo Mocenigo holding a torch aloft in one hand in order to see, and be seen: look, no feet! It gave him great satisfaction to defeat Angelo Mengaldo when the latter challenged him to a swimming contest, partly because the man was a hero who had performed a gallant crossing of the Danube under fire, partly because, in swimming the course from the Lido to the Grand Canal, he could strut before all Venice with no risk of tripping. When it came to water, he was literally in his element, unlike Shelley, the non-swimming boatman.

By the time the affair with Teresa began, the first canto of *Don Juan* had already been sent to England, where Scrope, Hobhouse and Kinnaird, on whose worldliness Byron had reason to think he could rely, were either scandalized or feared a scandal, should it be published. Byron protested that the poem contained nothing obscene: did not the poem's wit lie in putting the responsibility for what was read into it upon the reader? But his friends remained sure that his reputation would suffer. It has been suggested that Hobhouse, at the beginning of his political career, was anxious lest he should appear to be seconding an assault on moral standards, but such a view of Hobby lacks both generosity and acumen. His friends, aware of the increasing power of middle-class morality, were probably concerned to keep Byron's options open; he could still perhaps hope to return to England so long as he did nothing so egregiously offensive as publishing an immortal and immoral poem. Byron was sufficiently impenitent to invite Murray to publish his work exactly as it stood, 'indelicacies' and all, or not at all. Publishers will often honour obstinacy if it seems likely to be combined with success, and Murray abandoned his trimming objections. It was again agreed, however, that the first edition should be anonymous, though it is hard to believe that any but the most uninformed gossip or the crassest critic would not guess, from a very short list, who had written lines which, in the case of Donna Julia, a mathematical lady, were so waspishly *ad mulierem* as to be virtually trademarked '*Crede Byron*'. Shelley, scornful of London opinion and alert to genius, was the unambiguous advocate of uncut publication, despite – or because of – what his family and reputation had suffered from his own intemperance.

Count Alessandro Guiccioli was rich, cultivated and dangerous. He was rumoured to have poisoned his first wife, the Contessa Placidia Zinanni, on whose large dowry his own wealth was founded. She had objected to his fruitful liaison with one of their maids. Her reproaches led to sequestration in a remote villa from which she was reprieved, a sick woman, only just in time to make a will in favour of her husband before being carried off. Guiccioli promptly married his mistress, which spoke for a measure of softheartedness, but on the night of *her* death he went to the theatre as usual, which does not. He was a man of calculating temper who honoured the traditions of the society which his new money allowed him to dominate and patronize – he was a leading subscriber to the theatre in Ravenna, where he kept his main establishment – and he frowned no immediate disapproval when Byron became the *cavalier servente* of his pretty young wife. A politician who believed, in great things and in small, in playing a waiting game, he had the self-preserving opportunism of the Vicar of Bray, with a much more impressive living. He tended to the conservative cause and believed in collaboration with the Austrians, whose favourite he was. By marrying Teresa, however, he had, whether out of shrewdness or as the incautious consequence of his desires, effectively hedged his bets by becoming linked with a family, the Gambas, dedicated to the insurgent cause of the *Carbonari*. Guiccioli was a man who was always willing to wait and see, but because he waited it did not follow that he had not seen. Like Byron he had his pride and, in addition, a degree of ruthlessness which made it unwise to take unconventional liberties. A bare week after the clandestine meeting in Byron's *casino* where the romance was consummated, Guiccioli elected summarily to remove himself and his wife from Venice. They would travel home to Ravenna by way of his secluded estates along the way down the coast. Teresa seems already to have been as completely in love with Byron as any woman he had ever met and her piquant conjunction of unsqueamish urgency and fragile beauty had already worked on him, though he wrote cynically to Kinnaird of the likely duration of the episode. The tupped ewe lamb had embarrassed or perhaps alarmed him by rushing into the opera house, during a performance of Rossini's *Otello*, to bewail the news that she was being forced to leave Venice, but the naiveté of such unguarded affection (she was heard in public calling him 'mio Byron') was mitigated by agile recourse to the usual machinery of go-betweens to enable the lovers to correspond during her enforced absence. A private postal service run between a pliable priest and Teresa's personal maid allowed Byron to prove himself as Italian with sighs and compliments as the most flowery Romeo.

Love, rather than sex, sentiment rather than accountancy, returned to his life after two years of promiscuity. Teresa, he seems soon to have decided, was to be his 'Last Attachment'. Leslie Marchand, to whose dedicated industry anyone remotely interested in the poet must defer, points out that just before his involvement with Teresa, Byron had had an affair, under cover of the Carnival, with another young and seemingly unspoilt girl, Angelina, with whom his *passade* had been something less than a passion, but more than passing. Indeed, Angelina was eager to marry him (and willing to dispose of his wife when she discovered that he was married already), but her father called the police and she was restored to his obdurate custody. The similarity between Angelina and Teresa, and the temporal proximity of the two affairs, suggest that Byron had grown weary of the Medea type.

He had not, of course, ever felt obliged to restrict himself to a single type, or to a single sex, though how many of his ephemeral bedfellows had indeed been fellows no one can say. The debauchee rarely refuses whatever promises to stimulate him: what has been hired can always be fired. Though his defenders like to extract some desperate moral from his Venetian rut, Byron's jaded bragging does not necessarily give a true account of it. It is too much to argue that the succession of women was merely a screen for homosexual predilections, but the frenzy of those two years of rampant self-advertisement and compulsive tuft-hunting was an attempt to work off on women a more general resentment and also suggests that it was women, in particular, whom he resented. On the other hand, must the pleasure of sex require recherché explanation? Hedonism may be a shallow philosophy, but men do not always seek profundity: sheer self-indulgence may be nice work if you can get it, and Byron certainly could.

By the time he took up with Teresa he had satisfied himself, among others, that he had plucked all that could be offered in terms of sensual delectation. 'It's life, damme, it's life,' was the Regency epicure's unapologetic apology. Byron's hostility to cant insisted on the recognition of a common humanity which, in some respects, was established most incontrovertibly by cunt, that 'soft anvil', as the Earl of Rochester put it, on which all of us are forged. The truth, according to some, is what happens when you take your clothes off. Yet because of his pride, and his shame, his title and his crippled leg, Byron never really cared, or dared, quite to be on an equal footing with anyone; his good looks and his charm had to be braced by money and quarterings. The duality of which he was so conscious meant that almost everything he did, including his poetic work, had an inner and an outer sense. Hatred of cant was also love of exhibitionism. His imagination enabled him to see the contradictions in the conventional wisdom as well as to perceive how mutability kept the world in a state of flux so confusing that conventions might well seem the wisest recourse. The female who says she'll ne'er consent, and then consents, was the emblem of emotional instability and moral humbug. She was both delicious and dangerous; she deserved reward and punishment. His spectacular Venetian performance involved reduction of the largest possible number of women to a state of subjection. What better compensation for the early girls who remained enigmatic or indifferent, and what better gesture of contempt for Lady B.?

Even, and perhaps particularly, his catamites were evidence of his insatiable suspicions of the female sex, though the attraction of a change of potatoes should not be too officiously discounted. Shelley's distaste for what he saw, or guessed, of Byron's male lovers was probably sincere (not least because Byron's *ragazzi* were hired) but it also may have masked a certain fascination with homosexuality which he not only denied in himself but could not credit even in the ancient Greeks: when he translated Plato's *Symposium*, he elected to believe that the habits of which Sir Kenneth Dover has given us such an outspoken (if not unchallenged) anatomy were to be read in a purely metaphorical spirit, a likely story. But then Shelley was never in Greece.

It must have been particularly galling to him, after Byron had misconducted himself with such preening profligacy, when Richard Hoppner saw fit to pass the malicious word that Claire had become pregnant by Shelley and, having failed to procure an abortion, had farmed the resulting child out to the Foundling Hospital in Naples. The issue was further complicated by the fact that Allegra's quondam nurse, Elise, was the Hoppners' informant and that she herself was involved with a blackmailing servant in the Shelleys' employ. Claire Tomalin, in her monograph on Shelley, concludes that the rumour was probably largely true, though the motives for Shelley's behaviour remain obscure and, unless you reprehend the original adultery, not necessarily dishonourable. Whatever his capacity for self-deception or folly, Shelley was clear and clean in his condemnation of prostitution; his hostility to marriage, as the machine of sexual exclusivity and hypocrisy, was based not least on his revulsion at the merchandizing of women. In his view, Byron's aristocratic canker not only fouled his vision of the world but also explained the insouciance with which he made use of its sordid amenities. The Hoppners' complaisance over Byron's debauchery makes an ironic contrast with their officious malice towards Shelley, whose idiosyncratic morality would at least never allow him to assuage his sexual urges by proffering a few *soldi*.

Not only Byron's revels but also his Venetian sojourn came to an end by his falling in love with Teresa Guiccioli. At first he had been as callous in his report of the affair as he was tender in its pursuit: 'The charmer forgets that a man may be whistled anywhere before the essential business is completed, but that after . . . well, there is nothing very new before us.' Byron's lovesickness, once Teresa was on her way to Ravenna, smacks as much of decision as of passion: there seems to be an element of will no less than willingness in the hyperbolic Italian of his declarations. Of course, Shelley's description of Teresa as 'sentimental, innocent, superficial' addresses itself to the externals and may well tell more of her response to him than of her appeal to Byron, though she attributed to Shelley a poetic delicacy which blessed his no longer handsome face with 'remarkable beauty'.

Teresa has not fared particularly well with Byron's biographers, apart from the sympathetic portrait in Iris Origo's *The Last Attachment*, but she had qualities of courage and wholeheartedness which make her not only romantic but also touching. She was already pregnant, by her husband, at the time of her encounter with Byron in the little *casino* (her condition no doubt contributed to the perfunctoriness of her resistance to what she wanted) and the news now came that she had miscarried while on the way to Ravenna. She was seriously ill, but if Byron was concerned, it was not till June 1819 that he was moved to set out for Ravenna. Before quitting Venice, Marchand reminds us, he did two very typical things: he attempted to resume his courtship of the beautiful Angelina (during which escapade he fell into the Grand Canal) and he composed a long and passionate letter to Augusta, declaring once again how perfect and boundless had been, and remained, his devotion to her. 'The union of all passions and of all affections' had lacked the ructions of his other involvements, but it was, and must always have been, in some respects just as 'impossible'. It was distinguished not only by Augusta's scatty personality – that laughing and unpossessive loyalty no other woman ever offered – but also by the fact that it was a conspiracy of two against the accepted way of the world. It was perverse not because incest, especially of so 'technical' an order, is necessarily an intolerable vice (it has often been the privilege of princes) but because, in the circumstances of Christian England, it could never be tolerated.

Just as Shelley, in the midst of his emotional tangles, could dream of removing Mary to an Edenic retreat, so Byron, forever wishing that he were in 'mine island' (he almost certainly had Naxos in mind), could persuade himself that happiness had been denied him, after he and Augusta had been forced apart, when in fact his own appetite for publicity was always bound to jeopardize his fantasies of idyllic privacy. He never fastened his affections on a woman with whom there was any prospect of lasting and unthreatened felicity: he systematically connived at his own disappointment.

The liaison with Augusta, however gilded its memory, was in practice as fissile as any other. Only his marriage could have offered permanence; the savagely rueful reaction to its collapse proclaims how conscious he was that he had wasted a unique opportunity, though even here it can, of course, be argued that he designed his own chagrin by his self-punishing selection of a bride. The air of grievance with which he scented his letters from exile has something of the deliberate sulkiness which he adopted in Thorwaldsen's studio. What he always wanted was always the impossible; loving Augusta was in exquisite character with a man who never saw a rule without wishing to become the exception that proved it.

The Christian revenge which Lady Byron took by re-cruiting the once devil-may-care Mrs Leigh to the ranks of piety is not without its ironic gloss. If Augusta was the only person with whom Byron had ever felt truly at ease, it was partly on account of their similarity; Annabella, however hardened her heart, was still susceptible to Byron's power over her (she was much moved by the last canto of *Childe Harold* which Murray had been kind, or cruel, enough to send to her) and by making Augusta her kneeling companion she conscripted a penitent surrogate for her delinquent husband. By imposing on Augusta a régime of remorseful rectitude which made her almost incomprehensible to her absent and unrepentant brother, Annabella vanquished Byron in the more pliant person of his sister. She had the dual compensation of Augusta's resemblance to the man who had so excited and appalled her and of virtuous intimacy with a scapegoat on whom she could visit all her vengeful affection. In the most decorous way and for the most proper of motives,

Annabella was able to exact from Augusta the apologies refused her by Byron. In its chaste perversity, the relationship of the two women had something in common with the one which had so shocked Annabella in the first place: she gained an intimate hold over Augusta which, symbolically at least, could be held to be at once incestuous and homosexual. What had driven her from Byron's house was, in the sly way of such things, repeated in her own life: she may have forced Augusta to her knees only in prayer, but her exaggerated attention to that muddled lady's spiritual welfare has all the morbidity of an obsession. To manipulate Augusta was still to have *a* Byron to reproach and reform; while Byron's own Venetian rut can be read, in much the same light, as a re-assertion of the liberty Annabella had sought to confine or curtail.

However sweet and mettlesome Teresa seemed, Byron's following her to Ravenna marked a regression as well as a revival: he was again the lover of a married woman, girlish as she might be, and again he was pitting himself, under whatever licence of local usage, against a *marito* who, like William Lamb or even Lord Oxford, incarnated the wealth, dignity and power of the established order. The Last Attachment has been graced with a certain redeeming serenity, if only because Byron was as good as his word: he never fell in love again, at least not with a woman. The gallant rhetoric of his declarations and letters was never proved hollow, which seems to stamp it with sincerity, but the keen actor in him surely welcomed the kind of dashing adventure, dark with dangers and daggers, that he had imagined in *Beppo*. He was launched into a drama that both rejuvenated and alienated him, an emotional emigration which enabled him to turn his back on the family plot in which he had been for so long and so painfully embroiled.

As a guest in Guiccioli's fief, he accepted the position of a *cavalier servente* with all the courteous duplicities it involved. He acted, very convincingly, the part of the dedicated and patient lover (any impatience was largely Teresa's) in the stylized, if not always chaste, tradition of courtly love. Were there not *cicisbei* in Venice – the elderly Contessa Benzoni's lover was both paragon and doyen, having waited more than twenty years until she was free to marry him – who set an example at once touching and ridiculous of adherence to the *règle du jeu*? An English critic had recently advised Byron to set aside 'seven or eight years' for the composition of a masterpiece, and he had responded with spontaneous scorn;

such premeditation smacked of a 'scheme'. Now, however, he appeared to be committing himself to a protracted affair without any prospect of a happy ending either for himself or for his mistress. Once engaged, honour required him to prove to the foreigners that he could play their artificial games as well as a native: *Crede Byron*.

As an earnest of his seriousness, when they met again he showed Teresa a ring he had bought, containing a tiny cache of poison. He would have taken it, he promised, had she died from her miscarriage or its inept treatment (leeches had been set to sup on what was left of her blood). Teresa retorted that he should have bought a dose of the same poison for her, since she could not live without him. The fervour of her protestation was superior to its logic, but was it not prettily said? Byron, touched by her impetuosity, remained wary of her constancy. He half-expected her to let him down, or told Kinnaird he did, which may indicate his own lack of conviction: 'I doubt her liking anything for very long – except one thing and I presume she will soon arrive at varying even that.'

Teresa was, after all, at the beginning of her amorous career, whereas he had seen it all before, the likely future included. Although Byron does not seem to have suffered very cruelly from betrayal (at least in the years of his fame), the amorist often bemoans the infidelity of those to whom he looks forward to being unfaithful. Should Teresa's passion lose its panting call upon him, he would be free to quit Italy and make yet another fresh start; the Greek Committee in London was far from ready, either financially or militarily, to make any decisive move, but Greece was a spring at which he longed once more to drink. Teresa's whims were, for the moment at least, allowed to spin the coin of his heads-or-tails fate. He would not desert her, but if she did indeed proceed to vary her sexual diet, he was resolved not to be wounded: 'When a man has been for some time in the habit of keying a female, it is his own fault if being left in the lurch greatly incommodes him.' In fact Teresa displayed a fidelity which graces her foolhardiness; her Augusta-like willingness to laugh by no means implied that she was not serious. She had gone from secluded virginity to an arranged marriage with a dangerous man; her passion for Byron scarcely needs elaborate explanation (after all, he *was* Byron), but it allowed her to retrieve her bartered adolescence with none of the blushing reluctance expected of an untouched maiden. Her later history implies that she was highly sexed and had a stronger will and capacity for survival than her petite person suggested.

Ravenna threatened to lack either novelty or the kind of setting Byron favoured. He lived in a frowsty hotel, humiliatingly at the mercy of the Guicciolis' diary. The scintillating mosaics of Theodoric's capital afforded him small diversion; people rather than monuments were what interested him, and the Cardinal Legate and his cultivated and amiable secretary, Count Alborghetti, offered the kind of literate society which he endured but scarcely enjoyed. When Cardinal Malvasia, a conniving and worldly friend of Guiccioli and a priest said to have had a far from celibate youth, arranged a reception in Byron's honour, the poet gave impolitic offence by being too distracted to attend: anxious about Teresa's health, he was in an unusually febrile, even tearful, mood. Count Guiccioli's ambivalence gave the situation some menace. Teresa could swear that the ribald rhymes audible in the streets of Ravenna were not taken seriously by her husband, but then why did the Count decide peremptorily to take her on yet another voyage of inspection, this time to his estate in Bologna? Teresa had to go; Byron was persuaded to follow. Worried about Allegra's future and nagged by Murray's latest, spineless attitude to *Don Juan* (the anonymous publication of which was reported a flop), he was trundled about the Romagna – in his ageing coach – without fruitful purpose or desirable destination. He dreamed of an exile from exile itself in the form of an expedition to South America; if he could not be Washington or Aristides, perhaps he could be Simon Bolívar, who certainly thought he could be Byron. What was to be done with a mere pen but incite the English to giggle, which they seemed censoriously reluctant to do?

The visit to Bologna began with tears, when at a performance of Alfieri's *Mirra*, Byron was distressed by the seemingly ubiquitous incest theme; it ended with Guiccioli's complaisant agreement to the still sickly Teresa's travelling back with Byron to Venice in order to see a Dr Aglietti, in whom she had faith and whose place of business was conveniently distant from her husband's. Meanwhile, even when the Count invited Byron to move into an apartment in his own Bologna *palazzo*, his attitude was not wholly disinterested. The political situation remained finely balanced and might explode into violence at any moment. When the Count requested a personal interview, Byron may have been reminded of his ticklish confrontation with Wedderburn Webster (with whom he still corresponded amiably). Guiccioli no more demanded satisfaction than had Bold Webster: he wanted to be made British Consul in Ravenna. Diplomatic immunity might come in useful in case of civic disorder. Should it be beyond Byron's powers to procure him the full title, he would be content with the position of Vice-Consul. At the same time, like Webster, he asked Byron for a large loan, though his financial situation can scarcely have been perilous. If he attributed greater influence and wealth to the milord than he actually possessed, it was not beyond his subtlety to tax Byron merely to amuse himself at his guest's expense. Byron offered little satisfaction on either score; though a peer of England, it was not in his gift to influence the government or a Prince Regent with whom he had taken conspicuous pains to be at odds, and as for money, he was still a fortunate man without access to his fortune.

Guiccioli's complaisance was tested to destruction by the behaviour of his wife when she reached Venice. Despite the neat circumstance that her maid, Fanny Silvestrini, was the mistress of the Count's steward and informant, Lega Zambelli, whose loyalty was thus converted to Byron's side of the equation, it can hardly have escaped Guiccioli's ears that Teresa stayed first at the Palazzo Mocenigo – after a sniffy survey of the insalubrious accommodation reserved for her in the Palazzo Malipiero – and then at La Mira, where affectations of innocence (the lovers did have separate apartments) hardly convinced gossips of anything but the truth.

Her ill-health may have been genuine (she was said to have the piles and to be in danger of a prolapse) but her sexual expectations abated neither in urgency nor in regularity. Byron was once again the victim of a situation in which he could, in some respects, luxuriate but which put the initiative in the hands of others. He was a leading man who, time and again, took his cue from the other actors, or actresses. Guiccioli's patronizing ambiguousness degenerated suddenly into something close to panic when he joined the lovers in Venice at the beginning of November. They had returned to the Palazzo Mocenigo, where Teresa was nursing Byron in one of his feverish attacks, but it was now common knowledge that she had been more than mopping his lordship's brow and the Venetian nose for scandal was not averted by the friendly publicity with which the Count was welcomed into apartments in Byron's own house.

If Guiccioli chose not to quarrel with the man whose good offices he still hoped to procure, he was now openly and loudly angry with Teresa. At the climax of their quarrel he demanded whether she preferred to have a lover or a husband. If it was a cant question, it did not receive the cant reply. Mortified by Teresa's rejection, Guiccioli retreated in tears to Byron, who persuaded his mistress to do the right, or convenient, thing and return to Ravenna with her husband, though he had to promise to follow them shortly. He had teased himself with the prospect of Teresa's infidelity, but her fidelity was in some ways even more alarming. If she quit her husband, Byron was as good as married to her. He could not leave her without ruining her life; to stay with her meant a lifetime of carrying her fan. During October, before Guiccioli's return to Venice, Byron had been reminded of happier days in London by a visit from Tom Moore during which Teresa had granted him one night of leave in order to show his visitor the town. When Moore set off for England, with a clutch of Byron's newly written Memoirs in his keeping, his destination may well have excited no little envy. Italy was now knotty with problems, but some signal achievement was needed if Byron's return to his native land was to be anything but ignominious. The Memoirs, about which so much speculation has revolved ever since their incineration in the office fire at Murray's, were probably less scandalous or salacious than imagination would make them. Byron specifically declared that they were not confessions (Berlioz was to make the same distinction over his memoirs, and with verifiable justice), though we may still deplore the decision by Hobhouse and Murray – Moore dissenting impotently – to put them forever beyond assessment.

But if England tempted, it also intimidated: even the prosaic Hobhouse was in trouble for his political agitations. The protracted Westminster election campaign had ranged Hobby, Scrope and Kinnaird in a not altogether harmonious reformers' alliance against the Tories and, incidentally, Byron's pet hate, Sir Samuel Romilly. After the infamous massacre of Peterloo, in August 1819, Hobhouse's 'radicalism' reached its apogee and he was bold and unwise enough to demand in print, 'What prevents the people from walking down to the House [of Commons] and pulling out the members by the ears . . . ?' The Commons took his question for a revolutionary statement. Early in the new year of 1820 he was temporarily committed to Newgate prison for a putative breach of privilege, from which a dissolution of Parliament quite soon released him. If Byron never flinched from a fight (should there be real trouble in England, he promised to 'be among ye') the will was lacking for any dramatic flights. As for participating in electoral campaigns, he had already told his friends that a peer was obliged to be above such common activities. Byron was never a man to travel on a second-class ticket.

A pressing letter from Count Ruggiero Gamba, Teresa's father, in December 1819, may have been as timely as it was alarming: he had to leave Venice at once. Teresa's health had gone into another decline, though it rose with conspicuous speed once he re-entered Ravenna on Christmas eve. The enthusiasm with which Byron was welcomed, on all sides, flattered his vanity but it also reminded him of the soft shackles by which a sentimental Bonnivard might be constrained. Teresa's delight was touching; it was also triumphant. In Venice, he had been master in his own house; now he was lured into taking a vacant apartment in the Count's palace.

Teresa, having got what suited her, appeared less hostile to her husband (the proximity of her parents, however doting, favoured a return to familiar proprieties) and she was inclined to treat Byron as an entertainment rather than a commanding consideration. He had exchanged independence for the position of tenant and attendant. Marooned in provincial Ravenna, an emotional Crusoe, he was provoked to mill away at those he had left behind, since there was no punch bag closer at hand. He composed a flippant lampoon on Hobby's imprisonment (it was widely circulated by the sniggering Murray) and he took a prose poke at Wordsworth and company and especially at 'Johnny-piss-a-bed' Keats, that 'tadpole of the lakes', who had dared to disparage Pope and Dryden, his manifest betters. Hobhouse's understandable outrage was appeased by a joshing letter from Byron and his vanity restored by his election to the new House of Commons. The tepid reception of *Don Juan* had not improved Byron's temper – he may have been out of patience with Hobhouse not least since Hobby was one of the first to wrinkle his nose – but he was already working on the next two cantos, despite his confession that it was more from habit than inspiration. Whatever his disdain for Keats's mundane origins and blushful opinions, he had the broadmindedness to appreciate Pope's remark about upper-class versifiers:

But let a Lord own the unhappy lines,
How the wit brightens! How the style refines!

In fact, his output was no less impressive for its regularity. In the first half of 1820, he also worked on a translation of Pulci's *Morgante Maggiore*, finished *The Prophecy of Dante* and wrote most of *Marino Faliero*, a meta-Shakespearian drama celebrating the most unfortunate of Venetian doges, whose well-meaning 'reign' from 1354 to 1355 ended in disgrace and execution. In place of his portrait in the Great Council Chamber, where every other doge, ruthless or inept, is celebrated, there hangs the image of a black square, though his crime was less treason to the Republic than an attempt to break the oligarchy of the great families and give some say to the Venetian people. Byron's own long absence from Poets' Corner in Westminster Abbey may be taken as a petty repetition of the disgrace visited upon Faliero. Indeed the latter's tragedy was so amenable to Byron's gifts and such an appropriate metaphor of his own Quixotry, that it is regrettable that, after its unauthorized staging at Drury Lane in April 1821, the piece remains unperformed and, one fears, unperformable. The dream of an aristocrat who incurs the odium of his peers by putting his nobility at the service of the oppressed could not be exorcized in words; it was to have its practical enactment in the last gesture of Byron's life.

For the present, he lacked a cause good enough to engage his energies and to release him with honour from amorous subservience. Though the Austrian presence had grated on him from the moment of Polidori's contretemps at La Scala, it was not until his intimacy with the Gambas that he became involved with the Carbonari. Ravenna was much more tense than Venice, where the tradition of pleasure worked against revolutionary rigour. (The only shot fired during Byron's stay in Venice had been directed at a runaway elephant, put down at last by a cannon ball, to Byron's sentimental distress.) It was typical of his straddling sympathies that he maintained amiable relations simultaneously with Ruggiero Gamba, the revolutionary, and with his adversary, Count Alborghetti, whose taste for English literature and appreciation of Byron's place in it confirm that a writer rarely finds wholly deplorable the opinions of one who admires his work, even if he favours an inimical cause. A rash of graffiti, urging Italian independence and promising death to the Pope, whose temporal power depended on Austrian backing, polarized the two parties in Ravenna and put Byron's tact to the test. He had to reconcile courtesy towards Alborghetti with growing affection for the Gamba family. Old Gamba liked Byron's attentive forcefulness and also saw in him, as Guiccioli did, the prospect of financial and moral support in case of trouble, though he made no application to join the British consular service.

In May 1820, the uneasy equilibrium in the Palazzo Guiccioli was jolted by evidence that Guiccioli was spying on his wife (her writing desk had palpably been forced) and, no doubt, by the evidence that had been collected. The see-saw of Teresa's loyalty came down with a bump on Byron's side. The amour was being conducted with such flagrancy that it was only a matter of time before the lovers were caught 'quasi in the fact': the Count returned unexpectedly early from a *conversazione* and found what he had every reason to expect. Lack of more secluded opportunity had obliged them to adopt love's extatic postures behind casually closed drawing room doors. To lock them would be tantamount to confession of a guilty purpose, but if they had to remain unlocked, they did not lack keyholes for inquisitive eyes. In the face of the Count's bullying indignation, Teresa's father appealed to the Pope for an official separation, on the grounds that his daughter was unsafe in her husband's custody, a not implausible claim. Again the machinery of farce wheels into view, for it was only through the good offices of Count Alborghetti that the Pope's aid could be hastened. Meanwhile, Guiccioli had had enough of the comedy and informed Byron stiffly that he was no longer welcome under his roof, though he was not pressed to quit the rooms he had rented. In the event, he found himself stuck in them for a number of weeks.

Byron himself never denied that he was in the wrong, sneer as he might at Guiccioli's pretensions to satisfy a girl of nineteen. The monotony of his cavalieresque duties and the needling presence of the spies who dogged him (some on behalf of the Count, another, Torelli, on that of the *'Buon Governo'*) may have made the latest twist not wholly disconcerting. Teresa's incautiousness – an unwifely refusal to deny the truth was what had precipitated the marital rupture – suggests that the atmosphere in the Palazzo Guiccioli had become unendurable. In July, the Pope granted the separation. With the connivance of Alborghetti, Guiccioli was not apprised of it until Teresa had been spirited safely out of the house. The excitement of the escape, to the Villa Filetto, her father's country house some twenty-five kilometres from Ravenna, at least provided a galloping change of location for the romance; it also clinched Teresa's hold over her lover. The best, and the worst, had happened at last. Byron was now committed, by his too often pronounced word of honour, to stay forever what he had declared himself to be, her lover, her friend and ('when circumstances should permit') her husband. Whether through artful skill or artless instinct, Teresa had pulled every trick of the female trade. The man who had had his pick of all the cunts in Venice (the terminology of his correspondence did not lack monosyllabic directness) was now the pledged escort of a young woman who had absconded, albeit with a papal warrant and stipulated stipend, from her Italian husband in order to take up with a fugitive foreigner. Need Byron's love be counterfeit for his sighs to be genuine? Is it mere chance that Teresa's recklessness, with all its tethering implications, coincided with renewed political activity on Byron's part? There could be no further flight from his era by erotic means. Regenerative excitement or a worthy consummation must be sought elsewhere. In agreeing to collect evidence of the innocence of Queen Caroline in the face of George IV's accusations of adultery, during her tour of Italy, he once again rallied to the anti-Monarchist cause of his youth (thus suggesting that he had not aged) and also served notice on those at home that he had not lost interest in English affairs. He was also cocking a new snook at Henry Brougham, now the Queen's enemy and long his own. At the same time, his local ardour so recommended him to the Gambas that they proposed his admission to the fairly secret fraternity of the Carbonari. The aristocratic flamboyance of both Count Ruggiero and his son Pietro, Teresa's handsome and dashing young brother, was more to Byron's colourful taste than the beige activities of those like Hobhouse, whose rebellious bets were soon hedged with parliamentary prudence.

After his mistress's flight to Filetto, Byron found himself temporarily in the ludicrous position of being more wedded to Guiccioli than Teresa was; he dared not quit his apartments in the Palazzo in order to join her lest the Pope's indulgence be affronted by undisguised immorality. Byron wanted to rent a house close to the Gambas' villa, where he could be near, but not too near, his mistress (whose physical ministrations he was already missing) and where Fletcher,

Tita and the others would be exempt from the insults of the Count's servants, who feared Byron too keenly to direct them personally at him. The problem of Allegra, and the menace of her mother's calls upon him, continued to nag; rumours of war against the Austrians were preferable to the importunities of that 'damned bitch' Claire, the repeated story of whose clandestine baby suited his disparaging vision of her but could not recruit him to share Hoppner's prim opinion of Shelley. It was not until March of the following year, 1821, that he finally put into practice what had seemed a teasing whim when he first expressed it, and transferred Allegra to the convent school at Bagnacavallo, where she spent the rest of her short life. As regards Claire, he remained implacable: he would neither see her nor allow her custody of the child, but he did not oppose her having reasonable access. If he was truly touched by Allegra's personality, her Venetian lisp and her Byronic difficulty over pronouncing the letter 'r' (the seal of the paternity he had once been hectic enough, at Geneva, to question), her proximity emphasized how keenly he missed his legitimate daughter, Ada, whose picture he at last received in October 1820 and thereafter always kept on his table. He had requested it, in a sentimental letter to Lady Byron, at the turn of the previous year, when he was celebrating, with bitter self-reproach, the fifth anniversary of the fatal marriage. Hearing that old Joe Murray, who had accompanied him as far as Gibraltar on the 'pilgrimage', had died at Newstead, the exile was reminded once more of a time when all things seemed possible and all horizons open.

As winter set in, Teresa, pouting neglect, returned from Filetto to take up residence in her father's town house in Ravenna. Byron was cornered in an ingloriously narrow life, though the discipline of constraint led to prolific literary output. His correspondence was voluminous, his fancy as free as his freedom was limited. Having sided with Queen Caroline in order to faze her husband, he did not hesitate to lampoon her in the fifth canto of *Don Juan* when the rhyming occasion arose. He was to stay in Ravenna for almost as long as he had been in Venice, a period as sober as that on the Grand Canal had been splashy. He worked, he rode, he made faithful, circumspect love to Teresa. While he waited for public events to inspire a move he could not initiate for himself, he remained wary of 'entusymusy', the credulous partisanship of the zealot. Even as he succumbed to the *bel canto* rhetoric of the *Carboneria*, he recognized the odds against the success of a nationalist uprising to which the whole concert of Europe was hostile. Just as he may be accused of being a better writer of prose than of verse, so his prosaic judgment of men and situations was often shrewder and less wishful than his poetic calls to reckless action.

His aversion from callous factionalism was proved once more in December 1820, when the Commandant of the local troops, Luigi Dal Pinto, whom he had met socially at local *conversazioni*, was assassinated just outside his apartments. The bystanders stood paralysed with curious timidity; the famous foreigner alone had the courage and humanity to order the dying man to be carried inside. Byron's heterodoxy never prevented him from recognizing the manliness of his opponents or the vileness of shooting them in the back. The unreliability which Marx suspected in Byron surely stems from his want of systematic malice. He had not, he declared, embraced the cause of Italy in order to crook the knee to butchery. If Byron's tolerant attitude, no less than his amiable relations with Count Alborghetti, did not recommend him to the hard men among the Carbonari, he showed himself unequivocal in his readiness to turn his house into a fortress, should the hot occasion arise, and swore to defy the Austrians to the last. Meanwhile, he filled his ration of pages with cursive spontaneity; like his admirer Bertrand Russell, he believed that first drafts were best. He would never have defined genius in terms of taking infinite pains as did that other (temporary) admirer, Carlyle. His facility was an aspect of his open-handedness. Though he was to go through a phase of toying with avarice, or of teasing suppliants with it, it is difficult to dispute his generosity, not only when noblesse obliged its showy parade, but also in little matters; a Venetian storekeeper who had lost everything was once bailed out with fifty *louis d'or*.

And now Tom Moore was in trouble, forced into exile, like the luckless Scrope Davies, on account of his debts. When Byron finished a supplement to the Memoirs he had already entrusted to his old friend, he sent the new pages to Moore and authorized him to sell them for his own profit, which he did to the tune of a much needed two thousand guineas. The same Murray who would flinch from printing the full text was not slow to pay the price or to pass the juicier bits round his London circle. Byron might caricature his friends but he took them faults and all and he was never so loyal as when others had deserted them. He was no less trusting than he was reliable, with the result that men like his lawyer John Hanson could take advantage of his gullibility. (When, back in 1813, Hanson sought to better his family by marrying his young daughter to the widower Earl of Portsmouth, who was feeble-minded and fatuously sadistic, he persuaded Byron to dignify the occasion by giving away the bride.) To men and women alike, he was easily recruited; he had enough reserves of energy, as he had of wit, not to ration his response. As a result, it was sometimes hasty, partly on account of an excitable and resilient constitution, partly because, for all his posing, he did not have too lofty an opinion of himself to find any favour beneath his dignity or any gratitude too paltry to relish.

Despite Teresa's disapproval when she read a French translation of *Don Juan* (she had no English), he had finished the fifth canto by the end of 1820. He despatched it to Douglas Kinnaird to whom he had scrawled his dashing defence of the Don a year before: 'Confess, confess – you dog and be candid – that it is the sublime of *that there* sort of writing – it may be bawdy but is it not good English? It may be profligate but is it not *life*, is it not *the thing*? Could any man have written it who has not lived in the world? – and tooled in a post-chaise? – in a hackney coach? – in a gondola? – against a wall? – in a court carriage? – in a vis-a-vis? – on a table? – and under it? – . . . . I had such projects for the Don, but cant is so much stronger than c*** now-a-days, that the benefit of experience in a man who has well weighed the worth of both monosyllables, must be lost to despairing posterity.' Teresa's view that she would prefer 'the fame of Childe Harold for three years than an immortality of Don Juan' may have been decorous, but it shows scant understanding of Byron's progress. Her tone has the reforming severity of that tidy and familiar figure, the author's lady, who, resentful of his adventures without her, prefers to be the consort of a pruned celebrity rather than accept the hazards of a continuing, perhaps embarrassing, fruitfulness. Teresa's qualms did not put an end to the Don, but they had the stalling effect of an interim injunction.

Byron turned to his Ravenna Journal (a reflective attempt to make sense of his loud life) and to the composition of *Sardanapalus*. The Catullan principle of *variatio* kept him nimble as he moved from prose to verse, from poetry to drama, from life to letters. Like *Marino Faliero*, *Sardanapalus* was a tragedy 'not composed with the most remote view to the stage' and begins on a true Byronic note: 'He hath wrong'd his queen, but still he is her lord.' The play was dedicated to 'The Illustrious Goethe' and, whether or not it was designed to be acted, it has a palpably dramatic design on the spirit of its author: in form and content, it is an incantation calculated to rouse its hero from effeminate 'sloth and shame' and to prick him to play the manly part and 'head an army [rather] than to rule a harem'. In his response to William Bowles' critical revaluation of Pope, Byron commented cruelly on Keats's work as 'the Onanism of Poetry' (Keats was always 'frigging his imagination', he wrote to Murray), but mental masturbation is a charge the solitary creator can rarely escape; Pygmalions who are innocent of it seldom bring their work to life. The Hemingwayesque fear that action alone can prove a writer's virility suggests that Byron's slur on Keats reflects a more general doubt about the literary calling. Byron may have needed little sexual stimulation from his own hand (Keats's Fanny Brawne would not have been suffered to frustrate *him*), but Sardanapalus aches for a Napoleonic climax and is fraught with apprehensions of impotence.

During much of 1821, although less discomfited by Guiccioli's rancorous propinquity than might be expected and stimulated creatively by the regularity of routine, he was deprived of vigorous excitement, apart from gallops in the *pineta*. At the end of February, the craven collapse of the Carbonari's extravagant plans for a general uprising and the betrayal and arrest of many of their leaders revealed the gap between fine words and worthy actions. ('I always had an idea that it would be *bungled*,' Byron declared.) When those to whom he had furnished guns and ammunition rushed them back in a panic to his apartments, upon the *Buon Governo*'s threat of condign punishment for the clandestine possession of arms, he concluded that the Italians could achieve effective unison only in an operatic chorus. Disappointment did not entail total disillusion; his belief in the cause and courage of the Gambas was not shaken, but a petty instance had to suffice for an example of proper defiance. When Tita had a blood-curdling, bloodless quarrel with an officer called Pistocchi – weapons were flashed, not used – Byron lavished his indignant charm on the excellent Alborghetti in order to avoid the ex-gondolier's expulsion from the city. He was quick, and probably right, to read into the severity of the new legate, Cardinal Rusconi, a scantily veiled menace to his own privileges. Rusconi was less susceptible than his predecessor to the poet's reputation. Despite his popularity with the common people, a few commissioned graffiti actually advertised for Byron's assassination, but his renown made Alborghetti's master wary of open confrontation.

Then, during the second week in July 1821, Pietro Gamba was arrested and summarily banished. The authorities in the Romagna had decided to extirpate what was left of radical sentiment. Byron's rhetoric had secured the small sop of a reprieve for Tita, but it was useless to prevent Count Gamba and the rest of his family from soon suffering the same fate as Pietro. The Papal legate reckoned that Teresa would go after her father and Byron after Teresa; thus the whole skein of troublemakers would be drawn out of the province. Despite Teresa's reluctance to leave Byron, and his to leave Ravenna, the Cardinal's logic was valid. Teresa, afraid of being immured in a convent for immorality (her fate if she remained), quit Ravenna at the end of July; Byron, seigneurially snug with pets and furniture, as usual promised to follow but as usual proved in no hurry. The arrival of Shelley, at the beginning of August, although he was once again the emissary of Claire, was both a pleasure and a relief.

Adonäis, Shelley's obituary for Keats and the best evidence of his incautious genius, had shamed Byron into speaking better of the dead than he had chosen to speak of the living 'Cockney'. Shelley exaggerated in diagnosing death by critical lapidation, though few aggrieved poets would disagree with his view of the malignant critic as 'that second degree in the descending scale of the Academy of Disappointed Authors'. Despite his indignation on behalf of others, the tangle of his life, riven with premature deaths, and the cruel consequences of his ardent impracticality, rarely provoked Shelley to self-pity, though he referred to himself wryly as 'the spaniel of destiny'. Even now, galled by the Hoppners' story about him and Claire (which Byron accepted – rightly or wrongly – to be false, prompt though he had been to retail it), Shelley never flinched from his faith in the perfectibility of man. The two poets resumed an intimacy which, uninterrupted by vipers or vapours, came as both relief and stimulus. Shelley's conviction of the 'immortality' of the fifth canto of *Don Juan* was a welcome antidote to that female subjectivity which gave tears the last word in the vocabulary of aesthetics. Conversation apart, Ravenna had little appeal for Shelley; it was his considered view, after a visit to the mosaics of the Church of Saint Apolinaire, that it was 'one of the first effects of the Christian religion to destroy the power of producing beauty in art.' His gentle, gentlemanly company (he wrote once of 'the great and general laws of antique courtesy against which I never rebel') persuaded Byron to alter his plans to take Teresa and her family to Switzerland and, instead, to accept an invitation to join the Shelleys in Tuscany. A pantisocratic project was in hand aimed at forming an expatriate community of like-minded souls at Pisa.

Shelley returned to Pisa and secured Byron a 'large and magnificent house', the Casa Lanfranchi, on the Lungarno, in which his retinue and all the inmates of his menagerie fit to travel could be nobly accommodated. So, in October 1821, the domesticated Byron quit Ravenna as he had lived there, without enthusiasm; the place had lacked piquant diversions, but he had worked well. Fidelity to Teresa, present or absent, had been a steadying convenience no less than an occasional pleasure. Sexually, he had nothing left to prove and little to desire. The prospect of abandoning his habits at the Palazzo Guiccioli depressed him, though no one reading *The Vision of Judgment*, that satirical parody of Robert Southey's solemn celebration of the assumption of George III into Heaven, would guess that its author composed it in a state of feverish malaise. He was once more being evicted from agreeable surroundings but without the compensations of freedom. Like Bonnivard, he had come almost to love his confinement, but now, albeit released, he remained as good as married to Teresa, and what good had marriage ever been to him?

Not until the autumn of 1821 did he actually set out along slushy roads for Pisa, accompanied by his servants and his pets; the furniture wagons had gone on ahead. Solitude had prompted him to reflect on the meaning of life and on the immortality of the soul, to which he was now inclined to give credence. Man might be a 'sad jar of atoms' but sensuality seemed a fleeting solution to the problem of existence. The call to answer the questions of religion, once religion has been questioned, leaves every God-botherer bothered. He had once postponed 'sermons and soda-water' to the day after, but maturity or melancholy had advanced his calendar. He was always wary lest naiveté rumple the dandyish nonchalance in which he mantled himself, but the great mystery, of the meaning of life and death, haunted him, for all his procrastinating flippancy. Like those humorists who cannot write a joke unless admirers are there to laugh over their shoulders, Byron specialized in a kind of rhyming repartee, dependent on instant laughter (often his own) for its swing. His sociable reluctance to dwell on the grimness of mortality recalls that childhood promise, when his foot was being racked, that however much it hurt, 'you shall see no sign of it in me'. His last lonely days in Ravenna excited a mood which the presence of others might have aborted. The *Detached Thoughts* are a nervous mixture of anguished seriousness and sudden waggishness, as though his introspection had been surprised, like Onanism, by an eavesdropper for whom he had to flash camouflaging ironies.

How highly should one evaluate Byron's intelligence? His range of quotation is impressively wide, especially for one who maintained that he never liked *reading* verse. If he was not always as accurate as Bartlett, his apt allusiveness shows that, though he may have scanned more books than he read, his aversion from literary company betokens no fear of being found out. His naughtiness, like that of Ovid, another witty exile, is an ironic tribute to the standards it seems to flout; flippancy conceals the earnestness that dares not speak its name. Alone, he addressed himself to the great metaphysical issues and if his answers lack any elevating novelty, we can hardly expect satisfactory answers to unanswerable questions. His frivolity exasperates not least because it rings truer than his portentousness: may he not have been right in his vision of judgment as a kind of celestial college examination? He was, in short, very English, and Scottish, in his scepticism, a worthy compatriot of David Hume and Dr Johnson. Jerome McGann has argued that *Don Juan* should be read in a Wittgensteinian light: its profundity lies in its extension. On this view, Byron's genius was precisely for the surface of things, for the play of language (hence the irrepressible urge to pun and digress). In his penchant for the picaresque he was perhaps truer to reality than perhaps he knew, just as Wittgenstein's later method, though infuriating to those who insist upon conclusions, illustrated the systematic inconclusiveness of human thought.

52. *Margarita Cogni, 'La Fornarina', engraved by H. T. Ryall after the drawing by G. Harlow taken at the request of Lord Byron.*
'She was a fine animal, but quite untameable.'

53. *Byron's wax Carnival mask worn at Ravenna in 1820.*
'... fiddling, feasting, dancing, drinking, masking And other things which may be had for asking.

54. *Byron in the Palazzo Mocenigo.*
'Oh Venice, Venice ...
If I, a northern wanderer, weep for thee, What should thy sons do? ...'

55. Byron and his circle in conversation on a terrace overlooking the Venetian lagoon at sunset.

56. Countess Teresa Guiccioli.
'The Last Attachment.'

57. Contemporary French caricature of Byron and Teresa Guiccioli.

58. Palazzo Lanfranchi, Pisa.
'A famous old feudal palazzo . . . large enough for a garrison.'

59. A highly romanticized view of Shelley's funeral in 1822. Painting by L. E. Fournier, 1889.
'All of Shelley was consumed, except his **heart**, which would not take the flame, and is now preserved in spirits of wine.'

60. *Byron's arrival at Missolonghi in January 1824.*
'Arise, you sons of Greece.'

61. *The helmet Byron ordered in Genoa and wore in Greece.*

62. *Prince Alexander Mavrocordato, President of the Greek Government.*
'This fellow comes teasing me to give him money.'

63. **Oath of Lord Byron on the Tomb of Marco Botzaris, 1824.** *This Greek coloured print of the 1930s, a rather crude copy of the well-known nineteenth-century painting by Ludovico Lipparini, attests to Byron's continuing heroic status among the Greek people.*

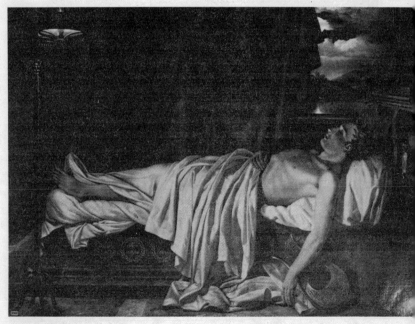

64. *A somewhat idealized drawing of the house where Byron lived and died in Missolonghi.*

65. **The Death of Byron** *by Joseph Odevaere, c.1826. 'O questa è una bella scena.'*

66. *Byron's coffin. The chest in front contains his brain, heart and other organs. To the right is the coffin of Lady Lovelace, his daughter.*

67. *Bronze memorial medal marking Byron's death in 1824.*

68. *Statue of Byron in the Zappeion Gardens, Athens. 'But I have lived, and have not lived in vain.'*

Yet Byron had an instinct for particularity; the specificity of his club-foot supplied inescapable testimony to the laming influence of the pettiest detail. At about the same time as he was trundling towards Pisa, he wrote that 'in the last nine years' he had seen himself compared to 'Rousseau, Goethe, Young, Aretino, Timon of Athens, an alabaster vase lighted up within, Satan, Shakespeare, Buonaparte, Tiberius, Aeschylus, Sophocles, Euripides, Harlequin the Clown, Sternhold and Hopkins, to the Phantasmagoria, to Pope, to Dryden, to Burns, to Savage, to Chatterton, to Michelangelo and to Raphael.' Some of the names on the list may be more appropriate than others, but the variety of flattery and accusation is harmonious with the skittering agility of his impersonations. *The Deformed Transformed*, of which Goethe spoke as warmly as its Advertisement speaks of Goethe, testifies feelingly to the poet's desire to escape from 'the tenement' in which his soul is 'mislodged'. The desire for change was not as superficial as Marx's suspicious allegation; it corresponded to an abiding discontent of which his foot was the objective correlative. His grudge against the world was subjective, but pride demanded that he take his appeal against the human condition to the highest quarters. The freak becomes the advocate of the maltreated and cures himself in the noble process. With a certain practical modesty, Byron never endorsed Shelley's legislative view of poetry; he could see that it was not writing which would change the world but practical politics. In this regard at least, he was more Marxist than his revolutionary friend.

As he travelled towards Pisa, on the road between Imola and Bologna, Byron met a revenant from his schooldays, the Earl of Clare, whom he had loved at Harrow and had not seen for several years. The two men stopped their coaches and spent an agitated few minutes together. 'I hardly recollect an hour of my existence which could be weighed against them,' Byron reported. It was said of one of the walks at Holland House that a man who, as he strolled, met his own image coming towards him, did not have long to live, a local version of the *doppelgänger* theme which Romantics were to embellish so pretentiously and with which Nabokov, in *Despair*, made such airy play. Nabokov, like Byron, was always alert to the patterns of chance. The more a writer takes into account – the more he can encompass in his art – the more he will read significance into the fortuitous; exulting in arcane duplicities he presumes, with the ultimate aristocratic arrogance, to be privy to a hidden, higher order of things. (Freud, in this sense, was almost a fellow spirit of Nabokov, who detested his ideas.) Wittgenstein, as sceptical of Kant as Byron was of Cant, hovered on the edges of mysticism and, like Byron, strained his eyes to divine the invisible.

The agitation of the chance meeting with Clare contrasted with a disappointing encounter, by appointment, at Bologna with Samuel Rogers, the old banker-poet who, by priming Caro Lamb with *Childe Harold*, could be accused of having initiated the loudest instance of Byron's by now countless ravishments. Despite his ear for belittling tittle-tattle, the vinegary tourist was impressed by the gawking gallery which saw Byron off from Florence, whither they had travelled together from Bologna.

Byron had made it a condition of his coming that Claire Clairmont not be of the party at Pisa: she would either stay away or wish she had. Shelley protested, but the warning had been taken seriously: on the road beyond Empoli Byron's unmistakable conveyance crossed the oncoming public coach from Pisa in which Allegra's mother was travelling to Florence. She saw him; he did not see her. It was their last, appropriately one-sided confrontation. The girl who had promised to cause him no trouble had been no end of a damned nuisance. She outlived him by many, many years and, in due course, her connection with the poet gave Henry James the *donnée* for *The Aspern Papers*, set in the Venice where she had waited in vain for an interview with her unloving lover. So Clare was followed by Claire with Rogers in between, a fortuitous epitome of Byron's English youth. If he invited Lord Clare to join him in Pisa, he doubtless recalled that many years before, on the day before he set out for Greece with Hobby, he had solicited the young man's company only for the Earl to prefer to go shopping with his mother and sisters. 'After the way the world has treated me, shall I not give them blow for blow?' Claire suffered a rejection that a glib accountant might balance against Clare's.

The Casa Lanfranchi suited Byron very well; it was grand and its owners' family had a murky history that chimed with his own. Pisa offered a more amiable climate than Ravenna and more amusing company. Byron was weary of Italian society, apart from the Gambas, and welcomed the company of his fellow-countrymen whom Shelley had either invited or attracted. The Shelleys, as usual, were modestly housed, in apartments on the other side of the deep bed of the Arno. The

Pisan circle was soon described: there were Edward and Jane Williams (she was the wife of one of Edward's brother officers in India, and had taken Williams' name to avoid embarrassment) and Shelley's cousin, Thomas Medwin, who had been in the same regiment as Williams; and they were soon joined by John Taafe, Jr., an Irishman like Tom Moore and a pretentious horseman, to whom Byron at once warmed. He was translating Dante, but he was no intellectual. Byron always preferred to see himself as a man of the world rather than as a littérateur, and his new acquaintances happily lacked Shelley's elevated notion of the poetic vocation and vocabulary; he could dispense with Parnassian circumlocutions and tactful asterisks. The newcomers had not heard his stories before and their amenable presence revived his zest for late nights of gossip and laughter.

The gaudiest tangent to the circle arrived in January 1822. Edward John Trelawny was a type not uncommon in artistic communities: the adventurer whose past is a pastiche of travellers' tales but contains enough hard experience to make writers feel (and fear) that he has something over them. The bearded ex-sailor claimed to have been a pirate, but seems actually to have had a depressingly well-behaved naval record. Trelawny encouraged Shelley's plan to acquire a boat and to spend the summer sailing in the Bay of Spezia. Byron, obliged to trump any ace idea, told Trelawny to spare no expense in commissioning a beauty for himself, which proved an expensive *carte blanche*. Byron's man-of-war was to have four guns, enough to make a devil of a noise and to grace some flamboyant excursion yet to be devised. The Greek Prince Mavrocordato's visit to the Shelleys (he stayed long enough to give Mary some Greek lessons) may have reminded Byron of the possibility of sailing towards the Turkish guns, but it is more likely that he was out to impress Trelawny, whose carefully composed resemblance to Byron's Corsair (he said he slept with the poem under his pillow) was calculated to flatter and fluster the celebrity. Eventually Byron was to say that they might yet make a gentleman out of Trelawny could he but be persuaded to wash his hands and stop telling lies, but in the meanwhile it was the Corsair who was encouraged to make a sailor of his lordship.

Life in Tuscany was easier and more entertaining than in the Romagna, but there were still spies and suspicions. The Englishmen were rich, however, and rumoured to be richer, and on that count both they and the Gambas were tolerated.

Byron was indeed enriched, to a marked degree, in February 1822, on the death of Lady Noel, whom he had once suspected of immortality; by the terms of his still valid marriage contract he was rewarded to the tune of some £6,000 a year. But he was not in gloating mood and, the servants in mourning, he showed himself correct and even sympathetic, when he thought of Annabella, in the light of his new circumstances and dignity. Since he was now entitled to style himself 'Noel Byron', his initials were identical with those of Napoleon. Though Marchand doubts whether he consciously vaunted himself on the coincidence, it is hard to believe that the ghost of his little Pagod did not pique him. Buonaparte's death, in May 1821, had surely reminded him of the brevity of the eagle's flight.

Byron's access of funds excited an early call upon them. Leigh Hunt, whose liberal 'democracy', like Godwin's, inclined him to believe that natural justice implied fair shares for all, but fairer for him, chummily importuned a loan to get him from England to his place in the Tuscan sun. He supposed that his jauntiness had an ingratiating candour, but Byron responded out of a sense more of obligation than of enthusiasm. He had visited Hunt in his cell when he was imprisoned for libelling the Prince Regent, but a visit from Hunt (and his family) was no great favour. The sale of Newstead and now his new inheritance had brought Byron wealth, and the prospect of security, much later in life than those accustomed to his expansiveness, mostly with borrowed cash, were likely to appreciate. Weary of wrangling with Murray and tired of the open-handedness with which others were prepared to dispense the fruits of hard work and good fortune, he advertised a sudden appetite for gold. Shelley (who had conscientiously turned his back on a huge inheritance) could never be accused of sponging, but he presumed sufficiently on Byron's goodwill for him to fear that he had been lured into a genial trap.

Claire, after a tactful retreat, had returned to Pisa, though she did not see Byron; her presence, whether or not he was directly aware of it, must have charged the atmosphere. Shelley was again her advocate for taking Allegra out of the convent at Bagnacavallo and bringing her to Pisa. Byron was suspicious of her excess of scruple with regard to the child and, though his petulance is not pretty, he had grounds for feeling put upon. Women could not live, he observed, without making scenes. Shelley's patience was exhausted. For all his repeated admiration for Byron, he was tempted to break with him for good; he was even tempted to strike him. There may have been an unconscious motive, no less than a clear incitement: Byron's presence, however keenly solicited and socially exhilarating, cast a blight on Shelley's creative powers. It was, he said, a case of the sun and the glow-worm. Mary Shelley sided with her husband, but she was, as she had been in Geneva, uncomfortably attracted to Byron (what woman was not?) and the good wife may have welcomed an insulating breach between her family and that disturbing presence. The 'nest of singing birds', of which Mary had been so proud when describing the Pisan circle to her friend Maria Gisborne, was soon less than harmonious, but the lineaments of solidarity were maintained. There were regular rides into the *campagna* where the men practised pistol shooting (forbidden within the city) and the ladies – Mary, Jane Williams and Teresa, who was not actually living with Byron, though she saw him constantly – went for walks, often in the vicinity of the Vaccà farm where the men had set up their butts. The rumour that Byron fancied a certain Maria (a dark and Segati-like peasant girl) kept Teresa vigilant.

On Sunday, 24 March 1822, they had been out as usual to the Vaccà farm and were riding back to Pisa when a soldier came galloping past at full speed and startled Taafe's horse. While that equestrian fought to retain his seat and dignity, Shelley and others gave chase. Catching the soldier at the city gate, Shelley was courteous; the cavalier was not. Byron, punctilious and prickly, flourished his card, assuming that the man was an officer and owed them satisfaction. (His propensity for challenges never actually took Byron so far as the duelling ground, but he was true to his proud image, as reflected in Pushkin, and had just called out Robert Southey, by letter, in reply to an offensive article.) A friend of his rackety youth, Captain John Hay, was visiting Byron and his gallant presence may well have required a more lordly show than usual: he would, after all, be reporting back to England. It emerged that the frantic horseman was in fact only a sergeant-major, Stefani Masi, whose haste had been impelled less by insolence than the fear of being late for roll call. There could be no question of duelling with a non-commissioned man, but the foreigners jostled him angrily and when Pietro Gamba, if indeed it was he, struck him with his riding crop, the infuriated Masi ordered the soldiers on gate duty to arrest the foreigners. All but Shelley, who was knocked unconscious for a time, managed to get through into Pisa without being apprehended, and Byron, combining prudence with a sense of dramatic occasion, first reported the incident to the police and then armed himself with a swordstick in case of any further affray. The servants at the Casa Lanfranchi had been alerted and when, after another shouting match, Masi clattered past the crowd which had assembled at the palace door, someone – probably Byron's coachman, Vincenzo Papi – thrust at him with 'a long-handled weapon'. Masi rode on, then collapsed and had to be carried to hospital; soon there came angry word that he was dead.

Teresa was distraught; Captain Hay had somehow received a nasty sabre slash across the nose and the crowd was turning ugly. Byron placated the Pisans with money and commissioned an English doctor to treat the wounded sergeant, the rumours of whose death had been exaggerated, but the foreigners found themselves isolated and resented. Tita and Papi were both arrested; the latter, almosty certainly guilty, was soon released; Tita, whose fierce beard and show of weapons announced him a villain, was held in prison and obliged to shave his beard, which he preserved in a napkin. The tension slowly subsided, after the recuperation of Masi and Tita's eventual release, but the circle remained fractious, especially since Taafe, left behind by the rush of events and horses, had dissociated himself from the rest of the Britons and made a separate peace with the authorities, thus earning himself the nickname 'Falstaff', false Taafe that he seemed.

From then on, little went right, in small things or in great. Samuel Rogers turned up on 20 April and Byron regaled the old gossip with a gross of stories for London ears, hoping perhaps that scabrous anecdotes would deflect him from bearing home discreditable accounts of the Masi affair. The truth was that both Byron and Shelley, for all their liberated and liberating sentiments, might as well have been a pair of high-handed Tories when it came to dealing with impertinent or misguided natives. (They had heard with horror, a few months previously, of the intention of the authorities at Lucca to burn a man at the stake for blasphemy and had hurried to the rescue, only to find that the heretic had already sought, and found, refuge in Florence.) It must have been clear to Byron, who had ensured that Tita was not abused by the other prisoners in the jail by sending them all a very good dinner, that only money and influence, rather than justice or high-mindedness, had prevented a very nasty incident indeed. After his release, Tita was exiled from Pisa and did not rejoin Byron's service until he removed to Genoa.

Rogers had been at the Casa Lanfranchi for two days (amusingly baited by Byron's bulldog, Moretto) when the news came that Allegra, who had been sick of a fever at Bagnacavallo, then better, had died. When Teresa brought him the news, Byron reacted with that sudden access of pallor which had been his only sign of emotion when his mother announced the marriage of Mary Chaworth. Claire was still in Pisa, though Byron did not know it, and when he told Shelley the painful news, it seemed best to remove her to Lerici, where the Shelleys were planning to spend the summer, before she was informed. Although a reproachful confrontation was avoided, she upbraided Byron bitterly in a letter. He was sufficiently punished by his own anguish to feel little guilt. ('It's God's will,' he said. 'Let us mention it no more.') Murray was asked to arrange for the child to be buried in Harrow Church; the Rector gave permission only when it was agreed that there should be no inscription on the gravestone. Byron had been prompt with an appropriate Biblical quotation: 'I shall go to her but she shall not return to me.' She had died on 20 April 1822; precisely two years later, his apt and gloomy prophecy was fulfilled.

The death of Allegra confirmed the demise of the Pisan circle, but scarcely caused it. Artists' colonies are always fissile and the case of the galloping Sergeant-Major had already strained relations among the foreigners and with the authorities, for whom it provided a pretext for bearing down on dangerous outsiders. It had needed all Shelley's now waning enthusiasm to hold the circle together, even though it had been drawn largely around Byron's alluring personality. The Leigh Hunts were already on their way to Italy and Shelley avoided any open rupture with Byron, prudent or preferable though he found it to withdraw from quotidian proximity. Byron too had found a summer place, the Villa Dupuy, a few miles south of Leghorn, to which hot-coloured retreat he removed, with the Gambas, in May 1822. Spied on meticulously by Torelli, a professional nark, the Count and his family never ceased to be regarded with vigilant suspicion by the Tuscan authorities. Teresa was living more or less openly with Byron, in breach of the terms of her separation. Her lack of caution was duly reported to Guiccioli and resulted in the abrogation of her allowance. Byron had always feared that she would be branded as an abandoned woman;

that status now seemed to be hers, with all it entailed of claims and charges.

Byron was diverted, when he reached the coast, to find a squadron of the American fleet at anchor. He contrived an invitation from the Commodore and was received with flattering reassurance as to his fame in New York. He seemed always to be a hero in places from which he was absent. On shore again, his spirits were flat. The delivery of his new boat did little to enliven them. He decided, unsubtle as a cigar advertisement, to name it after Simon Bolívar, the 'Byronic' liberator whose career in South America – a mixture of idealism and egocentricity, of action and rhetoric – mocked the inertia of his model. The authorities were as unamused by the boat's defiant name as they were uneasy at the guns with which she was to be furnished. They made such stringent rules concerning her use that Byron virtually lost interest in navigation. There was to be little question of 'O'er the glad waters of the dark blue sea,/Our thoughts as boundless, and our souls as free.' The *Bolívar* stayed at anchor and the Leigh Hunts, with their six children, arrived to stay with Byron. Although their presence was a call on his purse and his patience, he did his best to honour Hunt's hopes for *The Liberal*, a new magazine which they were to edit jointly with Shelley. 'Leontius', as Byron nicknamed Hunt, was both unctuous and uxorious and given to quoting the clever remarks of his wife, the sickly and sickening Marianne, whose determination not to be overawed by his lordship meant that she seldom said anything that her host was pleased to hear. (When asked what she thought about Byron's morals, she replied wittily that it was the first she had ever heard of them.) Literary conversation was, however, more to Byron's taste than his public school bluffness liked to confess, and Leontius, if no genius, was a well-read man whose lack of cash, though humiliating, was scarcely his fault. His intelligent companionship made a change from the squabbling of servants (Papi, the pugnacious coachman, had to be sacked temporarily after slightly stabbing Pietro Gamba when he sought to intercede during a quarrel) and it provided an antidote to Trelawny's windy braggadocio.

Shelley had also taken delivery of his more modest and decidedly capricious craft, which Trelawny proposed to christen 'Don Juan'. Shelley at first agreed to the name and then changed his mind. (Guy de Maupassant called his yacht 'Bel Ami', after his own novel, but no one wished the title on his friends.) Shelley can hardly be blamed for not choosing to sail literally under another poet's trademark (it had been inscribed on the mainsail), but its excision was an affront to Byron and the resulting sulks implied further discord.

In July 1822, Byron – reported by the Leigh Hunts to be unrecognizably fat – returned with Teresa to Pisa. The Count, her father, and the excitable Pietro had been moved on by the authorities, and were quartered in the hot little walled city of Lucca, inland from Viareggio. The Leigh Hunts were installed in an apartment in the Casa Lanfranchi which their modern children so defaced with dirty marks that Byron's Herodian streak was revived. He kept to his own rooms and was heard to demand of his bulldog, 'Don't let any cockneys pass this way.' Mrs Hunt, like so many principled spongers, judged her host by severe standards and held his concern for the fabric of the premises to be lacking in poetic largesse. By and large, however, Byron was in better heart back in the palace than he had been at the Villa Dupuy, not least because Teresa had agreed to rescind her embargo on the further adventures of Don Juan and the composition of the sixth canto was proceeding happily, with many bursts of laughter on the author's part as new jokes came off his pen.

With his friends' domestic arrangements apparently settled, Shelley joined Edward Williams at Leghorn with the intention of sailing their boat, now renamed *Ariel*, from there to Lerici. They cast off on 8 July, despite warnings of a storm and with an inadequate crew consisting only of themselves and a young Englishman, Charles Vivien. A few hours later, Trelawny was watching from shore as the squall roared into the bay. When it had cleared, there was no sign of *Ariel*. The word passed from Trelawny to Hunt, from Hunt to Byron and thus to Mrs Williams and Mary Shelley, who were at the seaside Casa Magni. A frantic search, of which Mary's anguished question *'Sapete alcuna cosa di Shelley?'* remains the poignant emblem, was conducted, fruitlessly, along the coast. Byron authorized the use of *Bolívar* in the operation, but there was never much hope. Shelley's curious obsession with the water and with boats, for neither of which he ever showed large aptitude, had reached its tragic climax. Just over a week after their disappearance, the bodies of Shelley and Williams were washed up on the shore near Viareggio. They were temporarily buried in the sand.

Mary and Mrs Williams were escorted to Pisa by Trelawny. Byron, as magnanimous now as he had been petulant before, was both courteous and tender. It was mid-August before permission was granted for the bodies of Shelley and his friend to be exhumed from their provisional graves and cremated on the beach where they had been tumbled ashore. Trelawny, who prided himself on his virile hardheadedness, officiated. Decomposition was seen to be repulsively advanced. 'Are we all to resemble that?' asked Byron. 'Why, it might be the carcass of a sheep for all I can see!' An old handkerchief was easier to recognize than the young genius. 'An old rag retains its form longer than a dead body. God, what a nauseous and degrading sight!'

Byron had often treated Shelley with impatience and he made amends by accusing the world of a misreading of which he too had been guilty: 'He was without exception the best and least selfish man I ever knew,' he wrote. 'I never knew another one who was not a beast in comparison. There is another man gone, about whom the world was ill-naturedly and ignorantly and brutally mistaken. It will perhaps do him justice now, when he can be no better for it.' The passion of his remarks, a cynic might think, suggests that he was rehearsing his own obituary as well as eulogizing the friend of whom Hazlitt had said, 'He has a fire in his eye, a fever in his blood, a maggot in his brain, a hectic flutter in his speech.' As at the executions he had attended, Byron forced himself to assist unblinkingly at the cremation but he plunged into the sea immediately after it, perhaps to purge his nausea, perhaps to prove his sang-froid. Trelawny hooked Shelley's hot heart from the pyre, since it would not burn. After their horrible duties had been concluded, Byron, Trelawny and the squeamish Hunt, who had remained in the carriage, went into Viareggio and drowned their sorrows. Later, in drunken high spirits, guffawing at the ghastliness of life and death, they rolled rollicking back to Pisa.

The Liberal had been intended to sustain that 'moral and political hope' to which Shelley, with pathetic irony, declared that he clung 'like a drowner to a plank,' but his death doomed the paper; it ran to four issues and then succumbed. Byron always knew that the others depended on his cash and cachet if the venture was to be successfully launched (his name on *that* masthead was unlikely to have been struck), hence resentments and huffs. But if he persisted because he felt that he owed Shelley something, his reluctant responsibility for the exigent Hunts was less compelling. It was no doubt unworthy to deplore their grubby and undisciplined brood and to count the pennies demanded for their maintenance in Hunt's jocular petitions, but even the most uncensorious patron may be soured by demanding presumptuousness on the part of pensioners. When Medwin visited Pisa in September, he found Byron very thin. Bouts of cosmetic self-starvation were a habit, but the appetites of his guests may have prompted an exemplary show of self-denial, though he did not curtail his intake of wine or watered gin, his prescription for poetic fertility. If Medwin thought him thin, Hobhouse – arriving in Pisa in mid-September – declared him fatter in the face: his mutability was apparently physical no less than mental.

Teresa and Byron seemed, after three years, still to be effusively fond of each other, but Hobby reported his old friend as saying that 'Cain was right to kill Abel, that he might not have the bore of passing two hundred years with him.' Constancy was not without its longueurs or its sarcastic temptations. If Hobhouse's visit began a little stiffly (Byron's gratuitous lines about 'Hobby O' still rankled), it ended warmly enough. Byron seemed older (he *was* older) but his ability to shock was apparently undiminished, if the obvious meaning is to be given to John Cam's reference to 'an adventure which gave me no high notions of the morals of the *contadine*'. (There were rumours that Byron had called a rural child *'figlio mio'* which may have been a joke, or a fact.) He speaks of not having indulged in any *costly* harlotry recently, suggesting that an occasional excursion, for small change, was not unknown. While Hobhouse was a guest during those last days in the Casa Lanfranchi, Nicolas Karvellas, a young Greek patriot whom they had met several times before in Switzerland and Venice, came to call. The visit was no casual social occasion. Hobhouse was active in the preparations to form a London Committee for the Liberation of Greece, and Byron's declaration of miserliness did not inhibit him from promising a lavish investment in the one cause of which he never wearied. Vexed by petty dissipations of his money – for instance Trelawny's splashing out on the *Bolívar* – he positively looked forward to investing his fortune in a single, showy enterprise. Like a flamboyant impresario enraged at petty peculation, he grudged nothing to the big scene.

At the end of September, after the usual loud packing up, the big coach quit Pisa, its library, according to unconfirmed reports, replenished with Shelley's books (they seem never to have been returned to Mary). It was followed by the usual wagons baronial with servants and belongings, including three geese, which had been due to be slaughtered at Michaelmas and were now accommodated in a specially commissioned cage that dangled behind one of the wagons. The soft-hearted poet (had he not called Augusta 'goose'?) proposed to submit the myth of their longevity to scientific experiment. Trelawny sailed the *Bolívar*, with a cargo of household belongings, to Lerici, where Byron and the Gambas came down from Lucca to meet him. It was now that a famous swimming competition took place. ('Let us test the waves that overpowered our friends.') Byron and Trelawny were to race to the *Bolívar*, lying three miles offshore. If Trelawny is to be believed (a considerable condition), Byron was so decisively beaten that the 'corsair' had time to order the 'edibles' before the author swam alongside. The competitors ate some food and then struck out for the shore. Byron vomited violently after they had gone a short distance (sunstroke or nausea from his opponent's postprandial cigar?) but fought off Trelawny's patronizing efforts to assist him to the boat. After a dose of brandy and despite Trelawny's prudent fear that the joke had gone far enough, Byron insisted on 'plumping in' and swimming back to shore. His determination to prove himself was as unwise as it was characteristic; he was very ill, in a miserable hotel in Lerici, for five days. The violent pains, biliousness and constipation suggest sunstroke, compounded by the manly brandy. Byron, who had been in such agony that he wanted to die, afterwards told an unsympathetic Trelawny that moving house always upset him; routine and bravado were the contrary horses of his soul.

At the beginning of October, health restored, Byron made himself at home with the Gambas, at the Casa Saluzzo in Genoa. The taxing Leigh Hunts had travelled with him, but he arranged for them to lodge with Mary Shelley at a mile's remove from the Casa Saluzzo, that he might be spared the 'Yahoos', and their mother, 'no great things' in his sour view. Nevertheless, the first number of *The Liberal* was now ready for the press, Byron's *The Vision of Judgment* prominent and provocative on its front page. The new cantos of *Don Juan* were passed down the hill to Mary Shelley, who was paid to make fair copies. Secretarial work distracted her from mourning and disguised charity as wages. Although Byron's voice continued to have a disturbingly seductive effect on Mary and his character pervades her fiction, the two of them were never easy together. Whatever attraction she may have felt was not returned except in the way of courtesy. *Don Juan* must have kept her busy, for new cantos were piling up: by the spring of 1823, there were no fewer than sixteen in all. John Murray's almost frantic revulsion from their outspokenness so incensed the poet that he broke once again with the 'tradesman' on whom he had lavished so much amusing ink.

When the grandly touring Earl and Countess of Blessington arrived in April, they found him lively and still boyish, though what was left of his hair was turning silver. Lady Blessington remarks that he drew attention to his lameness (he had accused Hobhouse on his last visit of 'looking at his foot') an indication that neither fame nor wealth had made up for his incurable, petty curse. Byron's garrulity with the Blessingtons suggests how eager he was for the company of his own class. He often appears the very antithesis of rectitude, but his want of delicacy (part of what lion hunters like the Earl and his lady expected of him) found its edge only when Shelley's 'great general laws of antique courtesy' were in force, and so could be daringly breached. The 'effeminate' accent ascribed to him by Lady Blessington may have been wished upon him by expectation (London gossip was shrill with homosexual innuendo) or it may have been the excited consequence of his awareness that whatever was said in the hotel would soon be repeated in England. Indiscretion before visitors is the exile's way of raising his voice high enough for it to be heard at home.

The prosecution of John Hunt, Leigh's London-based brother, for publishing *The Vision of Judgment*, which was alleged to be 'calculated to destroy the comfort and happiness of his present majesty', and not without justice, further widened the breach between Byron and the Hunts and thus between him and Mary Shelley, who felt a pious obligation to take their part. She now saw herself as the keeper of Shelley's flame, a role which, as widowhood extended into middle age, became an obsession until she could believe herself to have been the perfect wife of a perfect marriage, the tensions and tragedies of the children's deaths and the salacious rumours all forgotten. Byron's appetite for scandal – 'It is a sort of cayenne to the mind', he told Lady Blessington – and the delectable knowledge that, despite raised eyebrows, her ladyship enjoyed personal acquaintance with those he mocked (including his friends and hers), made him so eager for her regular company that Teresa became jealous, even though the ample Countess was never more than Byron's riding companion.

A more significant challenge to Teresa's peace of mind came from the blandishments of the Greek Committee, whose emissary, Edward Blaquiere, a retired English naval officer and busybody, made a recruiting call at the Casa Saluzzo in April with Andreas Luriottis, another Greek nationalist. In May came the news that Byron had been elected, with enthusiastic acclaim, a member of the Committee. Soon nominated to represent them in Greece itself, he was eager to accept the mission. Realizing that the *Bolívar* was both a financial burden and useless for serious military purposes (despite her pretty guns), he sold her to the departing Blessingtons, whose company had given him a taste of neglected flavours. He reverted, with a shifty conscience, to the adhesive Teresa who wanted (imagine!) to come to Greece with him; his fear of eventually letting her down only encouraged him to do it as quickly as possible. He was happy enough with her to claim that, married, they would have been paragons of conjugal felicity. But they were not married. Her sighs distressed and irritated him. He had never been a smug adulterer and, whether because it would have been easier for him or better for her, or both, he still believed that she might return to her husband. Yet he delayed the new Greek expedition even as he made preparations for it. Except in rage or frustration, he was never wantonly cruel and now that his sexual appetite was less peremptory, he was even more sentimental. Teresa's brother Pietro was, of course, eager for adventure and Trelawny might be expected to strike an attitude as near the limelight as possible.

In June 1823, the 120-ton brig *Hercules* was commissioned to take the party to Greece; its complement included Lady Blessington's favourite mount, Mameluke, which Byron had bought from her in part exchange for *Bolívar*. More practical cargo took the form of medical supplies for a thousand men, supervised by Francesco Bruno, another newly graduated young doctor who, unlike Polidori, had not even had time to kill his first patients yet. While *Hercules*, no beauty, was being loaded, Byron arranged for Homeric helmets and other glamorous accoutrements to be made to his and Pietro's measure. The excitement attending the approach of his glorious opportunity doubtless displaced onto the Hunts and Mary Shelley his furtive impatience with Teresa's tears. She was the living proof of his unremarkable epigram about love being woman's whole existence, of man's a thing apart, and if he could not reproach her for her taste in lovers, her wholehearted woe scarcely improved his temper. Hunt was demanding, both for himself and for Mary, whose new, haughty refusal to take Byron's money smacks of a ploy to make him take more notice of her. By passing the money through Hunt's account, he did his best to do her a good turn without expecting credit for it, but the widow was determined to be affronted: she wanted fine speeches as well as cash and Byron reserved those for Teresa.

His expeditionary brief was far from warlike; the reconnaissance – it was never intended to be more – was planned to last a few months at the outside. The agony of Teresa can be decked with mournful apprehensions, but at the time there was small likelihood that the heroics would match the helmets. Hindsight sees Byron sailing to a final rendezvous with redemption, some Hellenophile Hector quitting Andromache for the battle that must be fought, and the death that must be faced, but the funds he was carrying from the London Committee were exiguous and his mission more of organization than of derring-do. The Turks were facing noisy insurrections, not a full-scale war, and they had responded with systematic savagery. Byron's essential task was diplomatic rather than military: dissension among the Greek factions was as great an impediment to their cause as the dispositions of their enemies. Homeric swagger would have to wait upon an unsentimental assessment of how best to deploy the funds, about £9,000, so far delegated to him by the Committee, or procured, on his own account, through the good offices of Douglas Kinnaird.

Teresa's despair was touching and intolerable. In affectionate mood, he asked her to sit to a miniaturist, that he might have her picture always with him; in his impatience, he dreaded 'Lady Carolining and Lady Byroning', more tales of ill-usage and abandonment. It came as a relief when the Gambas' enforced exile was rescinded and they were declared free to return to Ravenna. Teresa did not want to leave, but as Byron's sailing date came closer, she agreed that she would quit Genoa with her father, and go back to her native city. Byron pledged eternal love while still rather hoping that, by acceding to her husband's clamorous claims upon her, Teresa might leave him the wounded (and unencumbered) party.

On 13 July 1823, after spending a painful last afternoon with her, he left his sobbing mistress in Mary Shelley's care and went aboard *Hercules*. He was free of them all. Whatever his ambivalence over Teresa, he had certainly had enough of Leigh Hunt, Marianne and their six reminders of the uncertain future of the human race. Hunt lamented the falling out of those who 'might have walked across the world triumphant as the sun' and so, in his way, did Byron, but a new sun was rising and he was eager for its dawn. Alas, 14 July was so calm that not a sail stirred. Anti-climax put them ashore again and Byron was as depressed and dejected as Teresa, now that she was inaccessible. (The cynic is often a sentimentalist who is ashamed of his own emotions.) 'What is happening in the heart of another,' Shelley once wrote, 'rarely escapes the observation of one who is a strict anatomist of his own.' Longing to abandon the whole expedition (delayed again, the next day, this time by a sudden storm that terrified the stalled horses), he declared that it was only the fear of being laughed to scorn that made him cleave to his resolve.

They reached Leghorn on 21 July and received a thirteen-gun salute from an Ionian ship whose captain, George Vitali, was to take passage with them to Greece. Byron scribbled a few lines to Goethe, 'the undisputed Sovereign of European literature', promising to visit Weimar one day, and a few more to Charles Barry, his banker and admirer in Genoa, thanks to whom the preparations had gone so smoothly, and a quick note to Teresa. Then, epistolary duties performed, he was ready for Captain Scott, a veteran seaman of an amiable but cautious character, to set *Hercules* on course for the (Western) Isles of Greece. Once at sea, Byron's spirits rose. He was now glad to be done with 'that cursed Italy'. He and Trelawny swam regularly and once dived overboard together, each with one arm in Captain Scott's new waistcoat, the lads. He also practised fencing with Pietro Gamba (a sighing Fletcher brought bottles of Burton's ale by way of refreshment) and was unassuming and excellent company. As they passed the island of Ponza, he remembered that the 'damned Huns' had dumped the Neapolitan revolutionaries there and swore that when they were done with Greece, they would return and 'have at' the Austrians. It seemed that the horizon of life was broad again. The wandering boy once more, he even considered reviving Childe Harold.

On 2 August, the brig docked at Argostoli, on the island of Cephallonia, part of the British protectorate of the Ionian Islands. A warm welcome and no good news awaited them.

Colonel Napier, the Governor, had had his benevolence taxed by a contingent of Harold's old friends, the Suliotes, who had been thrown out of their mainland fastnesses by the policing Turks and had sought refuge on the islands. They greeted Byron with what he took to be a clamour for arms but proved to be a clamour for gold. His steward, Lega Zambelli, once Guiccioli's man, sat immovably on the treasure chest, while Byron, exhilarated by the Albanians' welcome, promised them more than was sensible or practical. The opportunism he recognized in prosaic Leigh Hunt he failed to suspect in those clad in more poetic panoply.

Napier alerted Byron to renewed schisms in the Greek camp. The quarrel between wily Mavrocordato and wild Kolokotronis, from whom the bespectacled Phanariote prince had had to flee for his life earlier in the year, seemed irreparable; but meanwhile Marco Botsaris was engaging the Turk to the north of Missolonghi and seemed the best of the 'generals', often no more than bandit chieftains, whose parochial ambitions were difficult to reconcile with the national cause. Control of the foreign funds gave Byron some tenuous leverage over those whose individual plausibility he would have to resist if unity were to be achieved. After his gullibility over the Suliotes, he conserved the war chest very shrewdly. He regarded the Greeks without illusions, but he never lost his confidence in the righteousness of their cause or in the eventual resurrection of their ancient virtues. He saw that to expect such a cross-bred crew instantly to incarnate the energetic qualities of the Athenians, or of the disciplined Spartans, was to do them too much honour. He tried to stay cool while they exemplified the ancient vices of their Balkan ancestors, of whom Herodotus wrote, 'To be unoccupied is most prestigious, to work the land most shameful; to live by warring and looting most honourable.' Byron's sense of humour and of captaincy was never more steadfast. 'We must not look always too closely at the men who are to benefit by our exertions in a good cause,' he reminded the less tolerant 'Franks' among his entourage, 'or God knows we shall seldom do much good in this world.'

Delays are ever a part of the Greek world. *'Siga, siga'* (there's no hurry) and *'kathiste'* (sit down) are the first phrases the urgent traveller hears. As a tourist Byron had been in no hurry, but now, eager for practical politics, he was obliged to a slow and sedate existence varied only by tourism and conversation. The Turks had set an almost unbreachable blockade on Missolonghi to the north, but it was Napier's well-informed and well-intentioned view (official British neutrality did not inhibit his off-duty partisanship) that Byron should not take the easier way south into the Peloponnese. To join Kolokotronis there would make Byron the tool of a dubious faction, and lose him the trust of the rest of the Greeks. On the other hand, the good Captain Scott was not prepared to challenge the Missolonghi blockade, much as he longed to be done with the 'damned Zodiacs' who swarmed all over his ship. The Suliotes were as light-fingered as they were heavily-moustached. (Even Byron's pistols were filched from his cabin.)

Byron showed his usual lively tolerance not only in the face of Trelawny's Corsairish posturing but also when Dr James Kennedy, the local health officer, an earnest evangelical, attempted to convert, or re-convert, him to Christianity. Byron's mutability always surprised those whom rumour had prepared for an impudent Satanist. He rarely matched the caricatures which malicious pens concocted (only Peacock, in *Nightmare Abbey*, graced exaggeration with acumen). Dr Kennedy was so startled by Byron's biblical knowledge that he quite revised his desperate diagnosis of the poet's soul. Despite his flippant claim only to want to 'giggle and make giggle', Byron's quest for metaphysical certainty was never as false as the frown he prepared for Thorwaldsen; had he found a convincing creed, he might have embraced it. His scepticism was more a specific against the temptations of credulity (he was always prey to superstition, which is a kind of spilled piety) than an earnest of incorrigible atheism. His doubts whether Christianity had improved the human condition might cut little ice with theologians, but was it not Jesus who had advised, 'By their fruits shall ye know them'? The Christian record, he reminded Dr Kennedy, was hardly a reassuring guide to the perplexed.

As for tourism, the possessor of those flashing helmets could scarcely refrain from a visit to nearby Ithaca, where his small Odyssey was marred by the sight of mainland refugees living in wretched conditions. He immediately created a fund for their alleviation and, as so often, personally helped a family, the Chalandritsanoi, who had suffered particularly. Loukas, their absent son, a handsome boy of fifteen, would accompany Byron as the last of his many body servants to Missolonghi. On the way back to Cephallonia, he had another violent attack of ill-health; an aquatic display and a hot crossing in an open boat had been followed by an unwisely large and Bacchic dinner. However, having spent a distempered night at a hill-top monastery near Samos, he made a quick recovery and parted from the Abbot with more courtesy than he had displayed on his feverish arrival, when he called him a 'pestilential madman'. During the night, Byron so despised his own trembling feebleness that he was persuaded to swallow one of Dr Bruno's pills only when, after saying that if it were poison he would not hesitate to take it, he was reminded that without him the common cause was lost.

Colonel Napier was an agreeable host and Byron established a gentlemanly routine in which literary work scarcely figured. (He confined himself to his usual dashing correspondence.) He craved action, not rhymes, and seemed on the point of finding it when a cogent despatch from Marco Botsaris, fighting in the hills to keep the Turks from breaking through to insurgent Missolonghi, urged him to join the resistance. Botsaris's summons had scarcely arrived when news came that its brave author had been killed in battle. His character was in honourable contrast to the greedy Byzantinism of most of the rest of the leaders. 'They are such damned liars,' Byron concluded, 'there never was such an incapacity for veracity shown since Eve lived in Paradise.' The rank and file were as grasping as their supposed betters and it was not long before the Suliotes were temporarily paid off, that they might not have to be paid more, on condition that they returned to the mainland to await further instructions, and subventions.

Trelawny and James Hamilton Browne, a Philhellene who had joined them at Leghorn, suspected Byron of deliberate dawdling. Browne had been dismissed from the British administration for his undiplomatically loud partisanship, and he echoed Trelawny's bellowing belligerence. Neither could accept that Byron's procrastinations were due less to cowardice than to a sane assessment of the issues. In early September, the fretful pair set off for the Morea (the northern part of the Peloponnese), with the air of those who knew how to sort out the men from the boys. Before Byron himself moved to the mainland, the best part of four months were to pass, during which his inexperience was relieved by the excellent Napier's soldierly advice.

Napier's place in the dictionary of quotations is based on his terse despatch, PECCAVI, after his capture of Sind, while campaigning in India in 1843, but the Laconic pun, and its classical provenance, suggest an entertaining as well as a practical counsellor. Byron's willingness to listen to those who knew more than he did, provided they did, argues against the view of him as a monologuist incapable of dispassionate modesty. The posturing poet yielded to the practical leader (though a few famous lines, almost by force of habit, did emerge from his last pilgrimage) and he paraded his personality only where its charisma might serve to shame, or embolden, those around him. Of all the literary figures who have hazarded life or reputation in the world's game, who was ever less pretentious or more purposeful? His means were limited, his lines of communication unreliable, his troops venal and undisciplined. He had no zest for bloodshed, but he drove himself forward with a resolution which only heroes might fairly criticize. If he had a fault, it was that he dreamed of a generous conclusion which would reconcile Turk and Greek, thus keeping Childe Harold's illusions intact by leaving the one with his fierce glamour, the other with his ancient liberty.

Life at Metaxata, on the Cephallonian coast facing the mainland, which he could see from his rented front door, was chaste but not unsociable. Dr Kennedy was still attempting to make good Byron's soul ('I shall begin the 17th canto of *Don Juan* a changed man,' the poet observed) and Napier continued to propose soldierly solutions to the unabated squabbles of the Greeks, though those with closer experience, like Frank Hastings, a British naval officer, were sceptical of attempting to impose foreign tactics, officers or equipment on the klephts and other irregulars who were wary of outsiders and unused to the parade-ground drill and fancy weaponry of Napier's formula.

The monotony of life was unsettled by the news that Byron's daughter Ada was ill (she soon made a good recovery) and by the October earthquakes which reminded them that Ithacan Odysseus' old enemy, Poseidon, the earth shaker, still held local sway. Visitors came and went: Greek Deputies with a show of plausible speeches and empty pockets; English Philhellenes, including another young doctor, Julius Millingen, whom Byron – ever partial to medical men – recruited as physician to the Suliote brigade he was still hoping to deploy on the mainland; Charles Hancock, a resident in the Ionian Isles, who handled Byron's complicated finances and who admired his readiness to add his own fortune to the common treasury, which so far contained little else. Various volunteers, including the sophisticated idealist George Finlay, who took a trio of German officers to join the fighting in the Morea, came and saw him and were, for the most part, conquered by his high spirits and unflagging optimism, despite the depressing fractiousness of the Greeks whose leaders, even under fire, could not be trusted to distribute patriotic funds to their hard-pressed men. James Hamilton Browne and two of the Greek Deputies had now gone to London where Edward Blaquiere was trying to raise a loan of £800,000 in order to give the Greek government, such as it was, some real weight and credibility, but so foolishly exaggerated were his claims that his blurb proved counter-productive. (He had told the bankers 'the prospect of wealth and prosperity is almost boundless.') Blaquiere covered his embarrassment by accusing the Jews in general, and the Rothschilds in particular, of conspiring with the Turks to procure the massacre of the Greeks. The London Greek Committee was blemished by this implausible rant: when a loan was eventually floated, the actual cash available to Greece was less than half the nominal value of £800,000, since the investors were sceptical of the lucrative dawn painted by the rosy-fingered Blaquiere. So long did these arrangements take and so ticklish was the problem of administering the funds that Blaquiere did not reach Zante with the first instalment until after Byron's death in April 1824. The British were wary of seeming to have bought Greece, nor were they willing to pay for it without a reliable receipt.

The arrival of another British colonel, Leicester Stanhope, a delegate of the London Committee, added strength to Byron's staff but little to his humour. Stanhope was a meliorist who believed in the printed word and, despite his military background, had something of Dr Kennedy's moralizing character. The bored Byron asked whether he had any new books with him and he came up with Bentham's *Springs of Action*, provoking the exasperated retort, 'What does the old fool know of springs of action? My — has more spring in it!' (Byron is so reported, but the cocky poet surely filled in the missing word with monosyllabic explicitness.) Bentham's philosophy had, in fact, been influential in the editorial policy of the first Greek newspaper, published in Vienna in 1784; Stanhope's faith in him was no casual eccentricity. Nor did Stanhope's staunchness go unappreciated, happy as Byron may have been when the 'typographical Colonel' went on ahead to Missolonghi at the beginning of December.

His own months of frustration were about to end. The landing of Prince Mavrocordato at Missolonghi, after the success of a small Greek fleet from Spetsai in temporarily dispersing an even smaller Turkish one, confirmed Byron's decision to throw in his lot, and his cash, with the forces in and around the marshy and unprepossessing town which he and Hobhouse had seen from afar on their first day in Greek waters. The victorious Greek fleet had disgraced itself by the pursuit of a Turkish warship into neutral waters where the crew was massacred during the pillaging of its treasure, but when, at last, the Greek legislative body formally requested Byron to go to Missolonghi, there seemed nothing to prevent him quitting Metaxata for the mainland except that the Greek vessel sent for them was turned back by the British authorities. Whatever their sympathies, His Majesty's representatives could not be seen to countenance another violation of neutrality. Byron thereupon hired two small boats, a 'mistico', in which he himself took passage with Dr Bruno, Fletcher and Loukas Chalandritsanos (as well as the bulldog that had terrified Rogers and kept the Cockneys in their quarters), and a 'bombard', a larger, slower vessel loaded with the horses and heavier impedimenta and supervised by Pietro Gamba. On the evening of 29 December, they put to sea.

At first the two boats kept close enough together for flights of patriotic songs to pass between them but then, as the mistico made better way, only the bang of excited pistol and 'carabine' shots carried from one to the other. The amateurs' first experience of the realities of war was nearly their last. The Turkish blockade had been reinstated. The Greek fleet, after their small and bloody triumph, cut and ran when the Turks again put out from Patras, across the water from Missolonghi. The Spetziot crews were without pay and lacked stomach for an even fight. Soon after midnight on 31 December, a man-of-war loomed out of the darkness athwart the mistico. Byron assumed she was Greek; his skipper knew she was not. Only an abrupt change of tack avoided capture and almost certain death, or worse. (Byron promised Loukas that he would save him, whatever happened, to which the charmless, practical Dr Bruno retorted, 'Better save me; a doctor matters more than a boy!') The bombard was clumsier and less fortunate. Pietro Gamba gave the most incriminating of the documents a quick burial at sea, but there was little he could do about the arms, provisions and other manifestly contraband supplies, let alone the horses. Only the happiest and most romantic moment of *anagnorisis* saved the bombard from being sunk and the crew from execution: the Turkish Captain recognized, at the last second, that the Greek skipper had once saved his life in the Black Sea. Chivalry asserted itself; the Greek, his friends and his suspect crew were taken into Patras whence, after a tactful exchange of gifts, they were permitted by the governor, Yussuf Pasha, to proceed to Missolonghi, a gesture to which Byron, when eventually he managed to find his way through the blockade, responded kindly, and in kind. One of his first acts after landing was to send four Turkish prisoners with an effusive letter to Yussuf Pasha; it was not the least of his preoccupations to mitigate the brutalities committed by both sides. He had been becomingly unpretentious about his Messianic mission. 'I am going . . . to electrify the Suliotes,' he wrote, 'as George Primrose went to Holland to teach the Dutch English, who were fond of it to distraction.' He had a notion that only one thing would electrify the natives and that with £100,000 more of it they might already be halfway to Constantinople. However, his welcome at Missolonghi was as fervent as his appearance, in his commissioned finery, was theatrical. The Greek ships which had shunned combat crept back to fire a salute as his circuitous boat, after negotiating the long shallows of the lagoon under cover of darkness, put in at the quayside on the morning of 4 January 1824. He was welcomed onto Greek soil by Mavrocordato and Colonel Stanhope, who had wasted no time in setting up the printing press which Pietro (arriving before Byron, despite everything) had already given into his typographical charge. 'Give me that honest right hand,' said Byron, quenching his scepticism over leading articles as a means of procuring the greatest good of the greatest number.

All the usual problems quickly declared themselves. The Suliotes had trooped into town and no sooner had Lega Zambelli unloaded the treasure chests into the spacious, sparsely furnished house which had been prepared for Byron than all hands were available, and outstretched. With Stanhope soon rolling off copies of the *Greek Times* and the irregulars regular only in their demands for payment, it seemed that Missolonghi was to be little different from Cephallonia, save that it was less healthy and more dangerous. Their welcoming salute proved to have spent the full splendour of the fleet; the sailors again preferred flight to fight when the Turks returned to the bay. It was a miserable time of year in a miserable town. The several thousand ill-assorted troops were as demanding as they were incapable of unified or effective action. Mavrocordato was a competent man, of large culture (he spoke several languages, including English), but his administrative background in the Turkish civil service gave him no authority over the motley captains who attended his councils of war. (He was a 'Prince' by courtesy, not by blood; there was no Greek royal family, which allowed the government to flatter their British bene-factor with rumours of post-war coronation.) Byron's Napoleonic fantasies are easily mocked, but he proved a popular leader; not only on account of being the paymaster. Elevation to generalship did not blind him to realities, rather it enabled him to face them with that leaven of make-believe without which no leader of an improbable cause can hope to keep his spirits up. He was commanding 'Byron's Blacks' at last; prodigies of valour were harder to procure. An ambitious plan was afoot to attack Nafpaktos, the fortified town then known as Lepanto, some forty kilometres along the coast east of Missolonghi. It was a propitious place to attack the Turks (in 1571, Don John of Austria had utterly destroyed the Turkish fleet in the neighbouring waters), but the operation had to be postponed for want of cohesive force. There was little to be done in the sullen, soggy town but listen to the sound of Stanhope's clattering press, drill the reluctant troops and wait for sufficient funds and fire power to mount a practicable campaign. The strict accountant, as ever, of his ration of years, Byron geared himself for the coming test of fire with the lines written on his thirty-sixth birthday, 22 January 1824.

> 'Tis time this heart should be unmoved,
> Since others it hath ceased to move:
> Yet, though I cannot be beloved,
> Still let me love!
>
> My days are in the yellow leaf;
> The flowers and fruits of love are gone;
> The worm, the canker, and the grief
> Are mine alone!
>
> The fire that on my bosom preys
> Is lone as some volcanic isle;
> No torch is kindled at its blaze –
> A funeral pile.

The hope, the fear, the jealous care,
The exalted portion of the pain
And power of love, I cannot share,
But wear the chain.

But 'tis not *thus* – and 'tis not *here* –
Such thoughts should shake my soul, nor *now*,
Where glory decks the hero's bier,
Or binds his brow.

The sword, the banner, and the field,
Glory and Greece, around me see!
The Spartan, borne upon his shield,
Was not more free.

Awake! (not Greece – she *is* awake!)
Awake, my spirit! think through *whom*
Thy life-blood tracks its parent lake,
And then strike home.

Tread those reviving passions down,
Unworthy manhood! – unto thee
Indifferent should the smile or frown
Of beauty be.

If thou regrett'st thy youth, *why live?*
The land of honourable death
Is here: – up to the field, and give
Away thy breath!

Seek out – less often sought than found –
A soldier's grave, for thee the best;
Then look around, and choose thy ground,
And take thy rest.

Critics have observed, with a certain glee, that the argument of these lines is somewhat lame. The rousing spell Byron seeks to cast on himself lacks convincing magic; belligerent affectations are belied by the weariness of the sentiments and their confused expression. But Byron was always reckless in his revelations (posturing is often a function of self-doubt) and it was almost a point of honour to give himself away. The wonder is that in the surly climate of disappointment and bickering, to which the mosquito-ridden town gave small relief, he managed to maintain his faith that Greece *was* awake and, painfully conscious of having reached the *mezzo camin'*, to present an encouraging face for others to see.

The Suliotes behaved no better now than they had before; their demands were various, but they had a single end: more cash. Byron thought he was paying soldiers and found himself subsidizing inflated numbers of wives and children. The affection he felt for Loukas Chalandritsanos echoed that for Nicolo Giraud back in 1810, but Loukas was more acquisitive and less fond, adding to Byron's fear that he was passé. Removed from the *mise en scène* of Italy, he was aware of how much of an act would be needed if he was to spring himself again on Teresa with undiminished ardour. Although we cannot but remember that he would be dead within three months of that thirty-sixth birthday and that his road, so far from having reached its halfway point, was nearly closed, it is omen-mongering to suppose that he was regretting more than a spent youth or that he had a premonition of his own fate. It is true that his verses toy with death, but he had always done that, ever since his first you'll-be-sorry poems. Yet it must be granted that he had reason at least to imagine death in battle: if the Greeks were to be electrified, it would have to be by a conductor who led them from the front.

The military situation was improved by the arrival early in February of a ship carrying William Parry, the 'firemaster', who turned out to be a thickset and capable professional soldier with practical experience and down-to-earth ideas. He had brought some artillery pieces and the mechanics essential to any serious attack on Lepanto, but he was aggrieved at the omission from his cargo of the Congreve rockets which had been promised by the London Committee, but not loaded. Parry was neither an officer nor a gentleman, but Byron took to him at once, snobbery banished by more important considerations. Parry knew his trade and had not hesitated to put his hand in his own pocket to advance money to the exigent crew he brought with him. The Suliotes, true to their capacity for lazy ingenuity, refused to help unload the supplies since they were soldiers, not porters. As for the native Missolonghiots, everything came to a stop while they celebrated a religious holiday. Greeks are not always easy to love. However, Parry's businesslike presence had a rallying effect and his supplies added muscle to the armoury, even if valuable space had been filled by a large consignment of Bibles. Some of the foreign gentleman-volunteers resented Byron's unhesitating appointment of Parry as overseer of all military matters; a Prussian called Kindermann led a deputation which held that it was beneath their dignity to serve under a non-commissioned officer. Byron chided him (and it might have been Shelley speaking) for introducing his prejudices into Greece and the Public Schoolboy shamed the Junker by stating that he himself was ready to serve as a common soldier, if it would further the cause. Parry remained in charge. His promotion was daring as well as prudent, since Byron's presence and his declarations had recruited gentlemen and officers from all over Europe – a sort of 'crusade in miniature', said Pietro Gamba – and it required nerve no less than judgment to give a ranker precedence over them. Parry established workshops in the old Seraglio, and his mechanics set about assembling the guns, though their idealism, too, proved to depend disappointingly on cash. The Suliotes, despite their inaction, thought it was time for promotions all round. They wanted to have two generals, two colonels, two captains and twenty lieutenants, as well as a hundred sergeants and two hundred corporals, all of them at appropriately enhanced rates of pay. Byron's patience snapped. The rascals had camped all around his house, scarcely less baleful than the hosts of Midian, and he now proceeded literally to boot them out. Realizing that they had gone too far, they begged to be re-engaged as common soldiers. Some banged their heads on the ground in repentance and abasement. A compromise was reached and a reduced force remained on the payroll, but Parry – fearful of a riotous assault – put some Swedish volunteers on twenty-four hour guard over the arsenal, while Lega Zambelli and Byron's other servants sat firmly on the treasure chest. 'Robbers all' no longer sounded so rapturous a rallying call. Byron's exasperation was neither amused nor transitory. Large sums had drained away on the maintenance of a rabble whose belligerence went no further than the intimidation of the Missolonghiots, one of whom had actually been shot dead by his lodgers while protesting at the billeting of Suliotes in his house. The hope of marching them against Lepanto had been sapped by Parry's assessment of military realities. The artillery was still inadequate and, for all the rumours of treachery available (for 40,000 dollars) within the fortress walls, how was one to get a sufficiently intimidating force within sight of them? George Finlay had come back with word from Trelawny and the Greek leader, Odysseus, to whom the Corsair had become a swaggering legate, bidding Byron to a conference at Salona, modern Amphissa, where they might attempt yet again to unite the factions. Finlay's Romanticism, like Byron's, underwent some disillusioned modifications on closer acquaintance with the Greeks, but he too never lost his affection for their cause.

On 15 February, the day after the final disillusionment with the Suliotes, Byron had a violent seizure and pitched into Parry's arms, his face distorted, his mouth 'drawn on one side'. By the time Pietro Gamba and the doctors Millingen and Bruno had reached him, he seemed better, but they guessed that he had had an epileptic fit, though there was no history of epilepsy in the family or in his early life. Pietro, who had himself been the target, not undeservedly, of Byron's testiness (he had spent extravagantly on Ruritanian finery), agreed with Parry that his exasperation had been compounded by a typical reluctance to take sensible nourishment. That beautiful pale face was plump and plain, Loukas' indifference the gauge of its decline. The doctors proceeded to sap rather than to supplement his strength by applying leeches. 'I am not afraid to die,' Byron said, as if he feared he was. Bleeding was easier to start than to arrest and the patient fainted from loss of blood. In spite of the medical attention, he began to recover.

On 17 February, word came that a Turkish brig with twenty-two guns had gone aground not far from the town. A financial deal had to be worked out before any unHomeric heroes could be mustered to ride out and capture her. By the time the Suliote party was ready to go, under Parry's impatient command, the Turks had spiked their guns and fired the ship. Parry, who had warned Byron's doctors on pain of death not to apply any new treatment to their patient while he was away, reported that the expedition resulted in nothing more than a good gallop, and an expensive one. On the 19th, there was more trouble. One of the Suliotes had quarrelled with a Swedish officer guarding the armoury and shot him dead. The Swede's name is said to have been Sass, though the only local tombstone bearing that name seems to be that of a Sass drowned in 1826. If the dead man was Adolph von Sass, he had already suffered torture and enslavement, apart from unspeakable sexual humiliation, after being captured by the Turks. That he should die at Greek hands is the most unpoetic injustice imaginable. After his death, his assassin was rumoured to have been killed, whereupon the Suliotes began to riot. It looked as though the arsenal was about to be stormed. Byron kept cool. Ordering the guns to be turned on the gateway, he dared the mutineers to break in. The volatile tribesmen backed down, though not before a tense meeting with their erstwhile benefactor who, despite his nervous prostration, confronted their mutinous yelling with an Harrovian sang-froid that impressed Colonel Stanhope.

The latter's chain of newspapers acquired a new link shortly afterwards with the publication of the *Telegrafo Greco*, which circulated his improving views to all, or at least a few, Italians in the Greek orbit. Fine sentiments were also being expressed in London, where Hobhouse wrote that Byron was a great hero and that *Don Juan*, over which he had displayed such prim reservations, was receiving 'the admiration and attention it has always deserved'. The sale of the Rochdale estates had been concluded and there was nothing, on either social or economic grounds, to prevent Byron from returning to England in style.

It needed no London amnesty to tempt him to leave Missolonghi where morale was now very low, indeed so low that, whatever the temptation, he could not possibly leave. An earthquake on 21 February at least gave him a laugh, when even Parry, who feared nothing on two legs, was so unmanned by the tremor which rocked the town that he was discovered, sheepish on all fours, hiding under a table. As so often, Byron revelled in the chance to keep his head while all around were afraid of losing theirs. Laughs were, in general, so hard to come by that they sometimes had to be procured by elaborately ribald means. Fletcher may not have missed his wife quite so much on this rough pilgrimage, but his sexual appetite made him an easy target for a practical joke involving a Suliote 'girl' (actually a young warrior in drag) whose 'brother', cued to irrupt into Fletcher's chamber as the seduction got under way, threatened the unfortunate valet with merciless revenge. Fletcher was less amused than his master; it had been one thing to have the laundry-maids of Athens run pins into him, it was another to be put to the curved sword by a raving foreigner. Yet the valet's loyalty was soon retrieved. When Byron was once again taken ill, he watched with impotent anguish as the doctors worked their ignorant will on the man whom he had served for so long with such crass devotion.

As the possibilities of effective campaigning dwindled away in futile diplomacy and every show of patriotism turned out to be a new way of presenting a bill, Byron had a right to wonder what good he was doing, or would ever do. The Turks still commanded the gulf and the march on Lepanto had had to be shelved, the Suliotes having decided that Arta, to the north, though of little tactical consequence, would provide easier pickings. Greek cohesion remained impossible to procure, with love or with money. Optimism in London over the effect of the loan being raised by Blaquiere and the others was hardly warranted by what was happening on the ground. Even though the garrison of Lepanto had come down to 25,000 dollars on the deal to surrender the town, the Suliotes – who had greeted the earthquake with a stupendous airing of fire-power – would not consent to make war against stone walls, at least at the going rate, and without them even the garrison's mercenary honour could not countenance surrender. Philip of Macedon used to boast that he could take any city, provided he could get an ass laden with gold up to its gate. Byron lacked the ass.

As soon as his health was partly restored, he resumed his routine of riding outside the despondent town. He was entertained by the presence of Finlay, whose conversation was less limited than Parry's, more astringent than Pietro's, and on whom anecdotes of high old times were not wasted. The meeting of Greek leaders which Finlay had come to propose was finally set for the end of March, though it had to be postponed, like so many things, on account of the unnegotiable weather (so much for Blaquiere's, and other absentee Hellenists', advertisements for the eternal sunshine of Greece). Though Byron made a good show of recovery from his seizure, he continued to suffer from vertigo and dreaded both a recurrence and its 'cure': he did not want to expire 'on a bed of torture' or terminate his days like Swift – 'a grinning idiot'. Superstition reminded him that a fortune teller had once warned him that he should 'beware his 37th year'. It had certainly begun unpropitiously. When Finlay finally left for Athens, Byron's depression deepened. He even dreamed of retiring to England and resuming life with Annabella and his daughter, whose picture was always in his view. If marriage seemed ambrosial once more, it was Loukas Chalandritsanos who inspired the last, rueful lines he ever wrote. 'Yielding my couch and stretched me on the ground' leaves little doubt that the ungrateful page was the subject of his poem: Byron had acted exactly as he described after Loukas caught a chill on one of their innumerable wet excursions. Alas, the unloving page was neither an Edleston nor a Nicolo, but another of those leeches which attached themselves to his purse and his heart. In the midst of a savage war, self-pity seems deplorable, but he also pitied the war's innocent victims, no matter to which side they belonged: he had recently sent a Turkish woman and her pretty little daughter to Cephallonia for Dr Kennedy to practise his Christianity upon.

The fractiousness of the Greeks was demonstrated yet again at the beginning of April, when a fracas between some Missolonghiot boatmen and a band of soldiers loyal to Karaiskakis, another of the 'generals', whose base was at neighbouring Anatolico, forced Byron to order out his gunboats to discipline the intruders. Once again, at this late stage, he showed himself as capable of effective decision as anyone could expect. Hindsight insists that authority and resolution were waning, but there is little reason to conclude that, given better luck, better weather, better food and better health (none of them out of the question), he could not have recovered his energy and command. True, he had achieved little, but who could have managed more? Distant, dewy eyes blessed the hybrid Greeks with direct descent from the ancient heroes, but their characters had been formed, as Byron's rallying calls never concealed from him, in a shifty school. The best of them – like Mavrocordato – had been obliged to learn the slyness of the Phanariotes, concealing their patriotism from the intimidating masters on whom their privileges depended, and the common people were so mercilessly beaten into submission that it was only through dissembling that they could remain true to themselves. The Suliotes may have been the most shameless of the Greek soldiery, but nearly all who fought against the Turks, often with selfless courage, had been recruited from robber bands whose economy was based on scavenging. What Byron romanticized as indomitable and rebellious spirit, when he observed it in the days of Ali Pasha's unsubtle despotism, he now perceived to be reckless and conscienceless immaturity. The slowness of progress towards the incorruptibility of the ideal state can hardly be blamed on Byron. What George Finlay called 'Homer, Plato and Co.' were scarcely common reading in the counsels of Greek brigandage. In any case, Plato's contemporaries had been caricatured in *The Republic* with much the same faults that Odysseus, Karaiskakis, Kolokotronis and Mavrocordato exhibited. Did Byron have an inflated idea of his own significance? Any leader in whom high hopes are placed must act as if he were capable of honouring them, or where is his leadership? There are times when too honest an estimate of one's own limitations looks less like modesty than defeatism. It was as unfortunate that Byron could not coerce or cajole the Greeks into unity as it was unlikely that anyone else could have done as much. It would be excessive to claim that, had he managed to reach Salona, either his golden charm or his demotic reproaches would have sealed a confederation of the Greek leaders, but his recent experience had purged him of all illusions, while the increase in funds, brought about by the realization of the belated loan, would certainly have given him new leverage.

As it was, the spring weather was foul and, stubbornly, he would go out in it; he resumed his rides in the persistent wet. Thus his militant zeal for keeping fit contributed to his final illness. On 9 April 1824, he was soaked through while riding with Pietro Gamba, and then, sweating from the exercise, he insisted on taking a chilly boat, as usual, across the lagoon to reach his house. He might have gone round on horseback but, playing the exemplary soldier, he refused the softer option. He was taken ill that same night, but went riding again the next day, despite considerable pain. He chided his American Negro groom, on his return, for putting the same damp saddle on his horse, though such negligence is more likely to have aggravated than caused the fever which now possessed him. He had had no happy history with doctors and he seems, understandably, to have been terrified of any resumption of his treatment by Drs Bruno and Millingen. He did his best to appear normal and when he could no longer conceal his condition either from himself or from others, he agreed to Parry's anxious suggestion that he leave for Zante by boat. Poseidon was not favourable; a storm blew up and there was no hope of sailing from Missolonghi. The doctors were now in attendance and the feverish Byron fought off their wish to bleed him once more. On 14 April, he struggled up, with a bad headache, as if to advertise an improvement he could not sustain. Parry was bluntly opposed to the doctors' treatment; as a result they did their officious best to keep him from their patient. Bleeding was the only known treatment for fever, apart from the antimony powder which had proved ineffective, and the doctors pleaded, plausible ghouls, for permission to resume it.

Byron had laughed at Polidori's paucity of patients years before, saying that he had none because he had killed them all, and now he found himself at the mercy of a brace of quacks as insistent as they were wrong-headed. 'The lancet,' he punned desperately, 'had killed more people than the lance,' but if they smiled at his literary objections, Bruno and Millingen were determined to add to the casualties of their trade, though Bruno became so distressed by Byron's condition that he was scarcely more use than Fletcher and Pietro, who were quite unmanned by the spectacle (Tita was the steadiest and most consoling of his entourage). Parry was the sole man whom Byron trusted, but he could only sit at the bedside and watch helplessly as the wind continued to blow and the fretful candle of Byron's life flickered and eventually went out.

Milligen finally persuaded the sick man to accept the knife by threatening him with the grinning idiocy he so dreaded; again the bleeding began. They drew off pint after pint of blood. Byron's agony was protracted and irreversible. His flitting imagination led him now to ask for the old witch, lest his illness be the product of the evil eye, and then to hallucinations of martial glory, a death where the fight was thickest. By 17 April, his condition was so bad that two more doctors were called in, including the shrewd Treiber, a German volunteer serving with the artillery, who later suggested that he would have followed a different course. At the time he lacked the firmness to prevent Millingen from continuing to drain away Byron's strength.

The 18th was the Greek Easter. As the gun-happy townspeople were tactfully persuaded to parade their explosive faith as far as possible from Byron's sickroom, the weeping of the servants and the long faces of the doctors alerted him to the gravity of his case. There began that long and moving delirium, not all of it by any means foolish or unworthy, in which he proved that, to the very last, he could stay in Protean character, never monotonous, never pompous, alert to the ironic comedy of his own situation ('*Oh questa è una bella scena!*') and of the gravity of its consequences for others. In spite of his weakness, he lamented – and sought to alleviate, belatedly – the fate of his servants and of the Greek cause. As for himself, he asked only that his body be not 'hacked' (a request which the doctors ignored in their *post mortem* party) and that it not be sent to England (which it was). He asked to be laid 'in the first corner without pomp or nonsense.' His dying garrulity was of a piece with his cursive abundance in the days of his fame. He could produce a skein of words for any situation; his capacity to put himself in anyone's shoes –

Jew, Mohammedan, Christian 'of every profession of faith' – gave his flippancy a sort of magnanimity beyond the province of those with decided views. He never pretended to certainty and he never settled for cant. He bequeathed his life and fortune to Greece, but he forgot neither Ada, his mathematical daughter, nor even Loukas, the greedy boy. He seemed reconciled to death: 'There are things,' he is said to have said, 'which make the world dear to me, for the rest I am happy to die.' If he blessed his servants and pitied his daughter, he flared up with something of his old spirit against the doctors who had indeed murdered him, though with the best possible intentions.

On Sunday, 18 April, bled, leeched, purged, he blurted out some scarcely coherent commands to Fletcher, asking him to give his blessing to Ada and to Augusta (and the children with whom he had played bears at Six Mile Bottom) and to tell 'every thing' to Lady Byron. Did he hope that, after all, she might at last think well of him? He tottered out to relieve himself and then, about six in the evening, he was heard to say, 'I want to sleep now.' He turned on his back and shut his eyes. The doctors, with their leeches, moved in for the kill. It was not until a day later that Fletcher noticed that Byron had opened his eyes and shut them again 'without showing any symptom of pain, or moving hand or foot.' 'Oh my God,' Fletcher exclaimed, 'I fear his lordship is gone.' The doctors felt his pulse and said, 'You are right – he is gone.'

The Gods had not favoured him with the wind that might have taken him to safety, but they made up for it with a famous thunder storm which announced his death to the superstitious and horrified townspeople. Bereft of his protection, they would have to take their chances under the unreliable aegis of their own people. The terrible massacre which was to be the fate of so many of them might not have been averted by Byron's generalship, but his death unquestionably muted the town's call on both cash and reinforcements. The mutilated body was embalmed and put in a tin-lined chest for transportation to England in very same boat that brought Blaquiere to Zante. The heart remained, literally, in Greece. The modern view of Dr Nolan Lewis, detailed by Marchand, is that the cause of death was uremia, complicated by his feverish chill and, of course, in no way mitigated by the huge loss of blood. Dr Lewis confirms that Byron was probably not epileptic. A rather ghoulish modern examination of his remains, which includes an impressed report of his sexual dimensions, may be found in Elizabeth Longford's little book on Byron.

The eviscerated body did not leave Missolonghi, on the *Floria*, until 24 May, by which time the doleful news had spread throughout Greece; May 5th was proclaimed a day of national mourning (the national leaders could at least agree on that) and the obituaries were as flowery as they were earnest. Greek bonds fell to well below their opening price as word reached London, but Byron's gallant death, though it did not take place in the thick of the fighting, served Greece well. His memory was better respected than his person had been. An excess of rhetoric did not imply a want of genuine grief. The Greeks, in their fashion, took him to their hearts as few foreigners are ever taken; his name is as secure in their folklore as in their formal monuments. Peter Levi tells, in *The Hill of Kronos*, that when the peasants at Delphi observed foreigners scrabbling among the ancient marbles, they imagined that this was a race called 'Milordi', the descendants of the ancient worshippers of idols, come back now to worship the same stones. Perhaps they were not so far wrong.

Many who had never known him were stricken by an almost inexplicable sense of loss (Alfred Tennyson would never forget the day in his boyhood when he heard the news). All who had been his friends, or his lovers (and even his wife), were as shattered as the fifth-century Athenians when they heard that the Sicilian expedition had ended in catastrophe: the summer had gone out of the year. The shock seemed so universal at the death of the 'noblest spirit in Europe', as the young Carlyle called him (perhaps to his later regret), that some grand show of national admiration, or at least forgiveness, might have been expected. There was a proposal to have the body buried in Westminster Abbey, but it was rejected. Augusta – who was the chief mourner – decided to have her brother buried in Hucknall Torkard church, where his mother had been taken while he boxed with young Rushton at Newstead. If London had been struck 'as if by an earthquake' when the news first came through, the aristocracy soon picked up the pieces of their cautious dignity and, despite Hobhouse's efforts to recruit a respectable show of mourners, Byron's fellow peers stayed away from the funeral procession. For form's sake, however, they sent their carriages to dress the scene, just as once they had sent their footmen to crave Byron's attendance at their *soirées*. Their empty, emblazoned coaches followed the hearse up Highgate

211

Hill, but left the body, and the small party of mourners, Colonel Leigh deputizing for the prostrate Augusta, to continue the journey towards Nottingham alone.

The whiff of scandal clung to the skirts of glory. Hobhouse, whose grief was very great and whose most distinct recollection was of that most perishable of all personal attributes, the dead man's laugh, was determined to do all he could to save Byron's renown from pollution. It was surely in this spirit that he sided with John Murray, against Tom Moore, in voting to burn the memoirs which, whatever they may have contained in the way of further naughtiness, could scarcely have disclosed anything that had not already been guessed or documented. Moore, to whom Byron had written the modest wish that he be remembered in your smiles and wine', probably lacked vigour in pressing his case for preserving the memoirs. His objections were scarcely strengthened by the fact that he had already taken money for the manuscript from Murray. We have the idea that the truth has been filched from us, but after the exhaustive researches of Leslie Marchand, Iris Origo and Doris Langley Moore, to name but those to whom one is most evidently obliged, it is improbable that any vital detail is missing. Only the enigma of the marriage continues to tease and it is improbable that any revelation by Byron would provide an acceptable last word on why Lady Byron had deserted him. (He told George Finlay, at Missolonghi, that 'the causes were too simple to be soon found out.')

Annabella, however much she may have been moved by the news of his death, remained unflinchingly self-righteous; her grievance and its high-minded advocates contributed to the poet's dubious reputation throughout the Victorian age, but they cannot be said to have caused it. Though he never lacked admirers (one is tempted to say 'friends', since he always excited a personal rather than an aesthetic response), he could hardly be expected to appeal to the sententious impostures of an imperial power. Abroad, his support for national self-determination, untinged by ideological affectations or vindictive animus, procured him an undiminished fame. Not only in Greece, but also in Poland and in Italy, he was a symbol of disinterested inspiration. The Portuguese, whose hygiene had not impressed him when he visited that country on Childe Harold's pilgrimage, were unique in their lack of enthusiasm. The Germans were willing to honour Goethe's belief in his genius, and applauded his in Goethe's; the Russians – most notably Pushkin and Lermontov – appropriated his gloomy pride, his erotic dandyism and his quirky sense of destiny. He was the finest example of the 'superfluous man', the misfit for all seasons. As for France, Professor Robert Escarpit remarks that Byron has been more talked about than read. The professor emphasizes Byron's influence on French Romantic rebels, from the time of his death at least until the death of rebellion on the barricades of the Commune, but his observation draws attention to the continuing paradox of Byron's poetic standing.

Even today, when the full spread of his peacock wit, gorgeous with insolent colour, can be enjoyed in the complete edition of his letters, his poetry makes the eulogist uneasy. Few deny its wit, not many turn to his verse as a whole with the confidence they have in its parts. There are those passages of enviable dexterity for which Auden's admiration is reference enough, and there are gloriously purple patches, but density of meaning and a tone of high seriousness are either missing or intermittent. Byron exemplifies much that T.S. Eliot insisted was deplorable: the swagger of genius and the cult of individuality. He promoted self-centredness – the nationalism of the individual, one might say – into a paramount virtue by equating self-indulgence with lack of cant and shamelessness with being true to oneself. He was, and is, talked about more for the glamour and glitter of his social and sexual escapades than for the inherent value of his work. He confused thought with his own personal opinions and anguish with attitudinizing. He at once paraded British virtues and lent his name to their subversion. He had surprisingly stubborn standards (and was capable of trenchant self-criticism) but he was susceptible to a slickness that abused the fame and squandered the opportunity he had created for himself.

Even those who are convinced of his genius are likely to be embarrassed at the campaign to equate him with Shakespeare (of whose works, he said, he never owned a copy, lest he be accused of plagiarism). His place in the English poetic pantheon is that of one who resists being neatly niched. Even the long, loyal resentment of his admirers at his exclusion from Westminster Abbey until the memorial installed there in 1969 is perhaps misplaced, for while few would deny him honour in his own country, there is little reason to think of the Abbey as his proper due, unless poets' ideas and behaviour are to be beatified by an undiscriminaing sentimentality. He was interested in religious topics not least, one suspects, out of a kind of metaphysical snobbery; conversation about – or with – God was not to be regarded as above his station. His attachment to the liberal cause, in the largest sense, allowed him to escape the contradictions of his own position. He loved being a lord and not even the most resourceful encomiast could make of him the revolutionary which some have seen in 'red' Shelley. He wrote and lived out his contradictions without ever resolving them, hence the dramatic tension which enlivens his work even when its pretentiousness or brilliance palls or pales. He dreamed of settling down, or of settling down *again*, but if he was only marginally a Romantic (as Jesus was only marginally a Christian), his was an energetic rather than a considered intelligence: a shark for sensations, when he lost velocity he could not feed, or function. His style and his manhood went so closely together that he could no more stand back from his work than stand back from his own shadow, hence his modernity, especially as a prose writer, despite the Corinthian capitals of his poetic vocabulary. As a verse novel, *Don Juan*, masterly and maddening, lacks the unity of *Eugene Onegin* but it surely has as unchallengeable a claim to greatness.

Byron may be attacked, he may be defended; those who attack him must concede his fluency and his generosity, not least as a source for biographical research and speculation, while those who defend him must allow that his genius could be as otiose as it is sometimes felicitous and that his behaviour, however entertaining to investigate, was not always exemplary. Modern biography may affect to be too sophisticated to care for moral judgments, but there is humbug in so swift a disavowal: if we relish Byron's vivid hedonism and ignore his bouts of self-hatred or fantasies of marital decorum, we are denying the complexity of the man's character in favour of seeing him as a simplified naughty boy in whose adventures we may vicariously and blamelessly share. It is possible, and probably right, to find pleasure in his company and his work while still remaining this side of idolatry in both respects.

SELECTED
BIBLIOGRAPHY

Bernard Blackstone *Byron, a survey*. Clear, perceptive account of the poetry.

Marguerite, Countess of Blessington *Journal of Correspondence and Conversations between Lord Byron and the Countess of Blessington*.

Henry Blyth *Caro, the Fatal Passion*. Caroline Lamb's brief life accessibly told.

T. A. J. Burnett *The Rise and Fall of a Regency Dandy*. Scrope Berdmore Davies, his soft life and hard times. Promotes the witty Scrope to the near centre of the Byron drama and includes material from the recent cache of Davies' documents. Very good on quotidian detail of Regency life.

Malcolm Elwin *Lord Byron's Wife*. Fairminded study of Annabella, pros and cons.

Bernard Grebanier *The Uninhibited Byron*. A study of Byron's sexuality full of detailed references to the work and lacking in prurience. Contains full text of *Don Leon* poems.

Peter Gunn *My Dearest Augusta*. The heart of the matter clearly anatomized.

Richard Holmes *Shelley*. Full-length study, short on Lit. Crit., if you miss it.

M. K. Joseph *Byron, the Poet*. A technical examination, for microscopticians.

Michael Joyce *My Friend H.* Hobhouse's long life sympathetically treated; dark horse and dull dog, John Cam.

John D. Jump *Byron*. Excellent literary study of the prose and verse, brisk and unassuming.

G. Wilson Knight *Lord Byron: Christian Virtues*. A pretty piece of hagiography.

—— *Byron and Shakespeare*. The highest claim for Byron's poetic genius; illuminating if finally unconvincing.

—— *Lord Byron's Marriage*. The first clear statement of the case for the relevance of the *Don Leon* poems. Controversial (Doris Langley Moore hot in opposition), often convincing.

Elizabeth Longford *Byron's Greece*. Picture book with informative text.

Jerome J. McGann *Don Juan in Context*. The editor of the definitive works examines Don Juan in the light of Wittgensteinian ideas: original, unpretentious.

Leslie A. Marchand *Byron*. The standard biography; thorough, unopinionated, pedestrian in style.

—— *Byron: A Portrait*. Condensed version of the above, livelier and taking new material into account.

—— *Byron's Letters and Journals*. The definitive edition, scrupulously edited and annotated and including some recent finds.

André Maurois *Byron*. A neatly shaped, dated but elegant view, weak on documentation and indifferent to the poetry, but still highly readable.

Thomas Medwin *Journal of the Conversations of Lord Byron*. Thin but authentic memoir of Pisan days.

Doris Langley Moore *The Late Lord Byron*. Splendid account of the dust that would not settle: the squabbles and controversies after Byron's death.

—— *Byron Accounts Rendered*. A poet and his finances reconstituted from his files to humorous and lively effect. Some men can be heroes even to their accountants.

Sir Harold Nicolson *The Last Journey*. Readable, tactful account of the progress from Venice to Missolonghi.

Iris Origo *The Last Attachment*. Definitive account of the Guiccioli affair: revealing and enjoyable, but perhaps overdoes Teresa's importance to Byron.

Peter Quennell *Byron, The Years of Fame*. Elegant, occasionally supercilious biographical treatment. Dated but not *dépassé*.

Charles E. Robinson *Shelley and Byron*. Subtitled 'The Snake and the Eagle Wreathed in Flight', a subtle, academic examination of the creative tensions between the two *frères ennemis* of 'Romantic' poetry.

William St Clair *That Greece Might Still Be Free*. The Philhellenes in the War of Independence. Rogues, adventurers and idealists in the Greek cause, Byron *primus inter pares*.

Percy Bysshe Shelley *Letters*. Shelley lacked Byron's devil, but his letters are vivid with sincerity and the Oxford edition is richly detailed with Frederick L. Jones's notes.

Margot Strickland *The Byron Women*. A gallery of portraits, taking the leading ladies seriously.

Claire Tomalin *Shelley and His World*. A brief, informative, illustrated life; notably clear treatment of the tangled relationship between Claire Clairmont and P.B.S.

Edward J. Trelawney *Recollections of the Last Days of Shelley and Byron*. The Corsair scoundrel *dans ses oeuvres*. You can't believe a word he says, yet the ring of truth echoes from the vessel of falsehood.

Paul Graham Trueblood (ed.) *Byron's Political and Cultural Influence in Nineteenth Century Europe*. A symposium of unequal worth with good essays by Douglas Dakin (the background), W. Ruddick (England) and Robert Escarpit (France).

LIST OF ILLUSTRATIONS

PLATE SECTIONS

Private collection. Photo courtesy Newstead Abbey, Nottingham Museums.

6. *Byron at the Age of Seven* 1795. Anonymous miniature. By kind permission of the Governors of Harrow School.

7. Surgical boots belonging to Byron. Collection John Murray.

8. The Old Grammar School, Aberdeen, as it was between 1757 and 1863. Photo from *Bon Record: Records and Reminiscences of Aberdeen Grammar School*, 1906.

9. *Byron at Harrow* 1801. Pencil sketch signed T.W. Whereabouts unknown.

10. *Mary Chaworth* (detail). Anonymous miniature. Newstead Abbey, Nottingham Museums.

11. *Annesley Hall*. Lithograph. The Mansell Collection.

12. *The big school-room, Harrow*. Aquatint from R. Ackermann's *Public Schools of Cheltenham, Eton, Harrow, Rugby and Winchester*, 1816.

13. *Lord Byron's elm, Harrow churchyard*. Lithograph after N. Whittock.

14. Neville's Court, Trinity College, Cambridge. Photo Edwin Smith.

15. *Byron*. *c.*1804. Anonymous miniature which bears an inscription on the back in the hand of Augusta Leigh. Private collection.

16. *Lord Byron as a cricketer*. Lithograph from Lord Byron's *Poems and Letters*, 1912. Newstead Abbey, Nottingham Museums.

17. *Lord Byron in travelling costume*. Plumbago drawing. Private collection. Photo Newstead Abbey, Nottingham Museums.

18. The 'Byron Screen' started in 1814 showing pugilists, including the mezzotint portrait of John 'Gentleman' Jackson. Collection John Murray.

19. *Highest Life in London . . . Almacks in the West*. Aquatint and watercolour by I. R. and G. Cruikshank for Pierce Egan's *Life in London*, 1823.

20. *The House of Lords*. Aquatint by Thomas Rowlandson from *The Microcosm of London*, 1810.

21. *Newstead Abbey, the seat of the late Lord Byron*. Coloured lithograph by A. Picker. 'In this print may be traced the profiles of the late Lord Byron, Ada (Lord Byron's daughter), Theresa, the Maid of Athens and the Countess Guiccioli'. Collection *The Greek Gazette*.

22. Byron's bedroom at Newstead Abbey. Photo The British Tourist Authority.

23. The tomb of Boatswain in the grounds of Newstead Abbey. Photo *The Evening Post*, Nottingham.

24. *Boatswain*, 1803. Painting by Clifton Thomson. Newstead Abbey, Nottingham Museums.

25. Lord Byron's inkstand. Newstead Abbey, Nottingham Museums.

26. The Temple of Poseidon, Cape Sounion. Photo Edwin Smith.

27. *The Capuchin Monastery, Athens*. Gouache by J. Stuart. The British Architectural Library, RIBA, London.

28. Byron's name incised on a pillar of the Temple of Poseidon, Cape Sounion. Photo J. Lewinski.

29. *The Maid of Athens*. Engraving by C. R. Cockerell from *The Byron Gallery*, 1833.

30. *Lord Byron's presentation at the court of Ali Pasha of Janina* (1809). *c.* 1832–33. Sepia wash attributed to Frank Stone. Private collection.

31. *Lord Byron reposing in the house of a Turkish fisherman after having swum across the Hellespont* (detail), 1831. Painting by Sir William Allan. By courtesy of Roy Miles Fine Paintings, Duke Street, St James's, London SW1.

32. *The meeting of Lord Byron and Sir Walter Scott in the drawing room of*

the publisher *John Murray, Albermarle Street, 1815, c.*1850. Watercolour by L. Werner. The people portrayed are from left to right: Isaac D'Israeli, John Murray, Sir John Barrow, George Canning, William Gifford, Sir Walter Scott and Lord Byron. Collection John Murray.

33. *John Murray II.* Painting by H. W. Pickersgill. Collection John Murray. The bust of Lord Byron by Bertel Thorwaldsen is in the background.

34. Part of the autograph manuscript of *Don Juan* canto I by Lord Byron, completed in Venice in 1818. The Pierpont Morgan Library, New York.

35. South side of Holland House, Holland Park, which was partly destroyed during World War II. Engraving after P. H. Delamotte.

36. *John Cam Hobhouse* (later Lord Broughton de Gifford), 1843. Miniature by W. J. Newton. Collection Sir Charles Hobhouse.

37. *Breakfast at Samuel Rogers's residence* (detail), 1815. Mezzotint by Charles Mottram. Standing left to right are Wallerfoote, James Mackintosh, Lansdowne, Sydney Smith, Washington Irving and F. Jeffrey. Seated left to right are Sheridan, Thomas Moore, William Wordsworth, Robert Southey, Samuel J. Coleridge, Samuel Rogers, Byron and I. Kemble.

38. *Lady Caroline Lamb dressed as a page.* Painting by Thomas Phillips. Reproduced by permission of the Trustees of the Chatsworth Settlement. Photo The Courtauld Institute of Art, London.

39. *A voluptuary under the horrors of digestion.* Hand-coloured stipple engraving by James Gillray.

40. *Melbourne House, Whitehall.* Aquatint by Thomas Malton. Melbourne House was taken over from the Duke of York by William Lamb and is now the Scottish Office.

41. *Fashionables of 1816 taking the air in Hyde Park:* Hand-coloured engraving by I. R. Cruikshank which depicts Lord Byron walking with an actress on each arm trying to out-stare Lady Byron who is shown to be pregnant and accompanied by Mrs Clermont.

42. *St. James's Street, London.* Aquatint from Thomas Malton's *Picturesque Tour through the Cities of London and Constantinople,* Vol. II, 1792. Brooks's Club is on the right and Boodle's on the left.

43. *Lord Byron.* Miniature by H. Kearney. Newstead Abbey, Nottingham Museums.

44. *Lady Noel Byron* (née Annabella Milbanke). Engraving by W. H. Mote after the painting by W. J. Newton. From Finden's *Illustrations to the Life and Works of Lord Byron,* Vol. I, 1833.

45. The gold betrothal ring of Lord Byron. The ring has the crest and motto of the Byron family and the words 'sans peur' are engraved on the inside surface. Newstead Abbey, Nottingham Museums.

46. *Augusta Leigh,* 1817. Miniature by J. Holmes. Private collection.

47. *Halanby Hall, Co. Durham.* Lithograph by F. Peake. The Hall was partly demolished in 1953 and the remaining wing is now used as offices.

48. *Augusta Ada Byron aged four.* Engraving by W. Finden after G. Howse depicting the miniature of Byron's daughter. From Lord Byron's *Childe Harold's Pilgrimage,* 1841.

49. *Claire Clairmont,* 1819. Painting by Amelia Curran. Newstead Abbey, Nottingham Museums.

50. *Mary Shelley,* 1831. Painting by S. J. Stump. The National Portrait Gallery, London.

51. *Lord Byron at the Villa Diodati near Geneva, 1816.* Lithograph by

Spengler and Company, Lausanne.

52. *Margarita Cogni*. Engraving by H. T. Ryall after the drawing by G. Harlow 'taken at the request of Lord Byron'. From Finden's *Illustrations to the Life and Works of Lord Byron*, Vol. I, 1833.

53. Byron's wax Carnival mask worn at Ravenna in 1820. Collection Keats-Shelley Memorial House, Rome.

54. *Byron in the Palazzo Mocenigo, Venice*. Coloured lithograph after John Scarlett Davis. Newstead Abbey, Nottingham Museums.

55. *Byron and his circle in conversation on a terrace overlooking the Venetian lagoon at sunset*. Painting by Friedrich Nerly, Jr. Photo courtesy of Sotheby Parke Bernet and Company, London.

56. *Countess Teresa Guiccioli*. Engraving by H. T. Ryall after a drawing by H. Brockedon from Finden's *Illustrations to the Life and Works of Lord Byron*, Vol. II.

57. *Les Amants Célèbres. Lord Byron et La Comtesse Guccioli (sic)*. Lithograph by J. Platier.

58. *Palazzo Lanfranchi, Pisa*. Photogravure after O. F. M. Ward from *The Works of Lord Byron*, 1898–1901 edited by R. E. Prothero.

59. *The Funeral of Shelley, 1822*, 1889. Painting by Louis Edouard Fournier. The Walker Art Gallery, Liverpool.

60. *Byron's arrival at Missolonghi where he is met by Prince Alexander Mavrocordato, 5 January 1824* (detail). Painting by T. Vryzakis, 1861. National Pinakothiki and Alexander Soutzos Museum, Athens.

61. The helmet Lord Byron wore in Greece. The helmet, made in Genoa before his departure, was probably done to Lord Byron's own designs. Newstead Abbey, Nottingham Museums.

62. *Prince Alexander Mavrocordato, President of the Greek Government*. Lithograph from Friedel's *Series of Greek Portraits*, 1827. Newstead Abbey, Nottingham Museums.

63. *Oath of Lord Byron on the Tomb of Marco Botzaris, 1824*. Popular Greek coloured lithograph based on a painting by Ludovico Lipparini, c. 1937. Newstead Abbey, Nottingham Museums.

64. *Lord Byron's House, Missolonghi*. Aquatint by T. Clark after a drawing by R. Seymour from W. Parry's *The Last Days of Lord Byron* 1825. Idealized view of the house, which was in fact on three floors. Byron occupied the second floor which had the bedroom where he died overlooking the sea and a sitting room with three other rooms which were for his servants, Suliote bodyguard and colleague Colonel Stanhope.

65. *The Death of Byron, c. 1826*. Painting by Joseph Odevaere. Byron is crowned with bay leaves and his lyre lies beside him with broken strings. Musée Gronginge, Bruges. Photo copyright A.C.L. – Brussels.

66. The coffin of Lord Byron with the chest in front which contains his brain and heart, etc. To the right is the coffin of Lady Lovelace, his daughter. The photograph was taken by P . W. C. Bullock when the Byron vault, in the Church of St Mary Magdalene, Hucknall Torkard, Notts., was opened in 1938. See T. G. Barber, *Byron and Where he is Buried*, 1939. Photo by courtesy of P. A. Bullock.

67. Bronze memorial medal marking the death of Lord Byron, 1824. By A. J. Stothard. Newstead Abbey, Nottingham Museums.

68. The nineteenth-century marble statue of Lord Byron being crowned by 'Greece' executed by J. A. J. Falguière, Zappeion Gardens, Athens. Photo Jorge Lewinski.

INDEX

Figures in italics refer to illustrations.

Frederic Raphael is the author of many novels, including *The Glittering Prizes*. This and the collection of short stories *Oxbridge Blues* were also successful as sequences of TV plays. As well as writing and adapting for television, he has written, adapted and directed for the cinema. His other writings include a biography of Somerset Maugham, a collection of views and reviews, a stage play and various translations.

This book arose out of a television special.

Frederic Raphael is a Fellow of the Royal Society of Literature.